FORMATIVE JUDAISM III

Program in Judaic Studies
Brown University
BROWN JUDAIC STUDIES
Edited by

Jacob Neusner,
Wendell S. Dietrich, Ernest S. Frerichs,
Alan Zuckerman

Number 46

FORMATIVE JUDAISM:
RELIGIOUS, HISTORICAL AND LITERARY STUDIES
Third Series

Torah, Pharisees, and Rabbis
by
Jacob Neusner

Formative Judaism: Religious, Historical and Literary Studies
Third Series

Torah, Pharisees, and Rabbis

by
Jacob Neusner

Scholars Press
Chico, California

FORMATIVE JUDAISM:
RELIGIOUS, HISTORICAL AND LITERARY STUDIES
Third Series

Torah, Pharisees, and Rabbis

by
Jacob Neusner

Publication of this book is made possible in part by the Friends of the Program in Judaic Studies, Brown University, through the good offices of Mr. Lyman G. Bloomingdale, patron of the Program.

© 1983
Brown University

Library of Congress Cataloging in Publication Data
Neusner, Jacob, 1932–
    Formative Judaism.

    (Brown Judaic studies ; no. 46)
    Includes bibliographical references and index.
    1. Judaism—History—Talmudic   period,   10–425—
Addresses, essays, lectures.
I. Title. II. Series.
BM177.N4724 1983   296'.09'015   83–8662
ISBN 0-89130-633-1

Printed in the United States of America

For

<u>William F. Buckley, Jr</u>.

who shows what one human being can do

CONTENTS

PREFACE

This book continues the pattern of its predecessors and requires only a brief introduction. Once more I offer religious, historical, and literary studies of formative Judaism, that is, that kind of Judaism defined by the myth of the two Torahs revealed to Moses at Sinai, one in writing and the other oral, and documented by the Mishnah, the two Talmuds, and the several collections of Scriptural exegeses, midrashim, produced by the same circles of authorities, called rabbis. Here we take up three distinct exercises.

The religious studies ask about the meaning of oral Torah, and, in consequence, of the word Torah. They go over a long-standing problem in an essentially fresh way. Chapter One provides a brief overview of the results. Chapter Two asks about the Mishnah as Torah, that is, the relationship of Mishnah-tractates to corresponding passages of the Pentateuch. Chapter Three reviews my most current results on how the word Torah took on the meanings it now bears.

The historical studies return us to the first century and raise the question of the relationship of the Pharisees and their immediate successors after 70 to the rabbinical movement attested in the larger canon at hand. Specifically, I review the passages in which Josephus refers to the Pharisees. Then I reconstruct a picture of the religious situation after 70. Finally, in Chapter Six, I trace the movement from Pharisaism to Rabbinism, each viewed as an ideal type, through the aftermath of the destruction of the Temple. The chapter covers issues of method and substance: how the sources should be read, what they mean when they are rightly read. This essay completes the survey represented by the account of Josephus's Pharisees, then the overview and perspective upon the period of Yavneh, that is, 70 to 100, in the history of Judaism.

The literary studies take up two closely related problems of literary description of the rabbinic canon. In the first, Chapter Seven, I attempt to characterize the Babylonian Talmud as a complete statement. In the second, Chapter Eight, I try to differentiate one sector of the larger rabbinic canon from another sector thereof. This I do by reviewing facts about the Messiah that occur in, first, the Mishnah and its associated

documents, Abot, the Tosefta, and some of the compilations of
exegeses and, second, in the Talmuds and their associated
documents, other compilations of exegeses in particular. I
show that the former sector of the canon knows and uses one set
of facts, while the latter, utilizing these same facts, introduces a much larger repertoire of its own. So while the
penultimate and ultimate chapters prove to be unrelated to one
another, both of them constitute experiments in the description
of rabbinic texts, that is, exercises of comparison, contrast,
and differentiation.

These papers originate as follows:

Chapter Two, "The Meaning of Torah shebe^cal Peh,"
in AJS Review I, 1976, pp. 150-170.

Chapter Four, "Josephus's Pharisees," in Ex Orbe
Religionum. Studia Geo Widengren Oblata (Leiden, 1972:
E.J. Brill), I, pp. 224-244. Editors are C.J. Bleeker,
S.G.F. Brandon, M. Simon, J. Bergman, K. Drunjeff, and H.
Ringgren.

Chapter Five, "Judaism after the Destruction of the
Temple," in John H. Hayes and J. Maxwell Miller, eds.,
Israelite and Judaean History (Philadelphia, 1977: The
Westminster Press), pp. 663-677.

Chapter Six, "The Formation of Rabbinic Judaism," in
Wolfgang Haase, ed., Aufstieg und Niedergang der roemis-
chen Welt. II. Principat. 19.2. Religion (Judentum:
Palaestinisches Judentum) (Berlin and New York, 1979:
Walter de Gruyter), pp. 3-42.

Chapter Seven, "The Babylonian Talmud," in Elie
Kedourie, ed., The Jewish World. Revelation, Prophecy,
and History (London, 1979: Thames and Hudson), pp.
108-119.

I thank the several copyright holders for permission to reprint
my essays in this book.

I hope that by collecting these occasional papers, some of
them not published, and presenting them as a group, I may
provide a more coherent and cogent account of my picture of the
formation of Judaism and to do so for a wider audience than is
otherwise possible. The diverse papers flow from a single
method and produce coherent results. The large-scale scholarly
works, rich in the detailed presentation and analysis of
sources and the patient sifting of evidence, by their nature
can attract only a limited audience. People standing at the
margins of the subject want to know the main points and how

they are reached, but forgo the details, being engaged by the details of their own studies. I mean to serve that sizable audience of colleagues and students through publishing these books of essays. The critical response suggests that my intention is not entirely without result.

I have tried to excise repetitions, though I fear that at some few points, I may go over the same matter twice. I beg the reader's indulgence. Each of the essays has its own integrity.

The dedication of this book is to one of our generation's most talented, but also effective, intellectuals. William F. Buckley, Jr., has done more to change the world in which he lives than most people who, like him, mainly read books, think about things, and sit at a typewriter before a blank piece of paper. He has long since transcended his origins, making full use of his rich gifts and expanding them. With wit, style, and ineffable class, he has reshaped the political thinking of many in our day, showing possibilities that had long since lain unperceived, raising forbidden questions, challenging conventions, asking why where nearly everyone else assumed we all knew the answer. His career in public discourse has shown what a person can do. I am one of the legion of those privileged to count him as a friend and prompt correspondent. His greatness lies in the life he has made for himself, in the example of achievement of mind and heart and soul he gives to us all. So let us now praise famous men, when they achieve liberality of spirit. Here is one of them. I pay my modest tribute.

To understand these papers, and all of my several other volumes, the reader will find helpful a brief statement of what I think I am doing. Essentially, I engage in a game of testing possibilities, sifting sources to make sense of the whole, finding ways to describe in the entirety what is perceived only in detail, to analyze at the heart and center what is dissected only in part, and to interpret how, in a large way, people's social lives relate to the ideas they hold. Peter Medawar, in Pluto's Republic, speaks for me when he describes scientific reasoning as "a dialogue between two voices, the one imaginative and the other critical; a dialogue... between the possible and the actual, between proposal and disposal, conjecture and criticism, between what might be true and what is in fact the case." The sources under study in this book have in general served an other than historical enterprise. They too long have lain in the hands of theologians, who care only for results reached long ago, for the imaginative, the possible, the proposal, the conjecture, and what might be true. We deal with treasures of the human imagination. The theologians think they hold the key to the strong box. But long ago they threw away the key and thought to leave the treasure inaccessible, except as people would listen to what they reported was in the box. All this is now over. The astonishing human achievements of the ancient sages of Israel now lie open for anyone who wants to see. The keepers of the treasury have been dismissed. For now they too have to meet the standards of rationality, criticism, actuality, disposal, and either show what is in fact the case or shut up. I have retranslated the Mishnah; translated the Tosefta complete for the first time; translated the Palestinian Talmud complete for the first time; and plan to do the same for the Babylonian Talmud. I have given my account of what I think all these things mean and add up to. Now let us hear from everyone who wishes to work on these same documents and to tell us what they are as literature, what they report as history, and what they mean to humanity as constructions of religion.

J.N.

Providence, Rhode Island, U.S.A.
March 28, 1983
14 Nisan, Ereb Pesah, 5743

Part One

RELIGIOUS STUDY OF FORMATIVE JUDAISM

Chapter One
THE MYTH OF THE TWO TORAHS
A PROLEGOMENON

The myth that when God gave the Torah to Moses at Mount
Sinai, he gave it in two parts, one in writing, the other not
in writing but formulated for memorization and then handed on
orally, comprises the theory of revelation represented by the
oral law, the Torah-that-is-memorized. The power of the myth
lies in its capacity to account for those beliefs, and the
books that contain them, emerging long after the close of the
biblical canon. The beliefs held authoritative yet not found
in the Hebrew Scriptures derive, it is then explained, from
that other, oral revelation. Books that present principles and
beliefs handed on through the oral law's processes of formulation and transmission then enjoy the status of the written
Torah. In this way, the conception of a canon of authoritative
books that is forever able to receive new works serves to make
room for the religious genius of Israel in all periods of the
history of the nation. Indeed, viewed from one perspective,
the effect of the conception of the oral law is to state, in
mythic terms, the position of Reform theologians concerning
progressive or continuing revelation. That is to say, God
speaks through the prophets and sages of each generation.
Revelation is not exhaustively contained only in Scripture, or
in Scripture and its rabbinic amplification, but goes on even
now. While the conception of the oral law would in principle
accord with that theological position, in fact the contents of
the oral law attain canonical status only within the consensus
of the sages. Revelation of Torah may prove continuous, but it
is not promiscuous.

The documents accorded the status of oral law in the
formative age of the rabbinic canon begin with the Mishnah, ca.
200 C.E. For its part, the Mishnah refers backward to no
source of truth other than the written Torah, and so lays claim
to constitute the second document, after Scripture, excluding
everything Israel had produced as writing down of God's message
from the close of the Pentateuch in the time of Ezra, ca. 450
B.C.E., to the Mishnah's own time -- a veritable burned library
of revelation. The Mishnah, for its part, contains no myth of

its own origin, and its authors lay down no claim that in
principle what they say comes from Sinai. They even ignore the
morphology, syntax, and word-choices, of biblical Hebrew. They
do not allege that what they say has reached them through
angelic or other revelation. They do not introduce the names
of authentic prophets, such as Jeremiah or Ezra, and they do
not call their book a torah, or revelation. These established
and conventional means by which the framers of earlier Israelite books had secured credence for their writings all proved
useless.

The Mishnah's first apologetic, Abot, for its part, does
say that Moses received Torah at Sinai and handed it on to
Joshua and onward. What is important in that passage is that
it ends up with the names of authorities of the Mishnah, such
as Hillel and Shammai, and Hillel's family (in the Mishnah's
day, allegedly continued in the figure of the patriarch,
Judah), on the one side, and Hillel's disciples (in the
Mishnah's time continuing on in the sages of the Mishnah
itself). Accordingly, the connection of the Mishnah to Sinai,
so far as the framers of the chains of tradition in Abot are
concerned, lies through the person of the sage, on the one
side, and the family of the patriarch, on the other. But that
claim does not also allege that the Mishnah, in particular,
either in actual formulation (which would have been incredible)
or in principle derives from Sinai. Nor do we commonly find
any such allegation in the documents that constitute the
Mishnah's sector of the canon of Judaism in its formative age,
from ca. 200 to 600. The myth of the two Torahs appears only
rarely, until we reach the two Talmuds, the one of the Land of
Israel, ca. 400, the other of Babylonia, ca. 600, as well as
the associated documents in the Talmudic sector of the rabbinic
canon.

In the Talmud of the Land of Israel we find, nearly fully
worked out, the myth of the two Torahs, though the last stages
in the expression of the myth are scarcely reached before the
Babylonian Talmud. But both Talmuds know full well that at
Sinai there was a double revelation, one in writing, the other
orally. While the Talmud of the Land of Israel scarcely
testifies to the actual language of Torah-in-writing and
Torah-in-memory, the distinction between revelation in writing
and revelation formulated and transmitted orally is well
established there. Some of the collections of biblical
exegesis ("midrashim") associated with the Talmudic sector of

the rabbinic canon also know the same facts. We may say with
certainty, therefore, that the myth of the two Torahs had come
to full expression by ca. 400 C.E.

The polemical and political utility of the myth hardly
requires much comment. Where, in the two Talmuds, we find the
most vigorous assertions that there were two Torahs, we
commonly deal with controversy-stories, e.g., Hillel, Shammai,
and the proselyte, at B. Shab. 31a, Yohanan b. Zakkai and the
Sadducees, at B. Men. 65a. Christian apologists had framed
their principal attack on Judaism in the claim that the Jews
falsified Scripture and did not understand its true meaning.
The credence claimed for the Mishnah and its successor-writings
on the part of the rabbinical movement -- then the effective
bureaucracy and government of the Jewish people in both the
Land of Israel and Babylonia -- offered a tempting target.
When, in the aftermath of the conversion of Constantine in the
early part of the fourth century, Christianity rose to the
position of dominant, then state-religion, and when, in 361,
Julian's promise to rebuild the Temple turned into a fiasco,
with the consequence that Christianity returned to power in a
militant and frightened mood and determined to wipe out
paganism and humiliate Judaism, the urgent utility of the myth
became apparent.

At that time Israel's leaders, the rabbis represented in
the Talmud of the Land of Israel and associated documents, had
for the first time to confront the reality of Christianity and
cease to delude themselves that they could place Christianity
in the undifferentiated, and unimportant, backdrop covered in
the word "paganism" (Abodah Zarah in general, or _minut_ in
particular). At that time we find two closely-connected
activities. First, the same authorities who produced the
Talmud of the Land of Israel also engaged in a second work of
exegesis, done along parallel lines. Just as, in the Talmud
itself, they systematically worked out an exegesis of the
Mishnah, so, in the earliest compilations of biblical exegeses
beyond the Tannaitic ones, they systematically worked out an
exegesis of principal books of the Pentateuch. In Genesis
Rabbah and Leviticus Rabbah they constructed discourse about
Scripture along precisely the same logical principles that they
followed in framing discourse about the Mishnah. The second
activity brings us to the present topic. The sages then
expressed, in their exegeses of both the Mishnah and Scripture,
the conviction about the oral law that we have briefly outlined

here. So the fully exposed myth of the oral law, that is, the conviction that at Sinai God had revealed to Moses a dual Torah, one written down, one formulated and transmitted orally and through memorization, served remarkably well to defend the Judaism defined by the sages of the Mishnah and the Talmud, to account for its origins, and to validate its message.

This was accomplished in the face of the glimmerings of the challenge, first from Christianity, then from Islam as well, that Judaism would have to confront for the remainder of the history of Judaism in the West: to justify and validate those teachings, and the books that contained them, that Jews alone held, beyond Scripture, to constitute God's Torah to Moses at Sinai. Judaism as we know it, that is, the distinctive Judaism of the doctrine of the two Torahs, therefore was born in the encounter with triumphant Christianity, just as, in its formative century, Christianity had come into being in the encounter with an established Judaism of Temple, land, and self-governing state.

It must be noted that this picture will puzzle the many faithful Jews who, accepting at face value the allegations of the Talmuds, believe that the oral law comes from Sinai. It also stands at variance with the convictions of scholars of an earlier period, that the concept of the oral law characterized the pre-70 Pharisees in particular, who were the teachers of the dual Torah. If, however, we did not know in advance that such a myth had circulated before 70, we should hardly find an unequivocal statement of it in any of the passages that are adduced in evidence. These speak only of traditions in addition to Scripture. For a formulation of the claim that extra-biblical traditions -- a commonplace among a whole range of Jewish groups -- constituted the oral Torah revealed to Moses at Sinai, we have to wait until the appearance of the Talmuds, four centuries later.

If we take seriously the fact that only much later do we find the doctrine fully exposed, we also realize that, when it first reached full formulation, the myth had to explain a particular fact, namely, the authority and standing of the Mishnah and associated writings. Then, as is clear, we have also to formulate our explanation in response to the circumstance that required the sages to account for their distinctive traditions, law and theology alike. The explanation derives, at first view, from the circumstance that precipitated it: the triumph of Christianity, the disappointment, after Julian's

fiasco, of the Jewish people, but also from the document in
which it first occurs as a fully exposed and commonplace myth,
namely, the Talmud of the Land of Israel, coming it is generally assumed forty years after 361. Once held authoritative,
the myth of the oral Torah, or, more precisely, of the dual
Torah, would serve to defend that very corpus of revealed law
and theology that defined and made Judaism distinctive, and
further to explain and justify the inclusion, within that
corpus, of the teachings of the authoritative sages of the
Torah, in every succeeding generation, down to our own day.

Bibliography:
1.   For the conventional view of the topic:
     George F. Moore, Judaism in the First Centuries of the
          Christian Era. The Age of the Tannaim (Cambridge,
          1927). I, pp. 3-124, 235-280.
     Ephraim E. Urbach, The Sages. Their Concepts and Beliefs,
          trans. by Israel Abrahams (Jerusalem, 1975), pp.
          286-314.
2.   For a picture of the Pharisees as sages of the oral Torah:
     Ellis Rivkin, A Hidden Revolution. The Pharisees' Search
          for the Kingdom Within (Nashville, 1978).
3.   For amplification of the thesis outlined in this chapter:
     Jacob Neusner, Judaism: The Evidence of the Mishnah
          (Chicago, 1981).
     _____, Judaism: The Evidence of the Yerushalmi
          (Chicago, 1983).
     _____, Midrash in Context. Exegesis in Formative
          Judaism (Philadelphia, 1983).
     _____, Torah: From Scroll to Symbol in Formative
          Judaism (Philadelphia, 1983).

Chapter Two

THE MEANING OF TORAH SHEBE^CAL PEH
WITH SPECIAL REFERENCE TO MISHNAH-TRACTATES KELIM AND OHALOT

I

WHAT IS ORAL TORAH

The central conception distinguishing rabbinic Judaism from all other conceptions of Judaism, past and present, is the belief in the myth of Moses as "our rabbi," and the conception that when God -- also conceived in the model of the rabbi -- revealed the Torah to Moses, he gave Torah in two parts, one in writing, the other as tradition handed on orally. The tradition handed on orally is now contained in the Mishnah and its cognate literature: Tosefta, Babylonian and Palestinian Talmuds, the various Midrashim, and the like. Accordingly, at the center of Rabbinic Judaism is the concept of the dual Torah and the fundamental conviction that the written Torah is not the whole record of revelation. Indeed, one may say that just as the New Testament is represented by Christianity as the completion and fulfillment of the Old Testament, so the Mishnah is understood by Rabbinic Judaism as the other half of Tanakh.

Accordingly, from the beginning of modern Jewish scholarship, one crucial problem in the study of the history of Judaism has been the nature or meaning, defined in particular terms of the origins and development, of Mishnah.

In traditional circles, this problem, of course, was readily solved. The contents of the Mishnah constitute Torah shebe^Cal peh (oral Torah); their history is coextensive with that of Torah shebikhtav (written Torah). That conception is phrased in historical language, and, when so stated, is hardly compelling. But, as I shall try to show, that conception, when viewed from another, a phenomenological, angle, is essentially correct and represents a wholly accurate interpretation of the nature and meaning of Oral Torah.

The reason that modern Orthodoxy phrased its conception of Torah shebe^Cal peh in historical, rather than theological, terms is that Orthodoxy had to respond to the claim, also phrased in historical language, of Jewish scholarship beginning in the nineteenth century, that the concept of Torah shebe^Cal

peh is to be defined in terms of beginnings and growth, understood in the light of origins and change. Since the Reformers
approached the reform of the tradition through historical
means, the traditionalists reaffirmed the convictions of
tradition in historical language. It was unavoidable. What is
it that the Reformers alleged concerning the origins and
meaning of Torah shebe^Cal peh?

The Reformers, beginning with Zechariah Frankel, saw the
Oral Torah as historical and contingent, not supernatural and
autonomous. Oral Torah was represented as the product of the
exegesis of the Written Torah. It had no independent existence, no autonomy as a separate corpus of revelation, correlative to Torah shebikhtav. The Mishnah is the end-product of
about six centuries of the exegesis of Scripture. Frankel held
that the scribes explained the commandments, then joined their
explanation to the written Scriptures. This, he said, is the
crux of the oral law. Only later on were materials organized
thematically, rather than exegetically, that is, by the formulation of abstract law, "law which was meant to explain an
issue of the Torah without being attached to the text of the
Torah." So the beginning of the Oral Torah did not lie in
remote antiquity -- the time of Moses -- but in the time of
Ezra and the scribes. The Mishnah in no way is to be regarded
as an autonomous and separate Torah, but merely as the end of a
long period of study and exegesis of the one written Torah of
Sinai. The Mishnah serves merely to organize vast quantities
of exegetically based laws.

It would carry us far afield to investigate the historical
circumstances, intellectual influences, and philosophical
necessities, which led Frankel, Brüll, and their successors to
the present day to stress the historical origin of Torah
shebe^Cal peh in the period from Ezra to the editing of the
Mishnah, accomplished through the process of exegesis. Rather,
let us test their most fundamental allegation, that Oral Torah
essentially is nothing more than the exegesis of Written Torah,
against the evidence of Mishnah itself. It seems to me that it
is only by an inductive inquiry into the actual interrelationships between Mishnah and Scriptural law that we shall come to
a sound picture of what classical, Rabbinic Judaism really
understood by Mishnah, that is, by Oral Torah.

I hasten to add that the issue is not felicitously phrased
in terms of Frankel's theory or of the traditional and Orthodox
conception either. That is to say, when we ask about the

relationship between Oral Torah, represented by Mishnah-Tosefta, and the written Torah, we stand wholly within the mythic framework established by the second- and third-century rabbis. In point of fact, so far as Mishnah and Scripture are related, it is because the one holds views diametrically opposite those of the other upon the same issue. As we shall see, Scripture -- Leviticus and Numbers -- takes for granted that cleanness is important only in the Temple. The oral Torah -- Kelim, also Parah -- takes for granted that cleanness interpenetrates the world outside of the Temple. Scripture assumes that the priests are in charge, the Oral Torah -- Negaim -- assumes that the sage is in charge. Scripture speaks of tents, places in which people live. Mishnah Ohalot, as we shall show, is about the Tent, a space capable of retaining, or interposing against, that which exudes from the corpse upon death. In other words, while Mishnah does much with the themes of Scripture, in the tractates under study it always rejects even the simplest suppositions of Scripture. Why then should we ask ourselves to analyze Mishnah in terms of the rabbinic myth of correlative and autonomous Torahs?

And there is a further consideration. Mishah-Tosefta, in the tractates before us (as in other tractates, except for Abot), is not a work which claims to constitute <u>Torah</u> at all. We do not come across a single sentence in Mishnah-Tosefta Kelim, Ohalot, or, for that matter, Negaim and Parah, in which Mosaic or Scriptural authority is claimed to stand behind or generate a rule. True, once in a while, particularly in Negaim, we find exegeses in which Scripture provides proof-texts for a proposition. But said proposition also is estab-lished <u>without</u> proof-texts. In any case, it is difficult to demonstrate either that laws were created by looking into Scripture (Negaim in fact is a special case, for reasons spelled out in my <u>History of the Mishnaic Laws of Purities. VII. Negaim. Sifra</u>); or that Mishnah-Tosefta for the trac-tates before us ever was conceived within the scheme of the two Torahs of Moses "our rabbi." That conception, I think, comes after the completion and promulgation of Mishnah, and does not stand at the outset of the process of the formulation of the law. I am inclined to think that the history of the myth of the two Torahs is separate from, though intertwined with, the association of that myth with Mishnah-Tosefta in particular. We may for the moment observe that our tractates are remarkably uninterested in Moses "our rabbi" and in his dual Torah.

The real problem facing modern scholarship of Mishnah is the _definition_ of Mishnah. The established framework of argument presents us with two choices: Mishnah is a law-code, or Mishnah is a school-book. But when we ask, What is Mishnah? in fact we take up the search for an appropriate analogy. Frankel's analogy had to do with the spinning out of Oral Torah by exegesis of Written Torah. The more recent analogies take Mishnah to be separate from the written Scripture. When it is said, "Mishnah is a law-code," however, what is meant is, "Mishnah is like a law-code, like other law-codes." And the same is so for the analogy to the school-book. Neither analogy is suitable. I am inclined to think Mishnah is _sui generis_. For when we examine other documents of the first and second centuries which deal with the same topics as are dealt with in one tractate or another, we find that the modes of thought and expression of Mishnah, quite apart from the utterly distinctive substance of the laws, are entirely without analogy or parallel in other documents. Since there are no literary or cognitive parallels, there also can be no compelling analogies. Whatever Mishnah may be, as represented by the tractates before us, whatever functions it is meant to serve, and whatever the purposes of those who created the law and compiled it -- these have to be discovered wholly within the limits of Mishnah itself. No court enforced the laws of cleanness, or much of the remainder of Mishnah-Tosefta, after 70, so we simply do not have a law-code in the ordinary sense. People did study the laws, and that is why we have them. But for what purpose? What are we supposed to mean by "school-book" or "text-book" when we can scarcely demonstrate that there were _schools_ for this purpose and cannot adduce evidence of other, similar sorts of parallel school- or text-books? The choices under debate are inappropriate and impoverished.

The reason for urgency of the question, what is Mishnah? is to phrase in secular terms the issue of analogies raised in mythic terms when Mishnah is made into part of Torah, the Oral Torah. That too is an analogy, an effort to define and explain the character of the strange and curious document which is the foundation of rabbinic Judaism -- therefore of all Judaism from the second century.

II

PURITY AND ORAL TORAH

We shall focus upon two tractates in Seder Tohorot, Kelim and Ohalot.[1] The reason is that the laws of purities in Scripture are substantial and important. Further, we know that the Pharisees believed those laws were operative in ordinary life, not only in the Temple. Therefore, if any corpus of Mishnaic law is apt to rest upon a considerable heritage of exegesis of the written Scriptures, we have to choose a corpus of law for which Scriptures to begin with provide abundant laws. At the same time, if any corpus of Mishnaic law is apt to derive directly and immediately from the Pharisaic authorities of the period before 70 and to represent what surely is the creation of Pharisaism, it will be the laws of purities, concerning which the Pharisees held distinctive beliefs.[2] My

---

[1] It may fairly be objected that the challenge to Frankel's notion ought to be conducted on a base larger than Kelim and Ohalot. I may say that nothing in Parah or even in Sifra to Negaim, that is, Parshiyot Nega'im and Mesora', change the picture. Frankel will find little support in Sifra's exegeses for Mishnah-Tosefta Negaim, for nearly all of them indicate knowledge of Mishnah-Tosefta Negaim; and a fair amount of Sifra cites the materials of Mishnah-Tosefta verbatim or nearly verbatim. Still, before us are forty-eight chapters of Seder Tohorot, 38% of the whole. Frankel himself held that our order is the oldest ("because it is the largest") in Mishnah. It is a good sample of the order he cited and allows a reasonable test of his supposition. But, it should be stressed, the purpose of our work is not to test old theories but to investigate the sources and their cognitive structure.

[2] But the several tractates are not necessarily Pharisaic at their beginnings or even comparable to one another in origins. Kelim assuredly is Pharisaic, because only the Pharisees held that the susceptibility to uncleanness of domestic utensils, not employed in the Temple, mattered. But, as we shall observe, Ohalot turns out to be a deeply philosophical tractate, engaged in a profound inquiry into the state of the soul after death, an inquiry which, phrased in philosophical and abstract terms, will not have proved alien to Hellenistic philosophy. Even its very title, "Tents," evokes a simile much used by the New Testament writers, in particular Paul and the author of Hebrews. So Ohalot need not lead us deep into the circles of pre-70 Pharisaism. Negaim is a quintessentially "rabbinic" tractate, beginning in the thought of Aqiva, though based upon a rich antecedent corpus of (probably Priestly) study of the laws of Leviticus 13-14. Parah is Pharisaic in its supposition that we create a realm of cleanness outside of the Temple, that is, the place in which the red cow is burned, but its subject-matter, the burning of the red cow, is not necessarily of interest to Pharisees only. We know that the Samaritans burned red cows and used their ashes for many centuries after the destruction of the Temple in 70 (which meant nothing to them anyhow), and we may assume that

argument is that we can fairly test the twin concepts, first, that Mishnaic law is generated by the conceptions of Scripture through exegesis, and, second, that Mishnaic law is the product of the period from Ezra to the second century. This I do, specifically, by examining laws which, we can agree at the outset, relate to major corpora of Scriptural legislation. These laws are Pharisaic,[3] that is, reflective of the distinctive convictions of authorities in the period of which Frankel and Brüll speak.

Our problem is in the history and morphology of ideas. On the one hand, we have to ask, what laws or principles lie at the very foundations of the two tractates under examination? And on the other, what concepts and fundamental ideas are contained within those laws, and how do those concepts and ideas relate to the written Scriptures? We shall answer these questions by asking, what is the verifiable datum, the ab- solute, minimum given, underlying the earliest assigned or attributed sayings in a given tractate of Mishnah? If we can trace the ideas and conceptions of Mishnah from the time of Rabbi backward to Usha, and from the time of the Ushan authori- ties, for instance, Meir, Judah, Simeon, and Yose, backward to the Yavneh rabbis, for instance Aqiva, Gamaliel, Eliezer, and Joshua, and if we further can discern that rulings assigned to those earliest named masters rely upon conceptions never under dispute and always taken for granted in all rulings, then I believe we have gone as far back as we are able in the analysis of Mishnaic laws after 70.[4] Since, it is generally assumed, the Houses of Shammai and Hillel come before the destruction of the Second Temple, we may further ask, What are the givens of legal problems and disputes even in the period of the Houses?

Temple priests had some interest in Numbers 19:1-20. Accord- ingly, the four tractates on which the work is done are hardly comparable to one another, and only Kelim is to be assigned, from its very beginnings, to Pharisaic thinkers.

[3]Only within the qualification of the preceding note.

[4]But what we claim to uncover is the history of the ideas of interrelated and correlative pericopae, not of the exact formulation of those ideas in the very words before us. A vast amount of restatement of pericopae of Yavneh went on at Usha, and I think still more of the formulation of Mishnah was done by Rabbi. The distinction between verbal formulation and cognitive content of pericopae should be kept in mind through- out. In my earlier volumes of Purities, I-V, I did not sufficiently stress this distinction.

In stating matters thus, I report the result of in inquiry
into the history of the Mishnaic law of purities, which has
shown that there is a fairly orderly sequence or progression of
legal and conceptual principles, one built upon the last, from
the time of the Houses and the earlier authorities of Yavneh up
to the time of the Mishnah. One generation does depend upon
and make use of the legal conceptions of the previous one.[5]
Accordingly, we can trace the history of the Mishnaic law
backward to the earliest named authorities and then, with
remarkably little speculation, state with some precision the
fundamental principles upon which the entire structure of
Mishnaic law is built. True, we shall not then know where or
how these fundamental principles originated. But we can, at
the very least, test the allegation that Mishnah -- <u>Torah
shebe^{c}al peh</u> -- begins in the exegesis of <u>Torah shebikhtav</u>.

III
THE GIVENS OF THE TRACTATES (I) KELIM

Let us begin with Kelim and ask, What is the absolute and
minimum given of the entire tractate? The pre-history of the
Mishnaic law of Kelim begins with the assumption that the
status as to uncleanness of utensils outside of the cult does
matter, is consequential. That is, extra-cultic utensils have
to be kept clean for any purpose whatever. If we have no
reason to consider the status of the utensils as to cleanness,
we also have no cause to begin with to investigate whether they
are susceptible to uncleanness or insusceptible to uncleanness. Since only the Pharisees, among those known to us,
thought someone who was not a priest had to keep pure outside
of the cult (the Essene community at Qumran is a special

---

[5]To be sure, not all Yavnean rules are taken up and
developed at Usha, and some pericopae attributed to Ushans deal
with subjects simply not touched by pericopae assigned to
Yavneans. We have therefore, to distinguish reliable attributions of historical sequences, those in which a primitive idea
is attributed to an earlier authority, and a development of
that idea and a refinement of its details are assigned to a
later one, from merely probable assignments of those pericopae
which do not stand in logical sequence to others, either
earlier or later. But it is pleasant to report that most laws
of Mishnah do exhibit such a correlation of developments of
logic with chronological sequences of attributions, and so our
history of legal ideas is upon firm grounds.

case),[6] we need not doubt that the fundamental conception of
Kelim is part of the primary structure of Pharisaism. The laws
of Kelim do not begin before Pharisaism in the formulation
given it by lay people pretending to be priests.

The one specific concept characteristic of the Mishnaic
law of Kelim, beginning to end, is that a utensil which is
susceptible to uncleanness is one which is whole, complete,
useful -- normal. That notion is to be discovered in Scripture. Leviticus 11:33 tells us that to clean an unclean
utensil, one has to break it, make it useless. Then a utensil
which can become unclean is one which is not broken, which is
useful. The same exegete can have understood a utensil -- a
KLY -- to be defined in the same place, "Every KLY made of any
material" refers to anything at all; "any KLY used for any
purpose" limits the foregoing to useful objects only. Autonomy, and distinctiveness follow in the wake of purpose.

A second important early concept is that utensils are
regarded as divided into their inside or inner part and their
outside or outer part.[7] The first implication of that
division is that something which has a "midst" or an inner part
or a receptacle is susceptible to uncleanness, and something
which does not -- which is flat -- is insusceptible. Leviticus
11:33 readily generated that concept. To be sure, that
Scripture in the first place need not have brought the idea
into mind. The importance of a receptable in containing
uncleanness may have derived from the larger notion of uncleanness. If one conceived uncleanness as a kind of gas of heavy
viscosity, which will flow every which way unless it is
contained within some receptacle -- a utensil or a Tent -- but
which then will be kept in that one place, then the importance
of the receptacle depends not upon Leviticus 11:33 but upon a
quite separate conception of the material qualities of uncleanness. Accordingly, the first major development in the forma-

------

[6]I have found no rules, e.g., in CD, relevant to Kelim.
On this subject, see now L. Schiffman, The Halakhah at Qumran
(Leiden, 1975).

[7]See "First Cleanse the Inside," in Method and Meaning
in Ancient Judaism. Third Series (Chico, 1981: Scholars Press
for Brown Judaic Studies), pp. 155-164. I try to show that the
Hillelite view, that the condition of the inside of the cup
determines the status of the whole cup, is later than the
Shammaite view on the same matter, and that the stories in the
Gospels on the matter presuppose that the status of the inside
has no affect upon the status of the outside, the Shammaite
view.

tion of the law of the susceptibility of domestic utensils stressed two points, (1) usefulness as the definitive criterion of what is a utensil which can be made unclean, and (2) the presence of a receptacle as the requisite for the containment of uncleanness. Other early rules or conceptions cannot be so readily formulated.

If we stand back from this first stage and ask what the Written Torah has contributed to the Oral Torah, the question may be simply answered. The Written Torah has said that those things which break the natural rhythm of life are unclean. The Oral Torah has said that those things which, among all objects, serve, or are part of, the normal course of life are susceptible to becoming unclean. The abnormal affects what is normal.

Our firm result is that the laws of Kelim could have begun their development at any point, from the redaction of Leviticus onward, at which someone opened the pertinent Scriptures and decided to apply them to utensils not involved in the cult, part of a larger intention to keep purity laws outside the Temple. No considerable exegesis was then required to demonstrate that the Torah required pretty much what the authorities before 70 and immediately afterward took at face value. While, as I said, the laws of Kelim could have begun their development any time from the completion of Leviticus to the first century, the greatest probability is that the laws of Kelim began their development shortly before the time of the Houses. It is only then that the traces of a secondary exegetical tradition are to be found, resting on something more complex than the simple and plain meaning of the Scriptures themselves.

The fundamental theory of Kelim thus is that what is normal and useful is susceptible to uncleanness. What is abnormal or useless is insusceptible. So susceptibility is to the unusual and abnormal, which are represented by the sources of uncleanness -- things which are out of the ordinary and regarded (for whatever reasons) as distasteful. These abnormal things affect their very opposite, things which are commonplace. To put it differently, the negative -- the out-of-the-ordinary and the disharmonious -- affects the positive, the whole and complete, but not the negative. Accordingly, for Kelim we may describe the relationship of <u>Torah shebe^{c}al peh</u> to <u>Torah shebikhtav</u> as follows: Kelim in Scripture tells us about the negative; Kelim in Mishnah describes the positive. Without Mishnah the Priestly Code describes only part of

reality. Mishnah therefore completes the partial conceptions
of Leviticus. And, a second major innovation in Kelim: while
Scripture speaks of the cult, Mishnah speaks of the world
outside the Temple. Scripture addresses itself to the realm of
the sacred, Mishnah, to the world and to the secular reality
outside the cult. Just as Scripture tells what must <u>not</u> affect
the cult, so Mishnah tells us what <u>does</u> affect ordinary things.

IV

THE GIVENS OF THE TRACTATES (II) OHALOT

The relationship between Mishnah-treatise Ohalot and
Numbers 19:11-21 is completely different from that between
Mishnah-treatise Kelim and Leviticus 11:33ff. Before briefly
outlining the history of the laws of Ohalot, let me focus upon
what is the crucial issue. What is the conception of a Tent
characteristic of Mishnaic law? If we list the most profound
presuppositions of Ohalot, held by the earliest named authorities, we find the following: (1) a Tent requires egress.
This, logically and concomitantly, links to (2) the sealed
tomb. But that presupposition should not obscure the conception upon which these statements, in their turn, depend.
<u>Corpse-uncleanness passes through a squared handbreadth of open</u>
<u>space. Its passage may be prevented, therefore, by a minimum</u>
<u>of a handbreadth of closed space</u>. The entire tractate of
Ohalot is founded upon a single conception, to which we may
refer, for the sake of convenience, as the standard measure.
And what imposes that "measure" is the trait of corpse-uncleanness. Everything else in one way or another is logically spun
out of that single, fundamental trait of that which exudes from
the corpse. In no way is that concept related to Scripture.
No exegete even tried to find Scriptural foundations for it.
And, as we recognize, what is at issue is not merely the
measurement of a handbreadth, but all which is expressed by
that simple measurement.

For what the "handbreadth in breadth, depth, and height"
means is that the Scriptural tent, a place where people
actually live, has been left far behind us. The Tent as
conceived by the Old Torah, culminating in Mishnah, is anything
but a place in which people dwell. So, while Sifre Numbers
seems to preserve important exegeses which originate before the

earliest laws of Mishnah-Tosefta Ohalot,[8] it contains no hint
that that tradition begins with the exegesis of Scripture, the
discovery in the Written Torah of the foundations of our
tractate. We have the Talmud's own statement to the same
effect: little Scripture, many laws. What, then, is the
conception of Tent laid out in the Oral Torah?

The Written Torah speaks of a tent or a house in which
people, while and healthy in body and soul, live. The Oral
Torah speaks of a Tent capable of containing that which exudes
from the body at the moment of death. A Tent which takes the
place of the body. It goes without saying that the laws of
Numbers 19:11ff. were not understood in this way by others who
make reference to them.

What therefore has the Oral Torah contributed? On the
surface, we have nothing more than a useful definition, a
filling out of the Scriptural law with some necessary additional information. What is this tent, referred to in Numbers
19:11? It is simply an enclosed space of a certain dimension.
And what is that dimension? A handbreadth of enclosed space.
If this were the primary conceptual contribution of Mishnah,
then our notion of the Oral Torah should be stated as follows:
The role of Oral Torah -- or Mishnah -- is to fill in some
unimportant gaps in Scriptural law, to supply some needed
definitions.

But a closer look at the basis of Mishnah's contribution
requires a revision of our conception of the Oral Torah. For
that squared handbreadth, which is at the foundation of
everything else, is nothing other than a brief and elliptical
way of referring to the space through which the contaminating
effects of the corpse will make their way. We observe time and
again that "a corpse is assumed to pass through four hand-
breadths, its contaminating effects through one." When,
therefore, we define a Tent as a handbreadth in height,
breadth, and depth, what have we said? We have defined a Tent
not as a house or a building in which people can live or even
in which a corpse will fit. We have defined a Tent as the
space occupied by the gaseous effusion of the corpse. This
self-evidently has nothing to do with the house or building

---

[8]That is to say, some exegeses in Sifre Numbers raise
questions logically prior to the suppositions of anything in
Mishnah-Tosefta, and the latter document builds upon the
results of those exegeses. In substance, therefore, the
exegeses in a few instances seem to come before the law of
Mishnah-Tosefta.

which people see and use. It has much, I think, to do with the
house or building in which the person has existed, the body.

More explicitly: when we say a Tent must measure a
handbreadth, either to prevent uncleanness from entering its
enclosed space, or to keep uncleanness within its enclosed
space (without regard to the nature of the enclosure -- walls
or no walls), what is the meaning of such an allegation? What
is this Tent to which reference is made in Ohalot? (Even if we
substitute house for Tent, when house is used in Ohalot, the
referent at some point seems to be burial niche, kokh, as much
as a real house.) And what is it that can be contained in the
Tent of which Ohalot speaks? The answer is not the body, for a
whole body cannot be contained in a Tent. The terms of the
answer, moreover, have to include that invisible viscous gas
which is uncleanness, because it is everywhere taken for
granted that uncleanness cannot penetrate a closed area of a
handbreadth or less, on the one hand, or will be prevented from
exuding by that same closed area, if it is enclosed by it.

Corpse-uncleanness is something which can be contained by
a Tent. A Tent is something which can contain or interpose
against corpse-uncleanness.

The one has -- in the nature of things -- to be defined in
terms of the other. Our definition of a Tent is curiously out
of phase with the simple meaning of Scripture. The issue of
Scripture is drastically revised, indeed, when Tent becomes
"that which can contain what exudes from a corpse." When,
therefore, we define Tent as we do here, and as is taken for
granted throughout the Mishnaic laws which depend upon the
simple definition before us, we mean something entirely
different from what Scripture means.

If the conception of death is that when a person dies,
something leaves, exudes from, the body, then the Tent serves
as the functional equivalent to the body, for it is able to
receive and contain that which exudes from the body. The Tent,
therefore, takes the place of the body, makes a place for that
which, in the body, leaves at the point or moment of death.
The Tent is to be understood as a surrogate for the body,
restoring the order which has broken with the exit from the
body, of that which exudes from it. Death has released this
effusion. The Tent then contains it. We have avoided naming
this thing which "exudes from the corpse at such a viscosity as
to pass through an open space of a handbreadth or more, but no
less." I see no point in calling it the soul and to allege

that the "uncleanness" of the corpse is the "soul" which is the
"spirit" surviving after death and requiring a new locale.
(Simeon b. Gamaliel does refer to corpse-uncleanness as
tum'at hanefesh, Tosefta to Mishnah Ohalot 11:1.) Philo seems
to have had just the same notion:

> Further, too, those who enter a house in which anyone
> has died are ordered not to touch anything until they have
> bathed themselves and also washed the clothes which they
> were wearing. And all the vessels and articles of
> furniture, and anything else that happens to be inside,
> practically everything is held by him to be unclean. For
> a man's soul is a precious thing, and when it departs to
> seek another home, all that will be left behind is
> defiled, deprived as it is of the divine image. For it is
> the mind of man which has the form of God, being shaped in
> conformity with the ideal archetype, the Word that is
> above all.
>
> Special Laws 3:206-207
> (Trans. F. H. Colson, p. 605)

Neither Kelim nor Ohalot begins in the Priestly Code. Neither
tractate develops the lines laid out therein. Indeed, the most
fundamental convictions of both tractates lie wholly outside of
Scripture. For Kelim the issue is the susceptibility and
insusceptibility to impurity of various noncultic utensils.
For Ohalot the issue is the nature and functioning of Tents
(and utensils). Scriptural law knows little of either issue.
The Mishnaic conception that we ask about the susceptibility of
one object as against that of another is utterly alien to those
few references to Scripture which are even relevant to the laws
of Kelim. The question, what is a Tent? would be ludicrous to
the authority behind Numbers 19:11-22, for he takes for granted
that a Tent is a tent.[9]

---

[9]In point of fact, Mishnah-Tosefta contains two distinct
conceptions of a Tent. One is formal. A tent interposes
against uncleanness if it is of a certain size and shape. The
other is functional. A tent is formed by any substance which
is insusceptible to, therefore can prevent the passage of,
corpse-uncleanness. The two names of the tractate, Ohalot for
Mishnah, Ahilot for Tosefta, preserve these two distinct
conceptions, ohalot, the substantive, treats that which bears
the shape and form of the tent, and ahilot refers to that which
functions to overshadow. Interestingly, Ushan thought on the
nature of the utensil also is divided among two groups, one
which defines a utensil in terms of materials, the other in
terms of the function and shape of a utensil—that which can
serve as a container or receptacle. Those interested in form,
in both Kelim and Ohalot, are not interested in materials and
their susceptibility; those interested in function, in both
tractates, stress the susceptibility of materials. In Kelim I
think both groups can find in sayings of Aqiva support of their

Proof of the irrelevance to the two Mishnaic tractates is contained in the exegetical compilations which purport to link the Oral Torah to the wholly Written one. Sifra has virtually nothing which, in conception, let alone in articulation, does not depend upon Mishnah-Tosefta as completed compilations. Sifre Numbers does have exegeses which clearly seem in conception prior to, and in formulation autonomous from, anything in Mishnah. But these accomplish virtually nothing in linking Scripture to the underlying conceptions of the Tent (which are far, far earlier than our tractate's inquiry). And even if, for both tractates, we had considerably richer collections of exegesis, we could hardly claim that many specific laws have been worked out in response to the exegesis (let alone eisegesis) of the Scriptures. The contrary is the case. Perhaps the exegetes took for granted that the bed-rock convictions of the laws also were assumed by the Scriptures. But they still have not shown us where, in Scripture, they locate those laws or principles, and I think the probable explanation is that they could not (and did not care to). That is why they remind us that Ohalot has much law but little Scripture.

When, therefore, we refer to Scripture in seeking the beginnings, the pre-Mishnaic history, of Mishnaic law, we commit an error of gross anachronism. To put it very simply: Kelim begins somewhere, but not in Leviticus. At some stage in its early history, however, the sages who formed the law responded to such verses in Leviticus as seemed relevant to it, though the law's datum, its basic assumption, comes before the inquiry into Scripture. The problem of Ohalot, of course, is somewhat different for the appended tractates, fore and aft, Mishnah Ohalot 1:1-3:5, Mishnah Ohalot 16:3-18:10, do little more than add some clarifications and explications to what Scripture tells us about corpse-contamination and modes by which corpse-contamination is conveyed. Yet the Tents, meaning the processes of overshadowing, of which Ohalot speaks, bear no relationship whatever to the tent, the real tent, in which a person has died, mentioned by Numbers 19:11, 14-16, etc. We have, consequently, to address ourselves first to what is everywhere taken for granted, and only second to what is found

---

respective philosophies. In Ohalot it is difficult to find Yavnean sources for the Ushan conceptions. Aqiva, for his part, sees the Tent not as passive and formal but as active, something which unites discrete bits of corpse-matter within its shadow and draws together and makes affective their contaminating potentialities.

pertinent in the Priestly Code to that datum of the law, its primary conception.

V

THE AUTONOMY OF THE ORAL TORAH

Implicit in the contents and concept of Oral Torah therefore is the notion of the independence and autonomy of that Oral Torah. If, as I have suggested, the Mishnaic law is separate from, and autonomous of Scripture, though in its unfolding it is made to interrelate, where it can, to Scripture, then we must wonder whether we have not simply stated in historical language what the ancient rabbis meant in speaking, to begin with, of two Torahs, one in writing, the other transmited orally. It certainly is a drastic misstatement of the facts to see these two Torahs as interrelated in their beginnings, so far as the pertinent and reciprocally relevant segments of Leviticus and Numbers, Kelim and Ohalot, are concerned. It is an accurate statement of the facts as they were in the third century to regard Leviticus and Numbers as one Torah, Kelim and Ohalot as another, separate but correlative, one. The authorities of Mishnah-Tosefta do not derive their laws from Scriptures. On occasion they do twist Scriptures to make them fit preconceived conclusions. The implicit question of the exegetical compilations on the law is, "How do we know X from the Torah," with X the given law or belief. The problem is, then, to justify it from Scripture, not find out what Scripture teaches about that subject. If we started with Scripture and asked what it taught, we should never, never, discover even the simplest datum of rabbinic law. When we start with the answers -- the rabbinic law -- and ask how Scriptures can be made to justify that law, the answers are anything but perspicuous. That the authorities of Mishnah-Tosefta understood these facts full well seems strongly implied by their conception of two Torahs, one written, the other oral.

Having carefully distinguished Mishnaic from Pentateuchal conceptions in respect to utensils and Tents, Kelim and Ohalot, we now see that there is virtually no fundamental and reciprocal relationship whatever. True, as I said, a few verses in Leviticus prove not only relevant to Kelim but also formative of elements in the basic stratum of laws, and the same seems so for Numbers and Ohalot. But the generative concept, the

mythopoeic event or force, from which the Mishnaic tractates
emerge is not Scripture, precisely as the rabbis of the second
and later centuries claim, but an entirely separate "Torah" --
"revelation" in theological language.

We have, therefore, to ask about the relationships between
the two "Torahs," Scripture and Mishnah, just as did the
third-century exegetes who stand behind much of Sifra and
Sifre. We eliminate one theoretical relationship at the
outset: the historical and exegetical relationship. Because
of their utter disparity, I cannot see how the two Torahs
relate in some causal and sequential way, the written one
first, which then originates or generates the oral one. And,
it follows, exegesis of the Written Torah, the Pentateuch, did
not create, and does not stand behind, the fundamental conceptions of the Oral one, the Mishnah, although once those primal
conceptions were in being, the Pentateuch obviously would shape
their articulation.[10]

---

[10]Since this is so obvious, I am at a loss to explain
why Frankel came to such a conclusion and why so many thereafter persisted in it. I look in vain for a twentieth-century
scholarly account of "Oral Torah," whether in encyclopedias or
in more sustained studies, which does not tell us about how
"the rabbis" from Ezra to the first century spun out through
the exegesis of Scriptures the laws now found in Mishnah. The
explanations of why we have no evidence that such "rabbis"
existed are diverse and very imaginative. And a further
curiosity in the intellectual history of modern Jewish scholarship is why the name of Sherira Gaon, who originally proposed
the theory of the exegetical foundation of Mishnah, is mentioned only uncommonly. I recommend, as by far the best
account of the established theory, Jacob Z. Lauterbach,
"Midrash and Mishnah" in his Rabbinic Essays, edited by Lou H.
Silberman (Cincinnati, 1951), pp. 163-258. Lauterbach does
credit Sherira (p. 166, n. 4). He himself states, "Modern
scholars have...recognized it as an established historic fact
that the Midrash was originally the exclusive form in which all
teachings of the Halakah were given." "Mishnah-form is of a
much later date" (p. 167). I think that, standing by itself,
that statement is valid. We have ample evidence of various
types of exegesis of Scripture -- none of it "rabbinic," to be
sure -- in the period before 70, while what Lauterbach calls
Mishnah-form is not apt to derive much earlier than the middle
of the first century A.D. The rabbinic traditions about the
Pharisees, for example, do not even allege that that form
pertains to sayings of authorities before Shammai and Hillel,
who are the first to be given an ample corpus of materials in
standard attributive form (X says...) for instance, not to
mention in the form of disputes (Statement of problem, X
says...Y says...). But, it is clear, the issue is not whether
there were exegeses, nor whether these exegeses are preserved
in forms given them before 70. The issue is the origins of the
fundamental conceptions of the "Oral Torah" now contained in
Mishnah. Since the exegetical compilations alleged to contain
the beginnings of the Oral Torah make no pretense of proving

The sole reciprocal relationship we can describe, therefore, is conceptual, or, in a loose sense of the word, metaphysical. And here the relationship is amazingly close. The two Torahs complement one another, are necessary to one another, balance and complete the conceptions of one another. The world-view of the one invites and instigates the reflections which lay the foundations of the other.[11]

Specifically, in the case of Kelim, we noticed that the sources of uncleanness specified in Scripture are things which break the natural and normal course of life, the unusual or the abnormal (or, that which was perceived in remote times of antiquity to be unnatural or abnormal). Objects which are abnormal or useless are not affected by these processes. Susceptible to the unusual and abnormal are things which are commonplace, normal, everyday, and useful. The negative, the out-of-the-ordinary and disharmonious, affects the positive, that which is whole and complete. There is a striking correspondence between the priestly conception, in Leviticus, of the sources of uncleanness and the Mishnaic conception, in Kelim, of objects susceptible to the uncleanness imparted by those sources.

For Ohalot, we may discern parallel correpondences. When someone dies, a change affects the economy of nature. The body which has housed the person lies lifeless. Scripture is clear that that body produces "uncleanness," specifying the various ways in which the uncleanness is transferred and the things affected by it. (This imbalance specified by Scripture uses the language "uncleanness" to refer to that which has taken place, and we do not have to diverge from that language.) What then happens to the uncleanness released from the body? Where does it go? What is it?

The Oral Torah's answer, suggested above, is that that uncleanness now will find a new container, something which will keep and contain it as the body has done. What will do so? Something a handbreadth in height, breadth, and depth, with adequate entry (thus: egress) for the effusion of the corpse

---

the most basic convictions of the Oral Torah, so far as our tractates are concerned, it is difficult to find much evidence in favor of the theory that those conceptions begin in exegesis. But, it is to be stressed, that is simply beside the point.

[11]But, I repeat, this is a _post facto_ judgment, not a claim as to the generative force behind our tractate.

to find a way in. This new "house," the Tent, takes the place
of the old, the body, thus restoring the natural economy and
order. It may be envisioned as a "house"/Tent, or it may be
seen as something far more abstract, simply as that which will
prevent the passage of uncleanness, keeping it in ("bringing
the uncleanness") or preventing its entry ("interposing against
the uncleanness"). The two processes, interposition or
containment, are one and the same thing. The point of interest
of the Oral Torah, therefore, is in righting the imbalance
specified by the written one, in explaining how the whole,
complete order or economy -- the whole house -- in reality is
to be conceived. The Written Torah tells about the unbal-
ancing, the Oral Torah records the restoration of the wholeness
and completeness, the order and perfect form, of reality. This
so for both Kelim and Ohalot.

I therefore affirm the view of Mary Douglas, who sees the
total structure of purity laws as a "symbolic system."[12] She
says, "A symbolic system consists of rules of behavior, actions
and expectations which constitute society itself. The rules
which generate and sustain society allow meanings to be
realized which otherwise would be undefined and ungraspable...
In the case of the Bible, purity and impurity are the dominant
contrastive categories leading to holiness. As in any social
system, these rules are specifications which draw analogies
between states. The cumulative power of the analogies enables
one situation to be matched to another, related by equivalence,
negation, hierarchy and inclusion... The purity rules of the
Bible... set up the great inclusive categories in which the
whole universe is hierarchized and structured. Access to their
meaning comes by mapping the same basic set of rules from one
context to another." Douglas argues that each set of purity
rules matches the next: "In this exercise the classification
of animals into clean and unclean, the classification of
peoples as pure and common, the contrast of blemished to
unblemished in the attributes of sacrificial victim, priest and
woman, create in the Bible an entirely consistent set of
criteria and values. The table, the marriage bed, and the
altar match each others' rules, as do the farmer, the husband
and the priest match each others' roles in the total pattern...."

---

[12]Stated in my Idea of Purity in Ancient Judaism
(Leiden, 1974), pp. 138ff.

Unintentionally, and in a very circuitous way, I have found the relationship between the conceptions of purity, the respective articulations of the rules, of the Written and the Oral Torahs, to supply an apt illustration of Douglas's proposition. She has argued that the purity laws are a set of expressions, in discrete materials, of a single set of cogent and coherent categories, each parallel to the next, all necessary for a complete, whole conception of reality. In much the same way, the two Torahs, Written and Oral, create an entirely cogent and consistent set of conceptions. If we had one without the other, our structure (our "metaphysics") should be partial and incomplete. We can say what constitutes the incompleteness of the one Torah without the other, just as Douglas can say what constitutes the uncleanness of the unclean animals and the cleanness of the clean. Just as she has told us about a whole symbolic system, so we have been able to discern elements in a vast expansion and completion of that same whole symbolic system, though only through discerning what must be a very tiny part of the metaphysic.

Yet that is not the whole story. Clearly, the people who stand behind those segments of the metaphysic we discover in Kelim and Ohalot (and expect to see elsewhere) have done a great deal of selection. Why, after all, should a handful of verses in Leviticus have produced so vast a tractate as Kelim? The uncomplicated picture of Numbers 19:11ff. has been made to yield the extraordinarily complex laws of Ohalot. So what has been selected is not merely the Scriptural themes. Someone at some point has seen as terribly important what Scripture at best alludes to, and then not in a conceptual framework remotely resembling what is before us in Oral Torah. A world-view is contained within the laws of the Oral Torah. As I said, that world-view not only corresponds to, but also complements and completes, the conceptions, such as they are, of the Written Torah. Yet the disproportions, the disequilibrium are such as to prevent our claiming anything like balance and correspondence.

Two massive and all-encompassing conceptions of reality -- the one now in the Priestly Code, the other far in the background of Mishnaic law -- existed, each with its distinctive areas of emphasis, special obsessions, deep concerns. These are seen by us to be complementary, but this is only after the fact. To begin with, they were not. Why not? Because to the Priestly legislator, what is in the center of things is the

cult. Utensils made unclean are not used in the cult. That is
nearly the whole story, and a very minor story at that. In
like manner, the person made unclean by a corpse cannot enter
the cult. The predicate expressing the ultimate value in both
cases is cultic. For the Oral Torah, by contrast, the obses-
sion is not with the cult, which rarely explicitly occurs, but
with the _fact_ of cleanness or uncleanness itself. Uncleanness
affects pots or houses, is contained or released, creeps
through windows and doors or is kept out. The laws before us
see cleanness and uncleanness not as contingent, dependent upon
the cult for their importance, but as important in and of
themselves. That does not mean that for the Priestly legislator uncleanness was relative and not absolute, immaterial and
not material. To him it was very real. But its _importance_ --
not its reality -- depended upon the cult. For the Mishnah, by
contrast, at times uncleanness may seem relative and immaterial, e.g., dependent upon a person's intention or conception
of usefulness or upon time and circumstance. But uncleanness
always is a given, a datum, assumed to affect _all_ of one's
affairs, not solely the cult or equivalent cultic activities.
The Priestly legislator _homogenizes_ all sorts and sources of
"uncleanness" within a single term, _tum'ah_. The Mishnaic
legislators _differentiate_ that simple "uncleanness," assigning
to it a rich vocabulary of highly articulated and definitive
words.[13]

Working with the same themes, and, I think, working partly
with the inherited materials of Scripture, the mind behind
Mishnaic law has given us something quite different from those
Scriptural materials. What is it?

It is the picture of the relevance and importance of
uncleanness as it must have existed _before_ the Priestly lawyers
took all modes and forms of uncleanness and turned them into a
single cultic concern. In Mishnah, as in the time before the
Priestly Code, uncleanness is everywhere consequential, not
merely in the cult. It is highly differentiated both as to

---

[13]I wholly accept the arguments of Baruch A. Levine, _In
the Presence of the Lord. Aspects of Ritual in Ancient Israel_
(Leiden, 1974) in behalf of the view that cleanness and
uncleanness were not relative but material and palpable
realities: "Underlying the priestly regulations relevant to
the purity of the sanctuary was a demonic conception of sin,
offense, and transgression." The contrary view, put forward by
W. Robertson Smith, _The Religion of the Semites_ (1889, repr.
New York, 1956) and copied by Y. Kaufmann, seems to me decisively refuted by Levine.

causes and as to effects. Mishnaic law seems, therefore, to carry us back to the situation prevailing before the Priestly reformulation of purity. It not merely complements Scripture but reverses and revises Scripture's basic assumptions.

I hasten to stress that in claiming our tractates give us the picture of the relevance and importance of uncleanness as these were understood before the compilation of the Priestly Code, in no way do I offer an historical statement, but rather, a phenomenological one. That is, we see clearly in P that the priestly lawyers have taken over a vast and differentiated variety of taboos and made all of them focus upon the Temple, even though, to begin with, many of them can have had little if anything to do with the cult in particular. The Pharisaic lawyers differentiate what was homogenized, as I said, and at the same time claim that cleanness and uncleanness are concerns of the home, the table, the bed, and much else, and not solely, or primarily, important in the cult. Accordingly, we may say that the traits of the Pharisaic and later rabbinic thought on cleanness and the supposition of the torahs of cleanness compiled and revised by the priestly writers of P are diametrically opposed, and that the priests of Leviticus and Numbers revised and rejected conceptions of the locus and meaning of uncleanness in no way alien, in principle, to those of the Pharisees and later rabbis.

So far as the second and third century rabbis were concerned, however, both Torahs, written and oral, came down from Sinai as one whole Torah. In a strange way we must now agree that the Oral Torah, contained in Mishnah-Tosefta, not only corresponds to but completes the Written Torah. The Oral Torah returns us to the conceptual world prevailing long before that time, restoring what was reformed by Leviticus. Perhaps a certain logic, inherent in the subject matter, dictated that there should have to be two Torahs, the written one for the cult, the oral, other one for the world outside the cult, one for the place of the holy, the other for the realm of the ordinary and profane. If indeed there is such an inherent logic, then it is that which we may conclude -- to speak in the language of rabbinic myth -- was truly revealed to Moses at Sinai, one whole Torah indeed, completing the sacred with the profane.

Chapter Three
FROM SCROLL TO SYMBOL
THE MEANING OF THE WORD TORAH

Judaism as we know it at the end of late antiquity reached
its now-familiar definition when "the Torah" lost its capital
letter and definite article and ultimately became torah. What
for nearly a millennium had been a particular scroll or book
thus came to serve as a symbol of an entire system. When a
rabbi spoke of torah, he no longer meant only a particular
object, a scroll and its contents. Now he used the word to
encompass a distinctive and well-defined world view and way of
life. Torah now stood for something one does, and knowledge of
the Torah promised not merely information about what people
were supposed to do, but ultimate redemption or salvation. The
shift in the use of the word, accomplished in a particular set
of writings out of Judaism in late antiquity, appears drama-
tically in the following tale:

> R. Kahana [a disciple] went and hid under Rab's [his
> master's] bed. Hearing Rab "discoursing" and joking with
> his wife...., [Kahana] said to [Rab], "You would think
> that Abba's [Rab's] mouth had never before tasted the
> dish." [Rab] said to [Kahana], "Kahana, are you here?
> Get out! This is disgraceful!" [Kahana] replied, "My
> lord, it is a matter of torah, and I have the need to
> learn" (B. Ber. 62a).

As soon as we ask ourselves what the word, torah, means in such
a context, we recognize the shift captured by the story. For
-- to state the obvious -- to study "the Torah," meaning the
Scriptures, one need not practice cultic voyeurism.

I

THE PROBLEM

If the word torah came to stand for something other than
the particular writings comprising the ancient Israelite
Scriptures, how do we trace the shift in usage and meaning?
Clearly, the progress of the word and its meanings, both
denotative and connotative, demands our attention. Within the

expansion and revision of the word, originally referring to a
set of books but in the end encompassing how one is to do even
the most intimate deeds, we uncover the formative history of
the Judaism for which the word Torah stands. That is the
Judaism of the "one whole Torah," both written and oral, of
"Moses, our rabbi," -- Judaism as it has flourished from late
antiquity to our own day.

When we take up the issue at hand, therefore, we confront
the symbol that stands for the kind of Judaism presented by the
Talmuds and related literature, defined by the authority of the
rabbis who stand behind those documents, and best described as
"the way of Torah." So far as outsiders supply the name of a
religion, the one at hand may be called "rabbinic Judaism," or
"talmudic Judaism," for its principal authority-figure or
authoritative document, or "normative Judaism," for the definitive theological status of the formulation at hand in the life
of the Jewish people. But so far as insiders name the religion, that is, find language to capture and encompass the whole
of what they do and believe, it is, as Kahana's statement tells
us, "torah," -- "and I need to learn..."

The Torah of Moses clearly occupied a critical place in
all systems of Judaism from the closure of the Torah-book, the
Pentateuch, in the time of Ezra onward. But in late antiquity,
for one group alone the book developed into an abstract and
encompassing symbol, so that in the Judaism that took shape in
the formative age, the first seven centuries A.D., everything
was contained in that one thing. How so? When we speak of
torah, in rabbinical literature of late antiquity, we no longer
denote a particular book, on the one side, or the contents of
such a book, on the other. Instead, we connote a broad range
of clearly distinct categories of noun and verb, concrete fact
and abstract relationship alike. "Torah" stands for a kind of
human being. It connotes a social status and a sort of social
group. It refers to a type of social relationship. It further
denotes a legal status and differentiates among legal norms.
As symbolic abstraction, the word encompasses things and
persons, actions and status, points of social differentiation
and legal and normative standing, as well as "revealed truth."
In all, the main points of insistence of the whole of Israel's
life and history come to full symbolic expression in that
single word. If people wanted to explain how they would be
saved, they would use the word Torah. If they wished to sort
out their parlous relationships with gentiles, they would use

the word Torah. Torah stood for salvation and accounted for
Israel's this-worldly condition and the hope, for both individual and nation alike, of life in the world to come. For the
kind of Judaism under discussion, therefore, the word Torah
stood for everything. The Torah symbolized the whole, at once
and entire. When, therefore, we wish to describe the unfolding
of the definitive doctrine of Judaism in its formative period,
the first exercise consists in paying close attention to the
meanings imputed to a single word.

II
THE PROBLEM OF THE MISHNAH

Upon its closure, the Mishnah gained an exalted political
status as the constitution of Jewish government of the Land of
Israel. Accordingly, the clerks who knew and applied its law
had to explain the standing of that law, meaning its relationship to the law of the Torah. But the Mishnah provided no
account of itself. Unlike biblical law codes, the Mishnah
begins with no myth of its own origin. It ends with no doxo-
logy. Discourse commences in the middle of things and ends
abruptly. What follows from such laconic mumbling is that the
exact status of the document required definition entirely
outside the framework of the document itself. The framers of
the Mishnah having given no hint of the nature of their book,
the Mishnah reached the political world of Israel without a
trace of self-conscious explanation or any theory of validation.
   The one thing that is clear, alas, is negative. The
framers of the Mishnah nowhere claim, implicitly or explicitly,
that what they have written forms part of the Torah, enjoys the
status of God's revelation to Moses at Sinai, or even systematically carries forward secondary exposition and application
of what Moses wrote down in the wilderness. Later on, I think
two hundred years beyond the closure of the Mishnah, the need
to explain the standing and origin of the Mishnah led some to
posit two things. First, God's revelation of the Torah at
Sinai encompassed the Mishnah as much as Scripture. Second,
the Mishnah was handed on through oral formulation and oral
transmission from Sinai to the framers of the document as we
have it. These two convictions, fully exposed in the ninth-
century letter of Sherira, in fact emerge from the references
of both Talmuds to the dual Torah. One part is in writing.
The other was oral and now is in the Mishnah.

As for the Mishnah itself, however, it contains not a hint that anyone has heard any such tale. The earliest apologists for the Mishnah, represented in Abot, know nothing of the fully-realized myth of the dual Torah of Sinai. It may be that the authors stood too close to the Mishnah to see the Mishnah's standing as a problem or to recognize the task of accounting for its origins. Certainly they never refer to the Mishnah as something out there, nor speak of the document as autonomous and complete. Only the two Talmuds reveal that conception -- alongside their mythic explanation of where the document came from and why it should be obeyed. In any event, the absence of explicit expression of such a claim in behalf of the Mishnah requires little specification. It is just not there.

But the absence of an implicit claim demands explanation. When ancient Jews wanted to gain for their writings the status of revelation, of torah, or at least to link what they thought to what the Torah had said, they could do one of four things. They could sign the name of a holy man of old, for instance, Adam, Enoch, Ezra. They could imitate the Hebrew style of Scripture. They could claim that God had spoken to them. They could, at the very least, cite a verse of Scripture and impute to the cited passage their own opinion. These four methods -- pseudepigraphy, stylistic imitation (hence, forgery), claim of direct revelation from God, and eisegesis -- found no favor with the Mishnah's framers. To the contrary, they signed no name to their book. Their Hebrew was new in its syntax and morphology, completely unlike that of the Mosaic writings of the Pentateuch. They never claimed that God had anything to do with their opinions. They rarely cited a verse of Scripture as authority. It follows that, whatever the authors of the Mishnah said about their document, the implicit character of the book tells us that they did not claim God had dictated or even approved what they had to say. Why not? The framers simply ignored all the validating conventions of the world in which they lived. And, as I said, they failed to make explicit use of any others.

It follows that we do not know whether the Mishnah was supposed to be part of the Torah or to enjoy a clearly-defined relationship to the existing Torah. We also do not know what else, if not the Torah, was meant to endow the Mishnah's laws with heavenly sanction. To state matters simply, we do not know what the framers of the Mishnah said they had made, nor do we know what the people who received and were supposed to obey the Mishnah thought they possessed.

A survey of the uses of the word "Torah" in the Mishnah to be sure, provides us with an account of how the framers of the Mishnah, founders of what would emerge as rabbinic Judaism, understood by that term. But it will not tell us how they related their own ideas to the Torah. Nor shall we find a trace of evidence of that fully articulated way of life -- the use of the word Torah to categorize and classify persons, places, things, relationships, all manner of abstractions -- that we find fully exposed in some later-redacted writings.

III

TORAH AS INDICATOR OF STATUS IN THE MISHNAH

The most striking step away from meaning by the word Torah or "the Torah," a particular thing or "something like a particular thing," occurs in the Mishnah's sense of Torah in which the word denotes a particular status. That status obtains either by itself or (more commonly) in contradistinction to another, lesser status. Specifically, the Mishnah will refer to a teaching that enjoys the standing or authority of the Torah, usually as distinct from a teaching that does not. The other, lesser teaching or rule rests upon the authority, not of what is written in the Torah, but of what is laid down by an (in the Mishnah) otherwise-unidentified class or caste, "the scribes." The clearest statement of the distinction will have both "Torah" and "scribes" juxtaposed, as "the words of Torah...the words of scribes..."

In the present context, I must stress, the meaning of "written Torah" exhausts the intent of all the passages that refer to "Torah...scribes...." Every instance understands that "the words of Torah" are written in Scripture, that is, derive from the Torah-scroll. So we stand well within the connotations attributed to the Torah-scroll as object, when we find this (evidently) secondary usage. Just as "the Torah" or "Torah" connotes "revealed doctrine," so the "standing" or "authority" of "the Torah" validates a particular rule or detail of the law. Accordingly, the connotative sense of the word, "Torah," easily encompasses the present usage. But we do observe that although the usage has not become entirely abstract, "Torah" here has lost all concrete and material relationship to a given book. For Torah here stands for something entirely abstract, namely, an imputed status. But the status imputed to a given rule or person in no way compares that rule or person to a book. So the abstraction is complete.

IV

WRITTEN AND ORAL TORAH IN THE MISHNAH

The distinction between the oral Torah and the written Torah does not occur in the Mishnah, nor do the formulations, torah shebikhtav and torah shebe^cal peh. No passage demands the meaning, "not-written-down-Torah." None makes clear reference to a corpus of doctrine external to the written Torah, yet bearing correlative authority, and thus "oral Torah." Quite to the contrary, the contrast between the status of Torah ("words of Torah") and the status of authorita-tive-but-not-Torah ("teachings of scribes") precludes the conception of two Torahs of equal standing and authority, both deriving from God's revelation to Moses at Mount Sinai. Let me restate a simple, probative fact. Every Mishnah-passage in which "the Torah" speaks, or in which people refer to "Torah" in either a denotative way or connotative setting, alludes to what is in the written Torah, either in general -- as a status -- or in particular, as a source of the given fact adduced in evidence.

Accordingly, in the Mishnah not only does "the Torah" or "Torah" not denote the myth of the dual Torah. It also in no way even connotes it. All the evidence of the Mishnah points to a single conclusion, in two parts. First, no one in the Mishnah has heard of any Torah revealed by God to Moses at Sinai except for the one in writing. Second, no one in the Mishnah imagines that the Mishnah, in particular, either derived from revelation at Sinai or even related to it. Whatever its authors thought the Mishnah was supposed to be, they never indicated that it enjoyed the status of Torah.

V

TORAH AS A SOURCE OF SALVATION IN THE MISHNAH

The Torah in the fully realized Judaism of the Palestinian and Babylonian Talmuds represents a source of salvation under one of two conditions. Either the individual, through study of the Torah and obedience to its teachings, achieves life after death, or the people Israel, through study of the Torah, is saved from this-worldly disasters of a national or local character, or, through the Torah, draws nearer the coming of the Messiah and the eschatological rewards of the age to come. The conviction that the individual is saved through the Torah

is amply expressed in Abot, where we see promises of direct
encounter with God through study of the Torah. The nation at
large in both Talmuds is promised salvation, through the
Messiah's coming, from all manner of troubles afflicting the
community. This salvation depends on loyalty to the Torah.
Studying the Torah acts under some conditions like repetition
of an incantation; and the Torah forms a powerful source of
supernatural or magical power. But none of these convictions,
broadly represented in both Talmuds and a few correlative
documents, makes its appearance in the Mishnah. I know of no
passage in which the Torah is other than a particular object,
on the one side, or an indicator of status, on the other. Just
as the Mishnah exhibits no myth of its own origins, so the
framers of the document fail to endow with mythic character the
Torah of Moses at Sinai. The scroll remains just that: a
document, its teachings, their secondary effects and nothing
more.

VI
THE MISHNAH AND THE TORAH

When the authors of the Mishnah surveyed the landscape of
Israelite writings down to their own time, they saw only Sinai,
that is, what we now know as Scripture. Based on the documents
they cite or mention, we can say with certainty that they knew
the pentateuchal law. We may take for granted that they
accepted as divine revelation also the Prophets and the Writings, to which they occasionally make reference. That they
regarded as a single composition, that is, as revelation, the
Torah, Prophets and Writings, appears from their references to
the Torah, as a specific "book," and to a Torah-scroll.
Accordingly, one important meaning associated with the word
Torah, was concrete in the extreme. The Torah was a particular
book or set of books, regarded as holy, revealed to Moses at
Sinai. That fact presents no surprise, since the Torah-
scroll(s) had existed, it is generally assumed, for many
centuries before the closure of the Mishnah in A.D. 200.

What is surprising is that everything from the formation
of the canon of the Torah to their own day seems to have proved
null in their eyes. Between the Mishnah and Mount Sinai lay a
vast, empty plain. From the perspective of the Torah-myth as
they must have known it, from Moses and the prophets, to before
Judah the Patriarch, lay a great wasteland. So the concrete

and physical meaning attaching to the word Torah, that is, the
Torah, the Torah revealed by God to Moses at Mount Sinai
(including the books of the Prophets and the Writings), bore a
contrary implication. Beyond The Torah there was no torah.
Besides the Pentateuch, Prophets, and Writings, not only did no
physical scroll deserve veneration, but no corpus of writings
demanded obedience. So the very limited sense in which the
words, the Torah, were used passed a stern judgment upon
everything else, all the other writings that we know circulated
widely, in which other Jews alleged that God had spoken and
said "these things."

The range of the excluded possibilities that other Jews
explored demands no survey. It includes everything, not only
the Gospels (by A.D. 200 long since in the hands of outsiders),
but secret books, history books, psalms, wisdom-writings,
rejected works of prophecy -- everything excluded from any
biblical canon by whoever determined there should be a canon.
If the library of the Essenes at Qumran tells us what might
have been, then we must regard as remarkably impoverished the
(imaginary) library that would have served the authors of the
Mishnah: the Book of Books, but nothing else. We seldom see
so stern, so austere a vision of what commands the status of
holy revelation among Judaisms over time. The tastes of the
Mishnah's authors express a kind of literary iconoclasm, but
with a difference. The literary icons did survive in the
Churches of Christendom. But in their own society and sacred
setting, the judgment of Mishnah's authors would prevail from
its time to ours. Nothing in the Judaisms of the Israelite
heritage from the Hebrew Scriptures' time to the Mishnah's day
would survive the implacable rejection of the framers of the
Mishnah, unless under Christian auspices or buried in caves.
So when we take up that first and simplest meaning associated
with the word Torah, "The Torah," we confront a stunning
judgment: this and nothing else, this alone, this thing alone
of its kind and no other thing of similar kind.

We confront more than a closing off of old possibilities,
ancient claims to the status of revelation. For, at the other
end, out of the Torah as a particular thing, a collection of
books, would emerge a new and remarkably varied set of meanings. Possibilities first generated by the fundamental meaning
imputed to the word Torah would demand realization. How so?
Once the choice for the denotative meaning of the Torah became
canonical in the narrowest possible sense, the ranges of

connotative meaning imputed to the Torah stretched forth to an
endless horizon. So the one concrete meaning, made possible
many abstract ones, all related to that single starting-point.
Only at the end shall we clearly grasp, in a single tableau,
the entire vista of possibilities. To begin with, it suffices
to note that the Mishnah's theory of the Torah not only closed,
but also opened, many paths.

VII

TOWARD A THEORY OF THE MISHNAH IN ABOT

Tractate Abot ("Founders") presents sayings assigned to
authorities from "the Men of the Great Assembly," otherwise
unidentified, to sages of the generation beyond Judah the
Patriarch. These latter figures are assumed to have lived in
the early part of the third century, so Abot will have come to
closure no earlier than 250. The prominence of the term Torah,
in the tractate demands that the reader review the entire
document and delineate not only the several usages, but also
the larger theory of the matter. This verbatim survey also
will point to what we do not find.

Abot provides no account of the origin and authority of
the Mishnah as a finished document. The framers make no
explicit reference to the Mishnah at all. But there is an
implicit message. For when they speak about Torah, their
composition encompasses sayings of principal figures of the
Mishnah. It must follow that the authors or compilers see a
connection between the Torah, specifically, revelation of God
to Moses at Mount Sinai, and the authorities of the contents of
the Mishnah, that is, things said by Mishnah's sages. So while
the Mishnah as such makes no explicit appearance, that is not
the whole theory of the matter. The chain of tradition from
Sinai extends through unknown and legendary figures, such as
the Men of the Great Assembly, to known and familiar ones, such
as Shammai, Hillel, and their disciples and heirs. Hillel's
successors comprise both his family, through his son and
grandson -- hence the patriarchal house of Judah itself -- and
his disciples, through Yohanan ben Zakkai. Henceforward, then,
we find such well-known and commonplace names as Joshua,
Eliezer, Aqiba, Meir, Judah, Simeon, and the like.

This means that the important authorities of the Mishnah
are placed in a direct line with Sinai. That should also carry
the implication that their opinions, assembled in the Mishnah,

enjoy the status of revelation. But Abot does not specify the
Mishnah as the principal vehicle for the transmission of the
Torah of Sinai, hence as part of the one whole Torah of Moses,
our rabbi. That vehicle, for Abot, proves personal and human,
namely, the sage himself. True, the sage is not called a
Torah, but neither is the Mishnah. The status of Torah appears
to encompass the sage. But the metaphor of the Torah does not
envelop the sages' book, the Mishnah. My guess is that for
Abot the Mishnah does not present a critical problem of apolo-
getics. Why not? Because the Mishnah for Abot has not yet
gained the standing of a completed and autonomous document
(whether orally published or otherwise). It is not "out
there," a distinct and authoritative text. The Mishnah still
forms a stage in the process of tradition in a chain made up of
human links, that is, of sages, and not of documentary ones,
that is, of completed books.

The importance of tractate Abot to our inquiry requires
specification. The claim that the Mishnah derives from Sinai
and forms the oral part of "the one whole Torah of Moses our
rabbi" generally refers back to the tractate at hand. People
find that assertion at Abot 1:1-18. In fact, Abot disappoints
those who seek in its apophthegms the source for the opinion
that, first, two Torahs came from Sinai, and, second, the
Mishnah and documents flowing from it constitute one of those
two Torahs. The document knows that it is important to study
Torah. It nowhere cites -- e.g., as a proof text -- a passage
of the Mishnah or in some other way represents the Mishnah as
Torah. The Mishnah as a whole is unknown to Abot; in it, not a
single line of the other 62 tractates merits even remote
allusion. Indeed, as an apologetic in behalf of the Mishnah,
the tractate at hand performs remarkably slight service. For,
as I have stressed, its connection to the Mishnah lies only in
the names of sages appearing both in Abot and in other tractates of the Mishnah. But the teachings that sages deliver in
Abot -- their wise sayings -- are not represented as Torah.
And, more decisively, those sayings do not square with anything
stated by the same sages anywhere else in the Mishnah. So Abot
demonstrates importantly something other than what has been
conventionally deduced from it.

VIII
TORAH AND SAGACITY IN ABOT

Abot draws into the orbit of Torah-talk the names of authorities of the Mishnah. But Abot does not claim that the Mishnah forms part of the Torah. Nor, obviously, does the tractate know the doctrine of the two Torahs. Only in the Talmuds do we begin to find clear and ample evidence of that doctrine. Abot, moreover, does not understand by the word Torah much more than the framers of the Mishnah do. Not only does the established classification-scheme remain intact, but the sense of the items we have surveyed essentially replicates already familiar usages, producing no innovation.

Yet Abot in the aggregate _does_ differ from the Mishnah. The difference has to do with the topic at hand. The other sixty-two tractates of the Mishnah contain Torah-sayings here and there. But they do not fall within the framework of Torah-discourse. They speak about other matters entirely. The consideration of the status of Torah rarely pertains to that speech. Abot, by contrast, says a great deal about Torah-study. The claim that Torah-study produces direct encounter with God forms the heart and soul of Abot's thesis about the Torah. That claim, by itself, will hardly have surprised Israelite writers of wisdom-books over a span of many centuries, whether those assembled in the Essene commune at Qumran, on the one side, or those represented in the pages of Proverbs and in many of the Psalms, or even the Deuteronomistic circle, on the other.

A second glance at our tractate, however, produces a surprising fact. In Abot, Torah is instrumental. The figure of the sage, his ideals and conduct, forms the goal, focus, and center. To state matters simply: Abot regards study of Torah as what a sage does. The substance of Torah is what a sage says. That is so whether or not the saying relates to Scriptural revelation. The content of the sayings attributed to sages endows those sayings with self-validating status. The sages usually do not quote verses of Scripture and explain them, nor do they speak in God's name. Yet, it is clear, sages talk Torah. What follows? It is this: if a sage says something, what he says is Torah. More accurately, what he says falls into the classification of Torah. Accordingly, as I said, Abot treats Torah-learning as symptomatic, an indicator of the status of the sage, hence, as I said, as merely instrumental.

The simplest proof of that proposition lies in the recurrent formal structure of the document, the one thing the framers of the document never omit and always emphasize: (1) the name of the authority behind a saying, from Moses on downward, and (2) the connective-attributive, "says." So what is important to the redactors is what they never have to tell us. Because a recognized sage makes a statement, what he says constitutes, in and of itself, a statement in the status of Torah.

To spell out what this means, let us look at the opening sentences: "Moses received Torah, and it reached the Men of the Great Assembly." The three things those men said bear no resemblance to anything we find in the written Scriptures. They focus upon the life of sagacity -- prudence, discipleship, a fence around the Torah. And, as we proceed, we find time and again that, while the word Torah stands for two things, divine revelation and the act of study of divine revelation, it produces a single effect, the transformation of unformed man into sage. One climax comes in Yohanan ben Zakkai's assertion that the purpose for which a man (an Israelite) was created was to study Torah, followed by his disciples' specifications of the most important things to be learned in the Torah. All of these pertain to the conduct of the wise man, the sage.

When we review the classifications among which we may divide references to Torah in Abot, we find the consequent catalogues merely perfunctory. In fact in those taxa we miss the most important points of emphasis of the tractate. That is why, as I said, we have to locate the document's focus not on Torah but on the life of sagacity (including, to be sure, Torah-study). But what defines and delimits Torah? It is the sage himself. So we may simply state the tractate's definition of Torah: Torah is what a sage learns. Accordingly, the Mishnah contains Torah. It may well be thought to fall into the classification of Torah. But the reason, we recognize, is that authorities whose sayings are found in the Mishnah possess Torah from Sinai. What they say, we cannot overemphasize, is Torah. How to we know it? It is a fact validated by the association of what they say with their own names.

So we miss the real issue when we ask Abot to explain for us the status of the Mishnah, or to provide a theory of a dual Torah. The principal point of insistence -- the generative question -- before the framers of Abot does not address the status of the Mishnah. And the instrumental status of the

Torah, as well as of the Mishnah, lies in the net effect of
their composition: the claim that through study of the Torah,
sages enter God's presence. So study of Torah serves a further
goal, that of forming sages. The theory of Abot pertains to
the religious standing and consequence of the learning of the
sages. To be sure, a secondary effect of that theory endows
with the status of revealed truth things sages say. But then,
as I have stressed, it is because they say them, not because
they have heard them in an endless chain back to Sinai. The
fundament of truth is passed on through sagacity, not through
already formulated and carefully memorized truths. That is why
the single most important word in Abot also is the most common,
the word "says."

At issue in Abot is not Torah, but the authority of the
sage. It is that standing that transforms a saying into a
Torah-saying, or to state matters more appropriately, that
places a saying into the classification of Torah. Abot then
stands as the first document of incipient rabbinism, that is,
of the doctrine that the sage embodies the Torah and is a holy
man, like Moses "our rabbi," in the likeness and image of God.
The beginning is to claim that a saying falls into the category
of Torah if a sage says it as Torah. The end will be to view
the sage himself as Torah incarnate.

IX

WRITTEN AND ORAL TORAH IN THE TALMUD OF THE LAND OF ISRAEL

The Mishnah is held equivalent to Scripture (Y. Hor.
3:5). But the Mishnah is not called Torah. Still, as I have
pointed out, once the Mishnah entered the status of Scripture,
it would take but a short step to a theory of the Mishnah as
part of the revelation at Sinai -- hence, oral Torah. But
sages recorded in this Talmud do not appear to have taken that
step.

In the Talmud at hand, we find the first glimmerings of an
effort to theorize in general, not merely in detail, about how
specific teachings of Mishnah relate to specific teachings of
Scripture. The citing of scriptural proof texts for mishnaic
propositions, after all, would not have caused much surprise to
the framers of the Mishnah; they themselves included such
passages, though not often. But what conception of the Torah
underlies such initiatives, and how do Yerushalmi sages propose
to explain the phenomenon of the Mishnah as a whole? The

following passage gives us one statement. It refers to the
assertion at M. Hag. 1:8D that the laws on cultic cleanness
presented in the Mishnah rest on deep and solid foundations in
the Scripture.

Y. Hag. 1:7.V

> [A] <u>The laws of the Sabbath [M. 1:8B]</u>: R. Jonah said R.
> Hama bar Uqba raised the question [in reference to M.
> Hag. 1:8D's view that there are many verses of
> Scripture on cleanness], "And lo, it is written only,
> 'Nevertheless a spring or a cistern holding water
> shall be clean; but whatever touches their carcass
> shall be unclean' (Lev. 11:36). And from this verse
> you derive many laws. [So how can M. 1:8D say what
> it does about many verses for laws of cultic clean-
> ness?]"
>
> [B] R. Zeira in the name of R. Yohanan: "If a law comes
> to hand and you do not know its nature, do not
> discard it for another one, for lo, many laws were
> stated to Moses at Sinai, and all of them have been
> embedded in the Mishnah."

The truly striking assertion appears at B. The Mishnah
now is claimed to contain statements made by God to Moses.
Just how these statements found their way into the Mishnah, and
which passages of the Mishnah contain them, we do not know.
That is hardly important, given the fundamental assertion at
hand. The passage proceeds to a further, and far more consequential, proposition. It asserts that part of the Torah was
written down, and part was preserved in memory and transmitted
orally. In context, moreover, that distinction must encompass
the Mishnah, thus explaining its origin as part of the Torah.
Here is a clear and unmistakable expression of the distinction
between two forms in which a single Torah was revealed and
handed on at Mount Sinai, part in writing, part orally. While
the passage below does not make use of the language, <u>Torah</u>-
in-writing and <u>Torah</u>-by-memory, it does refer to "the written"
and "the oral." I believe myself fully justified in supplying
the word "Torah" in square brackets. The reader will note,
however, that the word Torah likewise does not occur at K, L.
Only when the passage reaches its climax, at M, does it break
down into a number of categories -- Scripture, Mishnah, Talmud,
laws, lore. It there makes the additional point that <u>every-
thing</u> comes from Moses at Sinai. So the fully articulated
theory of <u>two Torahs</u> (not merely one Torah in two forms) does
not reach final expression in this passage. But short of
explicit allusion to <u>Torah</u>-in-writing and <u>Torah</u>-by-memory,

which (so far as I am able to discern) we find mainly in the
Talmud of Babylonia, the ultimate theory of Torah of formative
Judaism is at hand in what follows.

Y. Hag. 1:7.V

[D]   R. Zeirah in the name of R. Eleazar: "'Were I to
      write for him my laws by ten thousands, they would be
      regarded as a strange thing' (Hos. 8:12). Now is the
      greater part of the Torah written down? [Surely
      not. The oral part is much greater.] But more
      abundant are the matters which are derived by exe-
      gesis from the written [Torah] than those derived by
      exegesis from the oral [Torah]."

[E]   And is that so?

[F]   But more cherished are those matters which rest upon
      the written [Torah] than those which rest upon the
      oral [Torah]

[J]   R. Haggai in the name of R. Samuel bar Nahman, "Some
      teachings were handed on orally, and some things were
      handed on in writing, and we do not know which of
      them is the more precious. But on the basis of that
      which is written, 'And the Lord said to Moses, Write
      these words; in accordance with these words I have
      made a covenant with you and with Israel' (Ex.
      34:27), [we conclude] that the ones which are handed
      on orally are the more precious."

[K]   R. Yohanan and R. Yudan b. R. Simeon -- One said, "If
      you have kept what is preserved orally and also kept
      what is in writing, I shall make a covenant with you,
      and if not, I shall not make a covenant with you."

[L]   The other said, "If you have kept what is preserved
      orally and you have kept what is preserved in writ-
      ing, you shall receive a reward, and if not, you
      shall not receive a reward."

[M]   [With reference to Deut. 9:10: "And on them was
      written according to all the words which the Lord
      spoke with you in the mount,"] said R. Joshua b.
      Levi, "He could have written, 'On them,' but wrote,
      'And on them." He could have written, 'All,' but
      wrote, 'According to all.' He could have written,
      'Words,' but wrote, 'The words.' [These then serve
      as three encompassing clauses, serving to include]
      Scripture, Mishnah, Talmud, laws, and lore. Even
      what an experienced student in the future is going to
      teach before his master already has been stated to
      Moses at Sinai."

[N]   What is the Scriptural basis for this view?

[O]   "There is no remembrance of former things, nor will
      there be any remembrance of later things yet to
      happen among those who come after" (Qoh. 1:11).

[P]   If someone says, "See, this is a new thing," his
      fellow will answer him, saying to him, "This has been
      around before us for a long time."

Here we have absolutely explicit evidence that people
believed part of the Torah had been preserved not in writing
but orally. Linking that part to the Mishnah remains a matter
of implication. But it surely comes fairly close to the

surface, when we are told that the Mishnah contains Torah-traditions revealed at Sinai. From that view it requires only a small step to the allegation that the Mishnah is part of the Torah, the oral part.

At the risk of repetitiousness, let us consider yet another example in which the same notion occurs. The following passage moves from the matter of translating from the written Torah into Aramaic, so that the congregation may understand the passage, to a distinction between two _forms_ of the Torah. The same discourse then goes over the ground we have just reviewed. The importance of the issue to the larger argument of this essay justifies our reviewing the whole.

The first point is that when the Torah (the written Scripture) is read in the synagogue, the original revelation is reenacted. God used Moses as intermediary. So the one who proclaims the Torah (God) must not be the one who then repeats Torah to the congregation (Moses). This further leads, at J, to the explicit statement that parts of the Torah were stated orally and parts in writing. Here, however, the part that is oral clearly means the Aramaic translation (Targum). In context, we need not invoke the conception of two kinds of one Torah, let alone of two Torahs constituting the one whole Torah of Moses our rabbi. That does not appear. Then, Kff., comes the familiar discussion about two modes of one Torah. This passage then precipitates a statement of what constitutes that whole Torah, written and oral. Here, as before, "Mishnah, Talmud, and lore" join Scripture. The main point again is the assertion that whatever a sage teaches falls into the category of the Torahs of Sinai. That point, of course, is familiar and conventional. First, what the sage says is Torah. Second, the sage cites Mishnah. Third, Mishnah is Torah.

Y. Megillah 4:1.II

> [G] R. Samuel bar R. Isaac went to a synagogue. He saw someone standing and serving as translator, leaning on a post. He said to him, "It is forbidden to you [to lean while standing]. For just as the Torah was given, originally, in fear and trembling, so we have to treat it with fear and trembling."
>
> [H] R. Haggai said R. Samuel bar R. Isaac went to a synagogue. He saw Hunah standing and serving as translator, and he had not set up anyone else in his stead [so he was both reading and translating himself]. He said to him, "It is forbidden to you, for just as it was given through an intermediary [namely, Moses] so we have to follow the custom of having an intermediary [so that the same person may not both read from the Torah and translate]."

[I]   R. Judah bar Pazzi went in and treated the matter as
       a question: "'The Lord spoke with you face to face
       at the mountain ... while I stood between the Lord
       and you at that time, to declare to you the word of
       the Lord'" (Deut. 5:4-5).
[J]   R. Haggai said R. Samuel bar R. Isaac went into a
       synagogue. He saw a teacher [reading from] a trans-
       lation spread out, presenting the materials from the
       book. He said to him, "It is forbidden to do it that
       way. Things which were stated orally must be pre-
       sented orally. Things which were stated in writing
       must be presented in writing."
[K]   R. Haggai in the name of R. Samuel bar Nahman: "Some
       teachings were stated orally, and some teachings were
       stated in writing, and we do not know which of the
       two is more precious.
[L]   "But on the basis of that which is written, 'And the
       Lord said to Moses, Write these words; in accordance
       with these words I have made a covenant with you and
       with Israel' (Ex. 34:27), that is to say that the
       ones which are handed on orally are more precious."
[M]   R. Yohanan and R. Judah b. R. Simeon -- one said,
       "[The meaning of the verse is this:] 'If you have
       kept what is handed on orally and if you have kept
       what is handed on in writing, then I shall make a
       covenant with you, and if not, I shall not make a
       covenant with you.'"
[N]   The other one said, "'If you have kept what is handed
       on orally, and if you have kept what is handed on in
       writing, then you will receive a reward, and if not,
       you will not receive a reward.'"
[O]   [With reference to the following verse: "And the
       Lord gave me the two tablets of stone written with
       the finger of God; and on them were all the words
       which the Lord had spoken with you on the mountain of
       the midst of the fire on the day of the assembly
       (Deut. 9:10,] said R. Joshua b. Levi, "[It is writ-
       ten,] 'on them,'and on them,' 'words,' 'the words,'
       'all,' 'with all.' [These additional usages serve
       what purpose?]
[P]   "The reference is to Scripture, Mishnah, Talmud, and
       lore -- and even what an experienced disciple is
       destined to teach in the future before his master has
       already been stated to Moses at Sinai."
[Q]   That is in line with the following verse of Scrip-
       ture: "Is there a thing of which it is said, 'See,
       this is new'? He and his fellow will reply to him,
       'It has been already in the ages before us'" (Qoh.
       1:10).

Here again, the penultimate statement of the theory of the
Torah of formative Judaism lies at hand. The final step is not
taken here, but it is a short step indeed.

                              X

        TORAH AS A SOURCE OF SALVATION IN THE YERUSHALMI

        To define the category at hand, I point to a story that
explicitly states the proposition that the Torah constitutes a

source of salvation. In this story we shall see that because people observed the rules of the Torah, they expected to be saved. And if they did not observe, they accepted their punishment. So the Torah now stands for something more than revelation and a life of study, and (it goes without saying) the sage now appears as a holy, not merely a learned, man. This is because his knowledge of the Torah has transformed him. Accordingly, we deal with a category of stories and sayings about the Torah entirely different from what has gone before.

Y. Taanit 3:8.II

[A] As to Levi ben Sisi: troops came to his town. He took a scroll of the Torah and went up to the roof and said, "Lord of the ages! If a single word of this scroll of the Torah has been nullified [in our town], let them come up against us, and if not, let them go their way."

[B] Forthwith people went looking for the troops but did not find them [because they had gone their way].

[C] A disciple of his did the same thing, and his hand withered, but the troops went their way.

[D] A disciple of his disciple did the same thing. His hand did not wither, but they also did not go their way.

[E] This illustrates the following apophthegm: You can't insult an idiot, and dead skin does not feel the scalpel.

What is interesting here is how taxa into which the word Torah previously fell have been absorbed and superseded in a new taxon. The Torah is an object: "He took a scroll...." It also constitutes God's revelation to Israel: "If a single word...." The outcome of the revelation is to form an on-going way of life, embodied in the sage himself: "A disciple of his did the same thing...." The sage plays an intimate part in the supernatural event: "His hand withered...." Now can we categorize this story as a statement that the Torah constitutes a particular object, or a source of divine revelation, or a way of life? Yes and no. The Torah here stands not only for the things we already have catalogued. It represents one more thing, which takes in all the others. Torah is a source of salvation. How so? The Torah stands for, or constitutes, the way in which the people Israel saves itself from marauders.

In the documents surveyed up to this point -- Mishnah, Abot -- we look in vain for sayings or stories that fall into such a category. True, we may take for granted that everyone always believed that, in general, Israel would be saved by

obedience to the Torah. That claim would not have surprised
any Israelite writers, from the first prophets down through the
final redactors of the Pentateuch in the time of Ezra, and
onward through the next seven hundred years. But, in the
rabbinical corpus from the Mishnah forward, the specific and
concrete assertion that by taking up the scroll of the Torah
and standing on the roof of one's house, confronting God in
heaven, a sage in particular could take action against the
expected invasion -- that kind of claim is not located, so far
as I know, in any composition surveyed so far.

Still, we cannot claim that the belief that the Torah in
the hands of the sage constituted a source of magical, supernatural, and hence salvific power, simply did not flourish
prior, let us say, to ca. A.D. 400. We cannot show that, hence
we do not know it. All we can say with assurance is that no
stories containing such a viewpoint appear in any rabbinical
document associated with the Mishnah. So what is critical here
is not the generalized category -- the genus -- of conviction
that the Torah serves as the source of Israel's salvation. It
is the concrete assertion -- the speciation of the genus --
that in the hands of the sage and under conditions specified,
the Torah may be utilized in pressing circumstances as Levi,
his disciple, and the disciple of his disciple, used it. That
is what is new.

To generalize: this stunningly new usage of Torah found
in the Talmud of the Land of Israel emerges from a group of
stories not readily classified in established categories. All
of these stories treat the word Torah, (whether scroll, contents, or act of study) as source and guarantor of salvation.
Accordingly, evoking the word Torah forms the centerpiece of a
theory of Israel's history, on the one side, and an account of
the teleology of the entire system, on the other. Torah indeed
has ceased to constitute a specific thing or even a category or
classification when stories about studying the Torah yield not
a judgment as to status (i.e., praise for the learned man) but
promise for supernatural blessing now and salvation in time to
come.

To the rabbis the principal salvific deed was to "study
Torah," by which they meant memorizing Torah-sayings by constant repetition, and, as the Talmud itself amply testifies,
(for some sages) profound analytic inquiry into the meaning of
those sayings. The innovation now is that this act of "study
of Torah" imparts supernatural power of a material character.

For example, by repeating words of Torah, the sage could ward
off the angel of death and accomplish other kinds of miracles
as well. So Torah-formulas served as incantations. Mastery of
Torah transformed the man engaged in Torah-learning into a
supernatural figure, who could do things ordinary folk could
not do. In the nature of things, the category of "Torah" had
already vastly expanded so that through transformation of the
Torah from a concrete thing to a symbol, a Torah-scroll could
be compared to a man of Torah, namely, a rabbi. Now, once the
principle had been established, that salvation would come from
keeping God's will in general, as Israelite holy men had
insisted for so many centuries, it was a small step for rabbis
to identify their particular corpus of learning, namely, the
Mishnah and associated sayings, with God's will expressed in
Scripture, the universally acknowledged medium of revelation.

Especially striking in the utilization of the Torah in the
rabbinical doctrine of salvation is the blurring of boundaries
between the nation and the individual. Formerly, individuals
required one kind of salvation from one set of problems, the
nation a different kind of salvation from another. Now the
Torah, as source of salvation, was made to serve both sets of
needs. Let me explain. Suffering afflicted both individual
and nation. Catastrophe in the form of a historical, one-time
event, such as the destruction of the Temple, was juxtaposed
with personal suffering and death. Accordingly, while the
troubles the nation and its people must be saved from were
many, the mode of salvation would be one and the same. The
consequence for the theory of salvation was this. The Torah
might protect a person from suffering or death, and the Torah
might also (in due course) save Israel from its subjugation to
the nations of the world. So for both the Jewish individual
and Israelite society, Torah would save Israel _from_ sin and
suffering, _for_ a life of Torah in Heaven as much as on earth.
How so? Since Heaven was conceived in the model of earth, so
that the analysis of traditions on earth corresponded to the
discovery of the principles of creation (as made explicit in
Genesis Rabbah), the full realization of the teachings of Torah
on earth, in the life of Israel, would transform Israel into a
replica of heaven on earth.

We deal, therefore, with a doctrine of salvation in which
the operative symbol, namely, Torah, and the determinative
deed, namely, Torah-learning, defined not only how to attain
salvation but also the very nature of that salvation. The

system thus was whole and coherent. Entering it at any point, we find ourselves at once within the structure as a whole. We enter a great, well-ordered hall, the inside of a world fully visible all at once, a kind of Globe Theater of Torah and of Israel. It is important, then, to recognize, as we do, that the profound issues confronting Israelite existence, national and personal alike, here and now, were framed in terms of Torah and resolved through the medium of Torah. Stated simply: salvation would come from Torah; and Torah defined the nature of salvation.

It had been for a long time an axiom of all forms of Judaism that, because Israel had sinned, it was punished by being given over into the hands of earthly empires; when it atoned, it was, and again would be, removed from their power. The means of atonement, reconciliation with God, were specified elsewhere as study of Torah, practice of commandments, and performance of good deeds. Why so? The answer is distinctive to the matrix of our Talmud: When Jews in general had mastered Torah, they would become sages (rabbis), just as some had already become sages -- saints and holy men of a particular sort. When all Jews became sages, they would no longer lie within the power of the nations, that is, of history. Then the Messiah would come. Redemption then depended upon all Israel's accepting the yoke of the Torah. Why so? Because at that point all Israel would attain a full and complete embodiment of Torah, revelation. Thus conforming to God's will and replicating Heaven on earth, Israel, as a righteous, holy community of sages would exercise the supernatural power of Torah. They would be able as a whole to accomplish what some few saintly rabbis now could do. With access to supernatural power, redemption would naturally follow.

XI

THE PALESTINIAN TALMUD'S THEORY OF THE TORAH

The key to this Talmud's theory of the Torah thus lies in its conception of the sage, to which that theory is subordinate. Once the sage reaches his full apotheosis as Torah incarnate, then, but only then, the Torah becomes (also) a source of salvation in the present concrete formulation of the matter. That is why we observed the doctrine of the Torah in the salvific process by elaborate citation of stories about sages, living Torahs, exercising the supernatural power of the

Torah, and serving, like the Torah itself, to reveal God's
will. Since the sage embodied the Torah and gave the Torah,
the Torah naturally came to stand for the principal source of
Israel's salvation, not merely a scroll, on the one side, or a
source of revelation, on the other.

The history of the symbolization of the Torah proceeds
from its removal from the framework of material objects, even
from the limitations of its own contents, to its transformation
into something quite different and abstract, quite distinct
from the document and its teachings. The Torah stands for this
something more, specifically, when it comes to be identified
with a living person, the sage, and endowed with those particular traits that the sage claimed for himself. While we
cannot say that the process of symbolization leading to the
pure abstraction at hand moved in easy stages, we may still
point to the stations that had to be passed in sequence. The
word Torah reached the apologists for the Mishnah in its
long-established meanings: Torah-scroll, contents of the
Torah-scroll. But even in the Mishnah itself, these meanings
provoked a secondary development, status of Torah as distinct
from other (lower) status, hence, Torah-teaching in contradistinction to scribal-teaching. With that small and simple step,
the Torah ceased to denote only a concrete and material thing
-- a scroll and its contents. It now connoted an abstract
matter of status. And once made abstract, the symbol entered a
secondary history beyond all limits imposed by the concrete
object, including its specific teachings, the Torah-scroll.

I believe that Abot stands at the beginning of this
process. In the history of the word Torah as abstract symbol,
a metaphor serving to sort out one abstract status from another
regained concrete and material reality of a new order entirely. For the message of Abot, as we saw, was that the Torah
served the sage. How so? The Torah indicated who was a sage
and who was not. Accordingly, the apology of Abot for the
Mishnah was that the Mishnah contained things sages had said.
What sages said formed a chain of tradition extending back to
Sinai. Hence it was equivalent to the Torah. The upshot is
that words of sages enjoyed the status of the Torah. The small
step beyond, I think, was to claim that what sages said was
Torah, as much as what Scripture said was Torah. And, a
further small step (and the steps need not have been taken
separately) moved matters to the position that there were two
forms in which the Torah reached Israel: one [Torah-]-in-writ-
ing, the other [Torah-]-handed-on-orally, that is, in memory.

The final step, fully revealed in the Talmud at hand, brought the conception of Torah to its logical conclusion: what the sage said was in the status of the Torah, was Torah, because the sage was Torah incarnate. So the abstract symbol now became concrete and material once more. We recognize the many, diverse ways in which the Talmud stated that conviction. Every passage in which knowledge of the Torah yields power over this world and the next, capacity to coerce to the sage's will the natural and supernatural worlds alike, rests upon the same viewpoint.

The Talmud's theory of the Torah carries us through several stages in the processes of the symbolization of the word Torah. First transformed from something material and concrete into something abstract and beyond all metaphor, the word Torah finally emerged once more in a concrete aspect, now as the encompassing and universal mode of stating the whole doctrine, all at once, of Judaism in its formative age.

Part Two

HISTORICAL STUDY OF FORMATIVE JUDAISM

Chapter Four
JOSEPHUS'S PHARISEES
A COMPLETE REPERTOIRE

In 1956, Morton Smith published a landmark study of
Josephus's pictures of the Pharisees, "Palestinian Judaism in
the First Century," in Moshe Davis, ed., Israel: Its Role in
Civilization (N.Y., 1956), pp. 67-81. In more than twenty-five
years since 1956, his discoveries have not made a perceptible
impact on the historical understanding of pre-70 Pharisaism.
Indeed, Heinz Schreckenberg, Bibliographie zu Flavius Josephus
(Leiden, 1968) between 1956 and 1968, pp. 263-312 lists no
studies at all of Josephus's Pharisees, excluding the extensive
citations in my Life of Yohanan ben Zakkai (Leiden, 1962,
1970[2], pp. 2, 166-171).

Furthermore, when Smith's article is alluded to, it is not
accurately summarized. Louis H. Feldman, Scholarship on Philo
and Josephus (1937-1962) Studies in Judaica (N.Y., 1963), p.
41b, states,

> Smith... notes that the Pharisees hardly figure in
> J[osephus's] account in BJ [= War] (2:162-3), but that in
> AJ [= Antiquities], written some twenty years later, the
> Pharisees take first place in the discussion of the Jewish
> sects; this shift is due, he says, to a desire to win
> support from the Romans for the Pharisees against the
> Sadducees; but the picture of the Pharisees in BJ, we may
> note, is fully as favorable as and not much shorter than
> that in AJ.

Smith's point, however, is not that the picture in War merely
is shorter, but that it omits the most important claim made
first in Antiquities, namely, that Palestine is ungovernable
without Pharisaic support. Length does not figure in Smith's
case. But as a matter of fact, Antiquities does contain
substantial materials not present in War. Apart from Feldman,
who is presently revising Scholarship and may be relied upon
for a more judicious account of Smith's article, I know of no
significant effort to confront, let alone make use of, Smith's
discoveries.

Here I wish to review the several references to Pharisees in Josephus's writings[1] and to spell out the sources in such a way that Smith's study will both receive the attention it deserves and be shown to be wholly correct, therefore to necessitate the revision of our picture of pre-70 Pharisaism.

Four of Josephus's works, written in Rome, come down from ancient times: The Jewish War, Antiquities, Life, and a treatise, Against Apion. The War was first written in Aramaic, as an appeal to the Jews of the Parthian Empire not to blame Rome for the destruction of the Temple, which Josephus argues, had been caused by the Jews' own misdeeds, and as a defense of the Romans' administration of Palestine and conduct of the war. This was then translated into Greek, in a second edition, and published sometime between 75 and 79 A.D. Sixteen years later, in 93-94 A.D., he issued his Antiquities, a history of ancient Israel down to 70 A.D. The Life came still later, sometime after 100 A.D., and likewise Against Apion.[2]

I

LIFE

Josephus claims, in Life, that he himself was a Pharisee:

At about the age of sixteen I determined to gain personal experience of the several sects into which our nation is divided. These, as I have frequently mentioned, are three in number -- the first that of the Pharisees, the second that of the Sadducees, and the third that of the Essenes. I thought that, after a thorough investigation, I should be in a position to select the best. So I submitted myself to hard training and laborious exercises and passed through the three courses. Not content, however, with the experience thus gained, on hearing of one named Bannus, who dwelt in the wilderness, wearing only such clothing as trees provided, feeding on such things as grew of them-selves, and using frequent ablutions of cold water, by day and night, for purity's sake, I became his devoted disciple. With him I lived for three years and, having accomplished my purpose, returned to the city. Being now in my nineteenth year I began to govern my life by the rules of the Pharisees, a sect having points of re-semblance to that which the Greeks call the Stoic school.

---

[1] In my Rabbinic Traditions about the Pharisees before 70 A.D. (Leiden, 1971; three volumes), I have analyzed the largest corpus of traditions on pre-70 Pharisaism. The New Testament traditions are thoroughly discussed, most recently, in Wolfgang Beilner, Christus und die Pharisäer (Vienna, 1959).

[2] H. St. J. Thackeray, Josephus, I. The Life. Against Apion (Cambridge, repr. 1965), pp. vii-xii.

At the end of his life, Josephus thus claims he himself was a Pharisee. He repeatedly tells us that ancient Judaism was divided into three sects -- though we know of others -- and here he alleges he himself underwent the training imposed by each of them.

If so, the whole process of entering the three sects seems to have been compressed into a very brief period. He says he began to study the several sects at the age of sixteen. He then lived with Bannus for three years. Now he is nineteen. He next declares he chose to follow the Pharisaic rules. So the three years of apprenticeship with Bannus consumed the whole time devoted to the study of all the sects. And Bannus himself is not represented as one of those sects. In all, Josephus does not suggest he studied Pharisaism, Essenism, and Sadduceism for a considerable period. Indeed, he could not have devoted much time to the several sects, if he actually spent the whole three years in the wilderness. Pharisees generally required a training period of twelve months; as to the Sadducees, we have no information; and the Essenes likewise imposed a long novitiate. So Josephus's evidence about the sects and his story of what he himself did do not seem to correlate. What he wants the reader to know is that he knew what he was talking about -- that, and one further fact: he himself was a Pharisee. But nothing else in the story of his Life tells us what being a Pharisee meant to Josephus. Like Luke-Acts' similar allegation about Paul (Acts 22:3), it is part of his credentials.

We do, however, gain a picture of how the Pharisees functioned, from Josephus's story of his doings during the revolutionary period of his life. On the eve of the war, Josephus says, he opposed sedition, and therefore feared for his life. He sought asylum in the Temple court. "When... the chieftains of the... brigands had been put to death, I ventured out of the Temple and once more consorted with the chief priests and the leading Pharisees".[3]

Later, during Josephus's time as commander of Galilee, his enemies in Galilee sent a mission to Jerusalem to seek his removal as commander. The emissaries went to Simeon b. Gamaliel:

---

[3]Life, 21-2.

This Simeon was a native of Jerusalem, of a very illustri-
ous family, and of the sect of the Pharisees, who have the
reputation of being unrivalled experts in their country's
laws. A man highly gifted with intelligence and judgment,
he could by sheer genius retrieve an unfortunate situation
in the affairs of state...

Life, 191-3 (Trans. H. Thackeray, pp. 71-73)

Simeon received the embassy and agreed to remove Josephus from
office. The administration then sent a deputation "comprising
different classes of society but of equal standing in educa-
tion. Two of them... were from the lower ranks and adherents
of the Pharisees; the third... also a Pharisee, came from a
priestly family; the youngest... was descended from high
priests":

Their instructions were to approach the Galileans and
ascertain the reason for their devotion to me. If they
attributed it to my being a native of Jerusalem, they were
to reply that so were all four of them. If to my expert
knowledge of their laws, they should retort that neither
were they ignorant of the customs of their fathers. If
again they asserted that their affection was due to my
priestly office, they should answer that two of them were
likewise priests.

Life, 197-8 (Trans. H. Thackeray, p. 75)

The Pharisees invariably are represented as experts in the
law. Of greater importance, some Pharisees come before us as
important politicians, in charge of the conduct of the war,
able to make or break commanders in the field. In Jerusalem
they enjoyed the highest offices. Their leaders are men of
political experience and great power. So much for the Pharisees of Josephus's Life.

II

THE PHARISEES OF WAR

Josephus's first work, the War, presents an entirely
consistent picture: The Pharisees were active in the court
affairs of the Maccabean state. They constituted a political
party, which sought, and for a time evidently won, domination
of the political institutions of the Maccabean kingdom. In
other words, however they might hope to teach people to conform
to the Torah, they were prepared to coerce them to conform
through the instruments of government. As E.J. Bickerman says,

"Early Pharisaism was a belligerent movement that knew how to hate".[4]

When Alexander Jannaeus died, his wife, Alexandra Salome succeeded. Here is the point at which Josephus's Pharisees first enter the picture. Alexandra Salome put the government in their hands. They thereupon executed Jannaeus's counselors, who had been their enemies, and exercised power with a high hand. The anti-Pharisaic opposition now was led by the queen's second son, Aristobulus. When the queen died in 67 B.C., Aristobulus won the throne. His brother, Hyrcanus, allied to Antipater the Idumean, father of Herod, besieged Aristobulus in the Temple of Jerusalem. The Roman general in the Near East, Pompey, intervened and supported Aristobulus. But he found reason to change his mind and preferred Hyrcanus. The Romans then took Jerusalem, in the fall of 63 B.C., and the independent government of the Maccabean dynasty came to an end. A few years later, Herod was entrusted with the rule of Judea.

The Pharisees occur in three important passages of War. First, the Pharisees -- not introduced, or extensively described, but standing without a history -- suddenly make an appearance as the dominant power in the reign of Alexandra Salome. They later are alluded to in connection with the court affairs of Herod. And finally, in Josephus's long account of Jewish sectarianism, the Pharisees receive requisite attention.

1. The Pharisees and Alexandra Salome

Alexander bequeathed the kingdom to his wife Alexandra, being convinced that the Jews would bow to her authority as they would to no other, because by her utter lack of brutality and by her opposition to his crimes she had won the affections of the populace. Nor was he mistaken in these expectations; for this frail woman firmly held the reins of government, thanks to her reputation for piety. She was, indeed, the very strictest observer of the national traditions and would deprive of office any offenders against the sacred laws. Of the two sons whom she had by Alexander, she appointed the elder, Hyrcanus, high priest, out of consideration alike for his age and his disposition, which was too lethargic to be troubled about public affairs; the younger, Aristobulus, as a hot-head, she confined to a private life.
Beside Alexandra, and growing as she grew, arose the Pharisees, a body of Jews with the reputation of excelling the rest of their nation in the observances of religion, and as exact exponents of the laws. To them, being herself intensely religious, she listened with too great

---

[4]Elias Bickerman, The Maccabees. An Account of their History from the Beginnings to the Fall of the House of the Hasmoneans (N.Y., 1947), p. 103.

deference; while they, gradually taking advantage of an
ingenuous woman, became at length the real administrators
of the state, at liberty to banish and to recall, to loose
and to bind, whom they would. In short, the enjoyments of
royal authority were theirs; its expenses and burdens fell
to Alexandra. She proved, however, to be a wonderful
administrator in larger affairs, and, by continued
recruiting doubled her army, besides collecting a considerable body of foreign troops; so that she not only
strengthened her own nation, but became a formidable foe
to foreign potentates. But if she ruled the nation, the
Pharisees ruled her.

Thus, they put to death Diogenes, a distinguished man
who had been a friend of Alexander, accusing him of having
advised the king to crucify his eight hundred victims.
They further urged Alexandra to make away with the others
who had instigated Alexander to punish those men; and as
she from superstitious motives always gave way, they
proceeded to kill whomsoever they would. The most eminent
of the citizens thus imperilled sought refuge with
Aristobulus, who persuaded his mother to spare their lives
in consideration of their rank, but, if she was not
satisfied of their innocence, to expel them from the
city. Their security being thus guaranteed, they dis-
persed about the country.

War I, 107-114 (trans. H. Thackeray, pp. 53, 55)

The Pharisees are repeatedly represented by Josephus as
"excelling" in religion and in teaching the laws. But the
substance of their religion and of the laws they taught is not
described. The party has no history; Josephus does not take
for granted we know who they are, for he tells us they are "a
body of Jews with the reputation of excelling the rest..." But
their beliefs, doctrines, religious and social goals -- these
are ignored. They come to the fore as a "body of Jews"
(suntagma ti Ioudaion). They play upon the queen's reli-
giosity, take advantage of her credulity, gradually assume real
power. They moreover exercise that power to their own advantage. They murder their enemies -- which tells us they have a
sorry past to avenge in Maccabean politics. The allusion to
their enemies recalls that under Alexander Jannaeus, a rebellion took place, which led to the crucifixion of eight hundred
of the king's enemies: "Eight thousand of the hostile faction
fled beyond the borders of Judea" (War, I, 97). But Josephus
does not name the "hostile faction." Only now do we find
reason to suppose the armed rebels of Alexander Jannaeus's time
in fact were Pharisees. Thus under Alexandra Salome, the
Pharisees killed anyone they wanted, and eminent citizens took
refuge with Aristobulus, the heir apparent.

2. In Herod's Court

The king was furiously indignant, particularly at the
wife of Pheroras, the principal object of Salome's
charges. He, accordingly, assembled a council of his
friends and relations and accused the wretched woman of
numerous misdeeds, among others of insulting his own
daughters, of subsidizing the Pharisees to oppose him, and
of alienating his brother, after bewitching him with drugs.

War I, 571 (trans. H. Thackeray, p. 271)

What is interesting in this reference is the view that the
Pharisees, like any other poltical party, might be "subsidized"
to support one party and oppose another.

3. A Philosophical School

Of the first-named schools, the Pharisees who are
considered the most accurate interpreters of the laws, and
hold the position of the leading sect, attribute everything to Fate and to God; they hold that to act rightly or
otherwise rests, indeed, for the most part with men, but
that in each action Fate cooperates. Every soul, they
maintain, is perishable, but the soul of the good alone
passes into another body, while the souls of the wicked
suffer eternal punishment.
The Sadducees, the second of the orders, do away with
Fate altogether, and remove God beyond, not merely the
commission, but the very sight, of evil. They maintain
that man has the free choice of good or evil, and that it
rests with each man's will whether he follows the one or
the other. As for the persistence of the soul after
death, penalties in the underworld, and rewards, they will
have none of them.
The Pharisees are affectionate to each other and
cultivate harmonious relations with the community. The
Sadducees, on the contrary, are, even among themselves,
rather boorish in their behavior, and in their intercourse
with their peers are as rude as to aliens. Such is what I
have to say on the Jewish philosophical schools.

War II, 162-176 (trans. H. Thackeray, pp. 385,
387)

The foregoing account represents Josephus's Pharisees as of 75
A.D. We find no claim that the Pharisees are the most popular
sect and have a massive public following, or that no one can
effectively govern Palestine without their support. All we
hear is their opinion on two issues, Fate and the punishment of
the soul after death. The Sadducees are matched opposites:
they do not believe in Fate or in life after death. The
Essenes, who are described at far greater length (War II,
119-161), believe the soul is immortal, reward and punishment
follow after death, and they can foretell the future. Josephus

adds, "Such are the theological views of the Essenes concerning the soul, whereby they irresistibly attract all who have once tasted their philosophy." Later on, as we have already seen, he would claim he himself had been able to resist their philosophy and so had joined the Pharisees.

The whole passage about the Jewish sects is introduced after an account of Judaea as a Roman province under the procurator Coponius in 6-9 A.D. It is an entirely separate unit. Afterward, the sects are ignored; Josephus then turns to another subject entirely. The section is complete as it stands and could have been placed just as well in any other part of the narrative. It neither illuminates, nor is illuminated by, its setting.

Here the Sadducees and Pharisees address themselves to identical issues, and take the two possible, extreme positions. In context, the two parties are not very important. Neither one receives a significant description. The Pharisees occur not as a political party, but as a philosophical school. The phrase about their being "the most accurate interpreters of the laws" and "the leading sect" are all that link the Pharisees of the sectarian passage to the Pharisees of the history of Queen Alexandra Salome.

III

THE PHARISEES OF ANTIQUITIES

Twenty years later, Josephus greatly expanded his picture, adding both important details to familiar accounts, and entirely new materials as well. To understand the additions, we must recall that at the same time he wrote Antiquities, Josephus was claiming he himself was a Pharisee.

In Palestine in the twenty years from 70 to 90, the Pharisees who had survived the destruction of Jerusalem in 70 had established themselves as the dominant group. Led by Yohanan ben Zakkai, they had created a Jewish administration at the coastal town of Yavneh. This administration had assumed those powers of self-government left in Jewish hands by the Roman regime. By 90 A.D., the head of the Yavnean government, Gamaliel II, grandson of the Gamaliel mentioned as Pharisee in the Temple council in Acts 5:34, and son of Simeon ben Gamaliel alluded to in Josephus's Life as a leader of the Jerusalem government in 66 A.D., had negotiated with the Roman government for recognition as head of Palestinian Jewry. The basis for

settlement was the Yavneans' agreement to oppose subversion of
Roman rule in exchange for Roman support of the Yavneans'
control over the Jews -- that is, the same agreement offered to
Pompey in 63 B.C. The Yavnean authorities, called rabbis --
whence "rabbinic Judaism" -- thus continued the Pharisaic
political and foreign policies initiated at the end of Maccabean times. Now, however, the Pharisees met with no competi-
tion. The Herodian dynasty had long since passed from the
scene. The Essenes were wiped out in the war. The Sadducees,
who had controlled the country through their power in the
Temple government, with the destruction of the Temple lost
their power-base and evidently ceased to constitute an important political force.[5]

Without knowledge of the Life, but only upon reading the
War, one might have supposed Josephus took most keen interest
in the Essenes and certainly sympathized with their ascetic way
of life. That surmise would have received further support had
we known that he spent three years of his adolescence with
Bannus, whose way of living corresponded in important ways to
that of the Essenes, though Josephus does not call Bannus an
Essene. So one might have expected that the great historian
would regard the Essenes as the leading Jewish "philosophical
school." But he does not. The Essenes of War are cut down to
size; the Pharisees of Antiquities predominate. And what
Josephus now says about them is that the country cannot be
governed without their cooperation, and he himself is one of
them. Josephus in fact was part of the pro-Roman priestly
aristocracy before the war of 66-73. Nothing in his account
suggests he was a Pharisee, as he later claimed in his auto-
biography.

1. A Philosophical School

Antiquities has two 'philosophical school' passages. The
first is brief. It comes in the middle of Josephus's account
of Jonathan Maccabee's agreement with Rome of ca. 140 B.C.,
interrupting the narrative. The second coincides, as in War,
with the beginning of procuratorial government, in the beginning of the first century A.D. Josephus here alludes to a
rebellion led by Judas, a Gaulanite, and Saddok, a Pharisee,

---

[5]See my Life of Yohanan ben Zakkai (Leiden, 1970[2];
E.J. Brill), and below, pp. 99-144.

who together started a "fourth school of philosophy," in
addition to the three already known, namely, of people who
sought the destruction of Roman rule. The passage thus
corresponds in position and function to War II, 162-166 (no. 3,
above).

The two accounts are as follows:

> Now at this time were three schools of thought among
> the Jews, which held different opinions concerning human
> affairs; the first being that of the Pharisees, the second
> that of the Sadducees, and the third that of the Essenes.
> As for the Pharisees, they say that certain events are the
> work of Fate, but not all; as to other events, it depends
> upon ourselves whether they shall take place or not. The
> sect of Essenes, however, declares that Fate is mistress
> of all things, and that nothing befalls men unless it be
> in accordance with her decree. But the Sadducees do away
> with Fate, holding that there is no such thing and that
> human actions are not achieved in accordance with her
> decree, but that all things lie within our own power, so
> that we ourselves are responsible for our well-being. Of
> these matters, however, I have given a more detailed
> account in the second book of the Jewish History.
>
>   Antiquities XIII, 171-173 (trans. R. Marcus,
>   pp. 311, 313)

Fate, or providence, thus is the primary issue. The three
'schools' take all possible positions: fate governs all, fate
governs nothing, fate governs some things but not everything.
The Pharisees enjoy the golden middle. In the War the Pharisees are given the same position, but there, the issue of the
immortality of the soul is also introduced. The second
philosophical account is as follows:

> The Jews, from the most ancient times, had three
> philosophies pertaining to their traditions, that of the
> Essenes, that of the Sadducees, and, thirdly, that of the
> group called the Pharisees. To be sure, I have spoken
> about them in the second book of the Jewish War, but
> nevertheless I shall here too dwell on them for a moment.
> The Pharisees simplify their standard of living,
> making no concession to luxury. They follow the guidance
> of that which their doctrine has selected and transmitted
> as good, attaching the chief importance to the observance
> of those commandments which it has seen fit to dictate to
> them. They show respect and deference to their elders,
> nor do they rashly presume to contradict their proposals.
> Though they postulate that everything is brought about by
> fate, they still do not deprive the human will of the
> pursuit of what is in man's power, since it was God's good
> pleasure that there should be a fusion and that the will
> of man with his virtue and vice should be admitted to the
> council-chamber of fate. They believe that souls have
> power to survive death and that there are rewards and
> punishments under the earth for those who have led lives

of virtue or vice: eternal imprisonment is the lot of
evil souls, while the good souls receive an easy passage
to a new life. Because of these views they are, as a
matter of fact, extremely influential among the townsfolk;
and all prayers and sacred rites of divine worship are
performed according to their exposition. This is the
great tribute that the inhabitants of the cities, by
practising the highest ideals both in their way of living
and in their discourse, have paid to the excellence of the
Pharisees.

The Sadducees hold that the soul perishes along with
the body. They own no observance of any sort apart from
the laws; in fact, they reckon it a virtue to dispute with
the teachers of the path of wisdom that they pursue.
There are but few men to whom this doctrine has been made
known, but these are men of the highest standing. They
accomplish practically nothing, however. For whenever
they assume some office, though they submit unwillingly
and perforce, yet submit they do to the formulas of the
Pharisees, since otherwise the masses would not tolerate
them.

Antiquities XIII, 11-17 (trans. L. Feldman, pp.
9, 11, 13, 15)

This considerable account adds to the Pharisees' virtues their
simple style of living -- the asceticism Josephus later admires
in Life and deference to the elders; earlier he had said the
Sadducees were boorish. The issues of providence and life
after death, last judgment, and reward and punishment for deeds
done in this life are alluded to.

What is entirely new is the allegation that the towns-
people follow only the Pharisees. The Temple and synagogues
are conducted according to their law. Of this we have formerly
heard nothing. With the Temple in ruins for a quarter of a
century and the old priesthood decimated and scattered, it now
is possible to place the Pharisees in a position of power of
which, in Temple times, they had scarcely dreamed. The
Sadducees, moreover, are forced to do whatever the Pharisees
tell them, for otherwise the people would ignore them -- an
even more extreme allegation. Later on it is alleged that the
followers of Shammai, the rival in Pharisaic politics to the
predominant leader, Hillel, know that the law really follows
Hillel, and therefore in all their decisions, they ruled in
accord with Hillelite doctrine. The allegation of Josephus is
of the same order, and equally incredible.

2. The Pharisees and John Hyrcanus

While in War, Josephus makes no reference to relationships
between the Pharisees and Maccabean monarchs before Alexandra

Salome, in <u>Antiquities</u>, he introduces a story, unrelated to the
narrative in which it occurs, about a break between John
Hyrcanus and the Pharisees. This same story, now told about
Alexander Jannaeus (= Yannai), furthermore occurs in the
Babylonian Talmud, first attested by a reference to the
narrative of a fourth-centry Babylonian master, Abbaye (d. ca.
340 A.D.). The two stories are as follows:

> As for Hyrcanus, the envy of the Jews was aroused
> against him by his own successes and those of his sons;
> particularly hostile to him were the Pharisees, who are
> one of the Jewish schools, as we have related above. And
> so great is their influence with the masses that even when
> they speak against a king or high priest, they immediately
> gain credence. Hyrcanus too was a disciple of theirs, and
> was greatly loved by them. And once he invited them to a
> feast and entertained them hospitably, and when he saw
> that they were having a very good time, he began by saying
> that they knew he wished to be righteous and in everything
> he did tried to please God and them -- for the Pharisees
> profess such beliefs; at the same time he begged them, if
> they observed him doing anything wrong or straying from
> the right-path, to lead him back to it and correct him.
> But they testified to his being altogether virtuous, and
> he was delighted with their praise. However, one of the
> guests, named Eleazar, who had an evil nature and took
> pleasure in dissension, said, "Since you have asked to be
> told the truth, if you wish to be righteous, give up the
> high priesthood and be content with governing the
> people." And when Hyrcanus asked him for what reason he
> should give up the high priesthood, he replied, "Because
> we have heard from our elders that your mother was a
> captive in the reign of Antiochus Epiphanes." But the
> story was false, and Hyrcanus was furious with the man,
> while all the Pharisees were very indignant.
>   Then a certain Jonathan, one of Hyrcanus's close
> friends, belonging to the school of Sadducees, who held
> opinions opposed to those of the Pharisees, said that it
> had been with general approval of all the Pharisees that
> Eleazar had made his slanderous statement; and this, he
> added, would be clear to Hyrcanus if he inquired of them
> what punishment Eleazar deserved for what he had said.
> And so Hyrcanus asked the Pharisees what penalty they
> thought he deserved -- for, he said, he would be convinced
> that the slanderous statement had not been made with their
> approval if they fixed a penalty commensurate with the
> crime -- and they replied that Eleazar deserved stripes
> and chains; for they did not think it right to sentence a
> man to death for calumny, and anyway the Pharisees are
> naturally lenient in the matter of punishments. At this
> Hyrcanus became very angry and began to believe that the
> fellow had slandered him with their approval. And
> Jonathan in particular inflamed his anger, and so worked
> upon him that he brought him to join the Sadducean party
> and desert the Pharisees, and to abrogate the regulations
> which they had established for the people, and punish
> those who observed them. Out of this, of course, grew the
> hatred of the masses for him and his sons, but of this we
> shall speak hereafter. For the present I wish merely to
> explain that the Pharisees had passed on to the people

certain regulations handed down by former generations and
not recorded in the Laws of Moses, for which reason they
are rejected by the Sadducaean group, who hold that only
those regulations should be considered valid which were
written down [in Scripture], and that those which had been
handed down by former generations need not be observed.
And concerning these matters the two parties came to have
controversies and serious differences, the Sadducees
having the confidence of the wealthy alone but no following among the populace, while the Pharisees have the
support of the masses. But of these two schools and of
the Essenes a detailed account has been given in the
second book of my Judaica.

And so Hyrcanus quieted the outbreak, and lived
happily thereafter; and when he died after administering
the government excellently for thirty-one years, he left
five sons.

> Antiquities XIII, 288-298 (trans. R. Marcus, pp.
> 373, 375, 377)

Abbaye said, "How do I know it [re the silence of a
husband in a case in which the wife is charged with
committing adultery by one witness only, that the husband
must divorce the wife if he remains silent]?"

As it is taught, the story is told (M'SH B):

Yannai the King went to Kohalit in the wilderness and
conquered there sixty towns. When he returned, he
rejoiced greatly, and invited (QR') all the sages of
Israel.

He said to them, "Our forefathers would eat salt fish
when they were engaged in the building of the Holy House.
Let us also eat salt fish as a memorial to our forefathers."

So they brought up salt fish on golden tables, and
they ate.

There was there a certain scoffer, evil-hearted and
empty-headed, and Eleazar b. Po'irah was his name.

Eleazar b. Po'irah said to Yannai the king, "O king
Yannai, the hearts of the Pharisees are [set] against you."

"What shall I do?"

"Test (HQM) them by the plate (SYS) that is between
your eyes."

He tested them by the plate that was between his eyes.

There was there a certain sage, and Judah b. Gedidiah
was his name. Judah b. Gedidiah said to Yannai the King,
"O King Yannai, let suffice for you the crown of sover-
eignty [kingship]. Leave the crown of the [high] priesthood for the seed of Aaron."

For people said that his [Yannai's] mother had been
taken captive in Modi'im. The charge was investigated and
not found [sustained]. The sages of Israel departed in
anger.

Eleazar b. Po'irah then said to Yannai the king, "O
King Yannai, That is the law [not here specified as the
punishment to be inflicted on Judah] even for the ordinary
folk in Israel. But you are king and high priest --
should that be your law too?"

"What should I do?"

"If you take my advice, you will trample them down."

"But what will become of the Torah?"

"Lo, it is rolled up and lying in the corner.
Whoever wants to learn, let him come and learn."

> (R. Nahman b. Isaac [ca. 375 A.D.] said, "Forthwith
> heresy (Epicureanism ['PYQWRSWT]) was instilled in him
> [Yannai], for he should have said, 'That is well and good
> for the Written Torah, but what will become of the Oral
> Torah?'")
> The evil blossomed through Eleazar b. Po'irah. All
> the sages of Israel were killed.
> The world was desolate until Simeon b. Shetah came
> and restored the Torah to its place.

>   b. Qid. 66a

The italicized words are in Aramaic, the rest in Hebrew. It is
as if a well-known event is referred to at the end: Simeon b.
Shetah made peace between the Pharisees and Yannai (or he
overcame Yannai). But we do not know what actually is attrib-
utable to Simeon, for what he said or did is left unexplained.

A persistent tradition on a falling out between the
Pharisees and Alexander Jannaeus evidently circulated in later
times. One form of the tradition placed the origin of the
whole difficulty at the feet of Simeon b. Shetah himself,
holding that the king believed he had been cheated by Simeon
(Y. Berakhot 7:2); therefore Simeon fled for a time, but later
on returned. A second, and different, set of traditions, of
which the above is one exemplum, held that difficulties between
Yannai and the Pharisees ("rabbis") as a group led to the
flight of many of them to Alexandra. Simeon managed to patch
things up -- we do not know how -- and therefore summoned the
refugees to return. But the two traditions cannot be reconciled or translated into historical language, nor can we
profitably speculate on what "kernel" of historical truth
underlay either or both of them. All we do know is that Simeon
b. Shetah was believed to have played a role in either the
difficulty, or the reconciliation, or both.

The Talmudic story is written in biblical, not Mishnaic or
rabbinic, Hebrew. In this respect one recalls the anachronistic, pseudo-archaic language of the Dead Sea Scrolls. It makes
use of the conversive waw, which no longer occurs later on, the
only such usage in all of Talmudic literature. Solomon Zeitlin
holds that the talmudic story is older than the version of
Josephus: it could have been written "only at a time when the
kings were not high priests, which was from the time of Herod
onwards."[6] At any rate, there is an important lacuna in the
talmudic version, for "that is the punishment" takes for

---

[6]Solomon Zeitlin, The Rise and Fall of the Judaean State
(Philadelphia, 1962), I, pp. 168-170.

granted the details available only in Josephus's account. It would seem to me that the talmudic narrator could not have had access to the Aramaic first-edition of Josephus War, since the story does not occur at all in War. So the relationship between the two versions is not clear. Either Josephus copied from a Hebrew source, or the talmudic narrator copied from Josephus, or both have relied on a third authority. At any rate, the story interrupts Josephus's narrative and contradicts it, for, after the disgrace, Hyrcanus lived happily ever afterward. One should have expected some more appropriate heavenly recompense.

Again we observe stress in Antiquities upon the Pharisees' enjoying mass support, while only the rich listen to the Sadducees. The difference between the two parties is, as was common in Hellenistic politics, between the wealthy few and the (virtuous) many. Whoever hopes to govern Palestine had best rely upon the leaders of the latter.

3.   The Pharisees and Alexandra Salome

The new version of the Pharisees-in-power story is strikingly revised in favor of the Pharisees:

> And when the queen saw that he was on the point of death and no longer held to any hope of recovery, she wept and beat her breast, lamenting the bereavement that was about to befall her and her children, and said to him, "To whom are you thus leaving me and your children, who are in need of help from others, especially when you know how hostile the nation feels toward you!" Thereupon he advised her to follow his suggestions for keeping the throne secure for herself and her children and to conceal his death from the soldiers until she had captured the fortress. And then, he said, on her return to Jerusalem as from a splendid victory, she should yield a certain amount of power to the Pharisees, for if they praised her in return for this sign of regard, they would dispose the nation favorably toward her. These men, he assured her, had so much influence with their fellow-Jews that they could injure those whom they hated and help those to whom they were friendly; when they spoke harshly of any person, even when they did so out of envy; and he himself, he added, had come into conflict with the nation because these men had been badly treated by him. "And so," he said, "when you come to Jerusalem, send for their partisans, and showing them my dead body, permit them, with every sign of sincerity, to greet me as they please, whether they wish to dishonor my corpse by leaving it unburied because of the many injuries they have suffered at my hands, or in their anger wish to offer my dead body any other form of indignity. Promise them also that you will not take any action, while you are on the throne, without their consent. If you speak to them in this manner, I shall receive from them a more

splendid burial than I should from you; for once they have
the power to do so, they will not choose to treat my
corpse badly, and at the same time you will reign se-
curely." With this exhortation to his wife he died, after
reigning twenty-seven years, at the age of forty-nine.

Thereupon Alexandra, after capturing the fortress,
conferred with the Pharisees as her husband had suggested,
and by placing in their hands all that concerned his
corpse and the royal power, stilled their anger against
Alexander, and made them her well-wishers and friends.
And they in turn went to the people and made public
speeches in which they recounted the deeds of Alexander,
and said that in him they had lost a just king, and by
their eulogies they so greatly moved the people to mourn
and lament that they gave him a more splendid burial than
had been given any of the kings before him. Now although
Alexander had left two sons, Hyrcanus and Aristobulus, he
had bequeathed the royal power to Alexandra. Of these
sons the one, Hyrcanus, was incompetent to govern and in
addition much preferred a quiet life, while the younger,
Aristobulus, was a man of action and high spirit. As for
the queen herself, she was loved by the masses because she
was thought to disapprove of the crimes committed by her
husband.

Alexandra then appointed Hyrcanus as high priest
because of his greater age but more especially because of
his lack of energy; and she permitted the Pharisees to do
as they liked in all matters, and also commanded the
people to obey them; and whatever regulations, introduced
by the Pharisees in accordance with the tradition of their
fathers, had been abolished by her father-in-law Hyrcanus,
these she again restored. And so, while she had the title
of sovereign, the Pharisees had the power. For example,
they recalled exiles, and freed prisoners, and, in a word,
in no way differed from absolute rulers. Nevertheless the
queen took thought for the welfare of the kingdom and
recruited a large force of mercenaries and also made her
own force twice as large, with the result that she struck
terror into the local rulers round her and received
hostages from them. And throughout the entire country
there was quiet except for the Pharisees; for they worked
upon the feelings of the queen and tried to persuade her
to kill those who had urged Alexander to put the eight
hundred to death. Later they themselves cut down one of
them, named Diogenes, and his death was followed by that
of one after the other, until the leading citizens came to
the palace, Aristobulus among them -- for he was obviously
resentful of what was taking place, and let it be plainly
seen that if only he should get the opportunity, he would
not leave his mother any power at all --, and they
reminded her of all that they had achieved in the face of
danger, whereby they had shown their unwavering loyalty to
their master and had therefore been judged worthy by him
of the greatest honors. And they begged her not to crush
their hopes completely, for, they said, after escaping the
dangers of war, they were now being slaughtered at home
like cattle by their foes, and there was no one to avenge
them. They also said that if their adversaries were to be
contented with those already slain, they would bear with
equanimity what had taken place, out of genuine devotion
to their masters; but if, on the other hand, these men
were to continue in the same course, let them, they
begged, at least be given their freedom; for they would
never bring themselves to seek any means of safety but

what should come from her, and would welcome death in her
palace so long as they might not have disloyalty on their
conscience. It would be disgraceful both for them and for
her who rules as queen, they added, if, being abandoned by
her, they should be given shelter by the enemies of her
husband; for Aretas the Arab and the other princes would
consider it of the utmost value to enlist such men as
mercenies, whose very name, they might say, had caused
these princes to shudder before they had heard it (spoken
aloud). But if this could not be, and she had determined
to favor the Pharisees above all others, let her, as the
next best thing, station each of them in one of the
garrisons, for, if some evil genius were thus wroth with
the house of Alexander, they at least would show themselves (loyal) even though living in humble circumstances.
     Speaking in this vein at great length, they called
upon the shades of Alexander to take pity on those who had
been killed and those who were in danger, whereupon all
the bystanders burst into tears. And Aristobulus in
particular made plain his sentiments by denouncing his
mother bitterly. But still they themselves were to blame
for their misfortunes, in allowing a woman to reign who
madly desired it in her unreasonable love of power, and
when her sons were in the prime of life. And so the
queen, not knowing what to do consistent with her dignity,
entrusted to them the guarding of the fortresses with the
exception of Hyrcanis, Alexandreion and Machaerus, where
her most valuable possessions were.

     Antiquities Xiii, 399-418 (trans. R. Marcus, pp. 429,
     431, 433, 435, 437)

We recall that in War, Alexandra listened to the Pharisees
"with too great deference," and they took advantage of her.
The picture is unfavorable. They ran the government, but she
paid. They wrecked terrible vengeance on their enemies, so
many had to flee. Now we have Alexander Jannaeus, arch-enemy
of the Pharisees, telling the queen to put the Pharisees in
power! Everyone follows them. Therefore, if she can win their
support, she can govern the country effectively. Josephus
waxes lugubrious on this very point. No longer do the Pharisees take advantage of the woman's ingenuousness. Now they are
essential for her exercise of power. Even Alexander Jannaeus
himself would have had a better time of it had he won their
support. "Let them dishonor my corpse if necessary!" And
above all, "do anything the tell you." In place of a credulous
queen, we have a supine one. In place of conniving Pharisees,
we have powerful leaders of the whole nation. The Pharisees
are won over, and they win over the masses -- even eulogizing
Jannaeus. What do the Pharisees do with their power? They
teach the people to live in accordance with "the tradition of
their fathers." John Hyrcanus's and Alexander Jannaeus's work
is undone. Exiles are called back. Prisoners are set free.

To be sure, the queen organized a professional army. Josephus adds that the Pharisees sought to avenge themselves upon their enemies. They killed one of them, and then more, and so the account of Aristobulus's protection of the Pharisees' enemies is included. Somehow, the Pharisees fell away from the account. The mass slaughter of War, in which the Pharisees killed anyone they wanted, is shaded into a mild persecution of the Pharisees' opposition.

4. In Herod's Court

The Pharisees now have a different, and more important, place in the account of Herod's reign. They have foresight. They seek to oppose Herod. No one now takes for granted that the Pharisees can be bribed. Their foresight, not their love of money, warned them that Herod's family was destined for a bad end (which everyone knew by 95 A.D.). The Pharisees are accused of corrupting people at court, not of being corrupted. Some of them are put to death on that account:

> There was also a group of Jews priding itself on its adherence to ancestral custom and claiming to observe the laws of which the Deity approved, and by these men, called Pharisees, the women (of the court) were ruled. These men were able to help the king greatly because of their foresight, and yet they were obviously intent upon combating and injuring him. At least when the whole Jewish people affirmed by an oath that it would be loyal to Caesar and to the king's government, these men, over six thousand in number, refused to take this oath, and when the king punished them with a fine, Pheroras' wife paid the fine for them. In return for her friendliness they foretold -- for they were believed to have fore-knowledge of things through God's appearance to them -- that by God's decree Herod's throne would be taken from him, both from himself and his descendants, and the royal power would fall to her and Pheroras and to any children that they might have. These things, which did not remain unknown to Salome, were reported to the king, as was the news that the Pharisees had corrupted some of the people at court. And the king put to death those of the Phari-sees who were more to blame and the eunuch Bagoas and a certain Karos, who was outstanding among his contempor-aries for his surpassing beauty and was loved by the king. He also killed all those of his household who approved of what the Pharisees said. Now Bagoas had been carried away by their assurance that he would be called the father and benefactor of him who would some day be set over the people with the title of king, for all the power would belong to him and he would give Bagoas the ability to marry and to beget children of his own.

> Antiquities XVIII, 41-45 (trans. R. Marcus and A. Wikgren, pp. 391, 393)

IV

CONCLUSION

The materials before us (except for the _Life_) have been
given in chronological order. They illustrate the definitive
judgment of Morton Smith:

> ...to which group within the Jewish tradition was he
> [Josephus] loyal? Here a comparison of the War with the
> _Antiquities_ is extremely informative. In the War, written
> shortly after the destruction of Jerusalem, Josephus still
> favors the group of which his family had been representa-
> tive -- the wealthy, pro-Roman section of the Priesthood.
> He represents them... as that group of the community which
> did all it could to keep the peace with Rome. In this
> effort he once mentions that they had the assistance of
> the chief Pharisees, but otherwise the Pharisees hardly
> figure on the scene. In this account of the reign of
> Salome-Alexandra he copies an abusive paragraph of
> Nicholas of Damascus, describing the Pharisees as hypo-
> crites whom the queen's superstition enabled to achieve
> and abuse political power. In his account of the Jewish
> sects he gives most space to the Essenes. (Undoubtedly he
> was catering to the interests of Roman readers, with whom
> ascetic philosophers in out-of-the-way countries enjoyed a
> long popularity.) As for the others, he merely tags brief
> notices of the Pharisees and Sadducees onto the end of his
> survey. He says nothing of the Pharisees' having any
> influence with the people, and the only time he represents
> them as attempting to exert any influence (when they ally
> with the leading priests and other citizens of Jerusalem
> to prevent the outbreak of the war), they fail.
>   In the _Antiquities_, however, written twenty years
> later, the picture is quite different. Here, whenever
> Josephus discusses the Jewish sects, the Pharisees take
> first place, and every time he mentions them he emphasizes
> their popularity, which is so great, he says, that they
> can maintain opposition against any government. His
> treatment of the Salome-Alexandra incident is particularly
> illuminating: he makes Alexander Janneus, Salome's
> husband and the lifelong enemy of the Pharisees, deliver
> himself of a deathbed speech in which he blames all the
> troubles of his reign on the fact that he had opposed them
> and urges the queen to restore them to power because of
> their overwhelming influence with the people. She follows
> his advice and the Pharisees cooperate to such extent that
> they actually persuade the people that Alexander was a
> good king and make them mourn his passing!
>   It is almost impossible not to see in such a re-
> writing of history a bid to the Roman government. That
> government must have been faced with the problem [after 70
> A.D.]: Which group of Jews shall we support? ...To this
> question Josephus is volunteering an answer: The Phari-
> sees, he says again and again, have by far the greatest
> influence with the people. Any government which secures
> their support is accepted; any government which alienates
> them has trouble. The Sadducees, it is true, have more
> following among the aristocracy... but they have no
> popular following at all, and even in the old days, when
> they were in power, they were forced by public opinion to
> follow the Pharisees' orders. As for the other major

parties, the Essenes are a philosophical curiosity, and
the Zealots differ from the Pharisees only by being
fanatically anti-Roman. So any Roman government which
wants peace in Palestine had better support and secure the
support of the Pharisees.

Josephus' discovery of these important political
facts (which he ignored when writing the Jewish War) may
have been due partly to a change in his personal relationship with the Pharisees. Twenty years had now intervened
since his trouble with Simeon ben Gamaliel, and Simeon was
long dead. But the mere cessation of personal hostilities
would hardly account for such pointed passages as Josephus
added to the Antiquities. The more probable explanation
is that in the meanwhile the Pharisees had become the
leading candidate for Roman support in Palestine and were
already negotiating for it...[7]

It therefore seems that the time has come to stop describing the Pharisees as the "normative" sect of pre-70
Palestinian Judaism. The sole source that explicitly claims
they predominated turns out to be post-70 propaganda. The
rabbinical traditions about the pre-70 Pharisees contain no
such claim, though, to be sure, they take for granted that
Pharisaic Judaism was identical with the Mosaic revelation of
Sinai. The rabbis do allege that the Pharisees ran the
Temple. But they tell no stories about how the Pharisees
governed Palestine, or how the Maccabean or Roman regimes in
Palestine had to rely upon Pharisees for help in controlling
the populace. They attribute to pre-70 Pharisaic masters no
laws about the administration of the country, no sayings about
how the government should be organized, no indication that they
believed, as did Josephus, that pre-70 times were marked by
Pharisaic political ascendency outside of the cult. The
picture of the Gospels is of a table-fellowship sect, whose
dietary laws -- careful tithing, ritual purity even at home,
outside of the Temple precincts -- were the main concern.

Smith, in my view, has placed into perspective the
distorted view of the pan-Pharisaic, pan-rabbinic scholars who
declare the Pharisaic viewpoint to be normative Judaism, and in
a fundamentalist, uncritical spirit cite Josephus as proof of
that proposition.

What, then, is to be learned about the historical Pharisees from Josephus? We obviously must discount all of his
references to the influence and power of the Pharisees, for, as
Smith points out, these constitute part of his highly tenden-

---

[7]Smith, "Palestine," pp. 75-6.

tious case in behalf of the Yavnean rabbis, the post-70 Pharisees' heirs, and not data about the pre-70 ones.

The picture of the War contains two important elements.

First, the Pharisees were a political party, deeply involved in the politics of the Hasmonean dynasty. They were opponents of Alexander Jannaeus, but we do not know why, and supported Alexandra Salome, who put them into power, but we do not know for what purpose.

In the first century A.D., individual Pharisees remained active in political life. Simeon ben Gamaliel and other Pharisees certainly took a leading role in the conduct of the war. But, strikingly, Josephus makes no reference to the sect as a party within the revolutionary councils, and one may fairly conclude that Simeon and others were members of the group, but not the group's representatives, no more than Judah the Pharisee represented the group in founding the fourth philosophy. The group itself probably was not an organized political force. Evidently the end of the Pharisaic party comes with Aristobulus, who slaughtered many of them, and was sealed by Herod, who killed even more. From that point forward, so far as Josephus is concerned, the Pharisees no longer play a role in the politics and government of Jewish Palestine.

Second, the Pharisees also constituted a "philosophical school." Smith's observation[8] that Jews thought of groups in their society distinguished by peculiar theories and practices as different schools of the national philosophy, helps us understand the foundations of Pharisaic policy. As a political party, the Pharisees stood for a particular perspective within the national philosophy. They presumably claimed they ought to rule because they possessed the true and wise doctrine. The specific doctrines alluded to by Josephus, however, seem to me unrelated to the political aspirations of the group. Why people who believed in fate and in the immortality of the soul should rule, or would rule, differently from those who did not, and how such beliefs might shape the policies of the state are not obvious. But evidently what characterized the group -- these particular beliefs -- and what rendered their political aspiratios something more than a power-grab presumably are inextricably related.

---

[8]Smith, "Palestine," pp. 79-81.

Josephus thus presents us with a party of philosophical politicans. They claim to have ancient traditions, but these are not described as having been orally transmitted, nor are they attributed to Moses at Sinai or claimed as part of the Torah. They are excellent lawyers. They are marked off from other groups by a few, relatively trivial philosophical differences. As a political party they function effectively for roughly the first fifty years of the first century B.C. While individuals thereafter are described as Pharisees, as a sect the group seems to end its political life with the advent of Herod and of Hillel.

Chapter Five
JUDAISM AFTER THE DESTRUCTION OF THE TEMPLE
AN OVERVIEW

The history of the Jews in the period between the destruction of the second temple in 70 CE and the outbreak of the
Bar-Kokhba War in 132 CE is to be divided into two parts,
political and social, and religious. In the writer's opinion,
one cannot improve upon the discussion of political and social
history by Salo W. Baron. I therefore shall concentrate on the
history of Judaism. This decision, furthermore, is justified
by the nature of our sources. They do not make possible the
description of the sequence of events of the history of the
period. We simply do not know, in a more or less coherent and
continuous way, precisely what happened from year to year or
decade to decade. It is important to specify the difference in
extant sources pertinent to the period before us and those
which preceded it.

Since Josephus provides extensive foundations for the
study of the history of the Jews and of Judaism, the period
before A.D. 70 is treated in narrative style. We are able to
tell a fairly continuous story. Indeed, the main outlines of
that story commonly consist of a paraphrase of Josephus. After
70 we have no such source; no continuous or narrative history
is possible. Instead, we have religious documents of various
kinds; we can never be entirely certain whom these documents
represent, all the more so to whom they spoke. Our own concerns naturally lead to stress upon the two groups in Palestinian Jewry between 70 and 132 who are seen by contemporaries
as 'spiritual' ancestors, the Christians, whether or not still
identified with the larger Jewish group, and the rabbis.
Apocalyptic writings, preserved under Christian auspices,
hardly yield considerable information on what was happening in
the country. While Talmudic and related sources contain many
stories about authorities assumed to have lived between 70 and
132, none of these stories can be shown to have been composed
during the period of which they speak. The laws of Mishnah-
Tosefta assigned to these same authorities, to be sure, probably do derive, in some instances even in their exact wording,
from this period. But they do not address themselves to those
subjects normally regarded as important in the writing of

history, for example, political, social, economic, and other
practical matters. Accordingly, it is not possible to supply
the continuous narrative of historical events, even those of
primarily religious interest, for the period under discussion,
in a way parallel to the narrative which pertains to the
Hasmonaean and early Roman periods.

Yet there is the firmly established fact of history, the
Bar-Kokhba War, from which many other historical facts flow
naturally. We know that between 132 and 135, a second major
war of rebellion against Roman rule was fought and lost.
Accordingly, a great many people thought that such a war should
be fought. It follows that they believed it was the time to
rebel, and we may from that fact infer that something in their
conception of the world led them to risk everything in such a
war. Exactly what they thought made such a war, if not pro-
mising, at least necessary, of course is difficult to say.
Speculation on that fact cannot be tested against the writings
of the leaders of the war, diaries or memoranda of people who
fought in, or opposed, it, reports of the course of the war
from apologists, of one side or the other, let alone reporters
or other objective onlookers, and memoirs of the war produced
by those who survived. All we have are a few references, of
later provenance and obviously polemical purpose, as well as
the trivial detritus uncovered (and vastly over-celebrated) by
Yadin. One fact is suggestive, again a fact of history.

Between the destruction of the temple in 70 and the
outbreak of the second rebellion in 132, three generations,
sixty-two years, had gone by; it may be that people expected
the legendary interval of seventy years between the destruction
of the first temple and the return to Zion to be reproduced.
Bar-Kokhba's war may have represented an effort to prepare for
the restoration of the temple by extirpating gentile, pagan
rule over the Holy Land. But this is only a surmise. A more
reliable surmise is that the same motives which produced the
first war produced the second, and these in some measure
included the view of the Zealots and others amply described by
Josephus. They assuredly thought they fought an eschatological
and messianic fight. Rabbinic stories about the period of
Bar-Kokhba similarly exhibit messianic motives. All of this is
at best reasonable speculation. If people fought a war, they
probably thought they had good reason, and the stated reasons
being unavailable, we can at best surmise that continuing
traits of the religious and cultural life of the country,

persistent expectations and enduring yearnings, may explain
that fact.

Accordingly, we may suppose that in the background of the
sources we do have are two facts, first, a profound sense of
disorientation because of the loss of the temple, second,
confusion about how it was to be restored. As to these facts,
we need speculate very little, since sources produced in this
period, e.g., II Baruch and II Esdras, are explicit that the
destruction of the temple produced a profound sense of mourning
joined to a deep yearning for restoration. To be sure, we
cannot demonstrate that these sentiments were widely held, but
the fact of history -- the war six decades later -- suggests
that there was a chronic cause of war, and, given the motiva-
tions for fighting the first one, we may suppose that the
second one in some measure came in consequence of those sentiments available to us in writings of just a few people of the
day.

I refer to the result of the destruction of the temple as
disorientation to state the problem in the broadest possible
terms. The full weight and meaning of the temple's destruction
and the cessation of the cult, the devastation of the Holy City
and the devastation of the priesthood -- these should not be
reduced to terms which, if not trivial, also do not comprehend
the matter's full implications. It is not merely that one form
of rite was lost and had to be replaced by another, or that one
set of religious leaders supplanted another.

What kind of issue faced the Jews after the destruction of
the temple? It was, I contend, a fundamentally religious
issue, not a matter of government or politics. For historians
of the Jews it is a common axiom that the destruction of
Jerusalem and its temple in 70 marked a decisive political
turning-point. For example, current rhetoric uses the year 70
as the date for the end of 'Jewish self-government.' Precisely
what is meant by that rhetorical flourish is difficult to
determine. If one means the end of Jewish independent government in Palestine, then that came to an end with the procura-
tors, and, one might say, even with the advent of Herod. So
the importance of the date must be located elsewhere. The Jews
continued to govern themselves, much as they had in procuratorial times, though through different institutions, long after
70. Patriarchal government finally ended at the start of the
fifth century -- a matter of Byzantine policy -- but by that
time large numbers of Jews had already left the land, and their

institutions of self-government persisted in the countries of their dispersion.

The significant event was the destruction of the temple. Still, long before 70 the temple had been rejected by some Jewish groups. Its sanctity had been arrogated by others. And for large numbers of ordinary Jews outside of Palestine, as well as substantial numbers within, the temple was a remote and, if holy, unimportant place. For them, piety was fully expressed through synagogue worship. In a very real sense, therefore, for the Christian Jews, who were indifferent to the temple cult, for the Jews at Qumran, who rejected the temple, for the Jews of Leontopolis, in Egypt, who had their own temple, but especially for the masses of Jews of the diaspora who never saw the temple to begin with, but served God through synagogue worship alone, the year 70 cannot be said to have marked an important change.

The Jews of the diaspora accommodated themselves to their distance from the temple by 'spiritualizing' and 'moralizing' the cult, as did Philo. To be sure, Philo was appropriately horrified at the thought of the temple's desecration by Caligula, but I doubt that his religious life would have been greatly affected had the temple been destroyed in his lifetime. For the large Babylonian Jewish community, we have not much evidence that the situation was any different. They were evidently angered by the Romans' destruction of the temple, so that Josephus had to address them with an account of events exculpating Rome from guilt for the disaster. But Babylonian Jewry did absolutely nothing before 70 to support the Palestinians, and, thereafter, are not heard from. The Babylonian and Mesopotamian Jews' great war against Rome, in Trajan's time, was the result not of the temple's destruction, but, in my opinion, of Trajan's evident plan to rearrange the international trade routes to their disadvantage. Nor do we hear of any support from the diaspora for Bar-Kokhba, so apparently no one was ready to help him re-establish the temple in a new Jerusalem. At any rate, the political importance of the events of 70 cannot be taken for granted. It was significant primarily for the religious life of various Palestinian Jewish groups, not to mention the ordinary folk who had made pilgrimages to Jerusalem and could do so no more.

We shall rapidly examine four responses to the destruction of Jerusalem, the end of the temple, and the cessation of the cult. The four responses are of, first, the apocalyptic

writers represented in the visions of II Ezra; second, the Dead
Sea community; third, the Christian church; and finally, the
Pharisaic sect. When the apocalyptic visionaries looked
backward upon the ruins, they saw a tragic vision. So they
emphasized future supernatural redemption, which they believed
was soon to come. The Qumranians had met the issues of 70 CE
long before in a manner essentially similar to that of the
Christians. Both groups tended to abandon the temple and its
cult and to replace them by means of the new community on the
one hand, and the service or pious rites of the new community,
on the other. The Pharisees come somewhere between the first
and the second and third groups. They saw the destruction as a
calamity, like the apocalyptists, but they also sought the
means, in both social forms and religious expression, to
provide a new way of atonement and a new form of divine service, to constitute a new, interim temple, like the Dead Sea
sect and the Christians.

The apocalypse of Ezra is representative of the apocalyptic state of mind. The compiler of the Ezra apocalypse (II
Esdras 3-14), who lived at the end of the first century, looked
forward to a day of judgment, when the Messiah would destroy
Rome and God would govern the world. But he had to ask, how
can the suffering of Israel be reconciled with divine justice?
To Israel, God's will had been revealed. But God had not
removed the inclination to do evil, so men could not carry out
God's will:

> For we and our fathers have passed our lives in ways
> that bring death... But what is man, that thou art angry
> with him, or what is a corruptible race, that thou art so
> bitter against it?... (II Esdras 8.31,34).

Ezra was told that God's ways are inscrutable (4.10f.),
but when he repeated the question 'Why has Israel been given
over to the gentiles as a reproach?' he was given the answer
characteristic of this literature -- that a new age was dawning
which would shed light on such perplexities. The pseudepigraphic Ezra thus regarded the catastrophe as the fruit of sin,
more specifically, the result of man's natural incapacity to do
the will of God. He prayed for forgiveness and found hope in
the coming transformation of the age and the promise of a new
day, when man's heart would be as able, as his mind even then
was willing, to do the will of God.

For the Dead Sea community, the destruction of the temple cult took place long before 70. That is why we consider that group, even though it did not survive the war. By rejecting the temple and its cult, the Qumran group had had to confront a world without Jerusalem even while the city was still standing. The spiritual situation of Yavneh, the community formed by the Pharisaic rabbis after the destruction of the temple in 70, and that of Qumran, are strikingly comparable. Just as the rabbis had to construct, at least for the time being, a Judaism without the temple cult, so did the Qumran sectarians have to construct a Judaism without the temple cult. The difference, of course, is that the rabbis merely witnessed the destruction of the city by others, while the Qumran sectarians did not lose the temple, but rejected it at the outset.

The founders of the community were temple priests, who saw themselves as continuators of the true priestly line, that is, the sons of Zadok. For them the old temple was, as it were, destroyed in the times of the Maccabees. Its cult was defiled, not by the Romans, but by the rise of a high priest from a family other than theirs. They further rejected the calendar followed in Jerusalem. They therefore set out to create a new temple, until God would come and, through the Messiah in the line of Aaron, would establish the temple once again. The Qumran community believed that the presence of God had left Jerusalem and had come to the Dead Sea. The community now constituted the new temple, just as some elements in early Christianity saw the new temple in the body of Christ, in the church, the Christian community. In some measure, this represents a 'spiritualization' of the old temple, and the temple worship was affected through the community's study and fulfilment of the Torah. Thus the Qumranians represent a middle point between reverence for the old temple and its cult, in the here and now, and complete indifference to the temple and cult in favor of the Christians' utter spiritualization of both, represented, for example, in the Letter to the Hebrews.

Because of their faith in the crucified and risen Christ, Christians experienced the end of the old cult and the old temple before it actually took place, much like the Qumran sectarians. They had to work out the meaning of the sacrifice of Jesus on the cross, and whether the essays on that central problem were done before or after 70 is of no consequence. The issue of August 70 confronted Qumranians and Christians for other than narrowly historical reasons; for both, the events of

that month took place in other than military and political
modes. But the effects were much the same. The Christians,
therefore, resemble the Qumranians in having had to face the
end of the cult before it actually took place, but they were
like the Pharisees in also having to confront the actual
destruction of the temple, here and now.

Like the Qumranians, the Christian Jews criticized the
Jerusalem temple and its cult. Both groups in common believed
that the last days had begun. Both believed that God had come
to dwell with them, as he had once dwelt in the temple. The
sacrifices of the temple were replaced, therefore, by the
sacrifice of a blameless life and by other spiritual deeds.
But the Christians differ on one important point. To them, the
final sacrifice had already taken place; the perfect priest had
offered up the perfect holocaust, his own body. So, for the
Christians, Christ on the cross completed the old sanctity and
inaugurated the new. This belief took shape in different
ways. For Paul, in I Corinthians 3.16f., the church is the new
temple, Christ is the foundation of the 'spiritual' building.
Ephesians 2.18-11 has Christ as the cornerstone of the new
building, the company of Christians constituting the temple.

Perhaps the single most coherent statement of the Christian view of cult comes in Hebrews. Whether or not Hebrews is
representative of many Christians or comes as early as 70 is
not our concern. What is striking is that the letter explores
the great issues of 70, the issues of cult, temple, sacrifice, priesthood, atonement, and redemption. Its author takes
for granted that the church is the temple, that Jesus is the
builder of the temple, and that he is also the perfect priest
and the final and unblemished sacrifice. It is Jesus who is
that most perfect sacrifice, who has entered the true, heavenly
sanctuary itself.' Therefore, no further sacrifice -- his or
another's -- is needed.

We know very little about the Pharisees before the time of
Herod. During Maccabaean days, as we saw above, according to
Josephus, our sole reliable evidence, they appear as a political party, competing with the Sadducees, another party, for
control of the court and government. Afterwards, they all but
fade out of Josephus' narrative. But the later rabbinical
literature fills the gap -- with what degree of reliability I
do not here wish to say -- and tells a great many stories about
Pharisaic masters from Shammai and Hillel to the destruction.
It also ascribes numerous sayings, particularly on matters of

law, both to the masters and to the Houses of Shammai and of Hillel. These circles of disciples seem to have flourished in the first century, down to 70 and beyond.

The legal materials attributed by later rabbis to the Pharisees before 70 are thematically congruent with the stories and sayings about Pharisees in the New Testament Gospels, and I take them to be accurate in substance, if not in detail, as representations of the main issues of Pharisaic law. After 70, the masters of Yavneh seem to have included a predominant element of Pharisees, and these rabbis assuredly regarded themselves as the continuators of Pharisaism. Yohanan ben Zakkai, who first stood at the head of the Yavnean circle, was later on said to have been a disciple of Hillel. More credibly, Gamaliel II, who succeeded Yohanan as head of the Yavnean institution, is regarded as the grandson of Gamaliel, a Pharisee in the council of the temple who is mentioned in Acts 5.34 in connection with the trial of Paul. In all, therefore, we may regard the Yavnean rabbis as successors (if not in all details continuators) of the Pharisees before 70, and treat the two as a single continuous sect of Judaism. (Chapter Six refines this judgment.)

What was the dominant trait of Pharisaism before 70? It was, as depicted both in the rabbinic traditions about the Pharisees and in the gospels, concern for certain matters of rite, in particular, eating one's meals in a state of ritual purity as if one were a temple priest, and carefully giving the required tithes and offerings due to the priesthood. The gospels' agenda on Pharisaism also added tithing, fasting, sabbath observance, vows and oaths, and the like, but the main point was keeping the ritual purity laws outside the temple, where the priests had to observe ritual purity when they carried out the requirements of the cult. To be sure, the gospels also include a fair amount of hostile polemic, some of it rather extreme, but these intra-Judaic matters are not our concern. All that can be learnt from the accusations, for instance, that the Pharisees were a brood of vipers, morally blind, sinners, and unfaithful, is one fact: Christian Jews and Pharisaic Jews were at odds.

The Pharisees, therefore, were those Jews who believed that one must keep the purity laws outside the temple. Other Jews, following the plain sense of Leviticus, supposed that purity laws were to be kept only in the temple, where the priests had to enter a state of ritual purity in order to carry out the requirements of the cult, such as animal sacrifice. They also had to eat their temple food in a state of ritual purity, but lay people did not. To be sure, everyone who went to the temple had to be ritually pure, but outside the temple the laws of ritual purity were not observed, for it was not required that non-cultic activities be conducted in a state of levitical cleanness.

But the Pharisees held, to the contrary, that even outside the temple, in one's own home, people had to follow the laws of ritual purity in the only circumstance in which they might apply, namely, at the table. They therefore held that secular food, that is, ordinary, everyday meals, must be eaten in a state of ritual purity as if one were a temple priest. The Pharisees thus arrogated to themselves -- and to all Jews equally -- the status of the temple priests and did the things which priests must do on account of that status. The table of every Jew in his home was seen to be like the table of the Lord in the Jerusalem temple. The commandment, 'You shall be a kingdom of priests and a hold people' (Ex. 19.6), was taken literally. The whole country was holy. The table of every man possessed the same order of sanctity as the table of the cult. But, at this time, only the Pharisees held such a viewpoint, and eating unconsecrated food as if one were a temple priest at the Lord's table was thus one major signification that a Jew was a Pharisee, a sectarian.

We see, therefore, that the Dead Sea Sect, the Christian Jews, and the Pharisees all stressed the eating of ritual meals. But while the Qumranians and the Christians tended to oppose sacrifice as such, and to prefer to achieve forgiveness of sin through ritual baths and communion meals, the Pharisees before 70 continued to revere the temple and its cult, and afterwards they drew up the laws which would govern the temple when it should be restored. In the meantime, they held that (b. Berakhot 55a), 'As long as the temple stood, the altar atoned for Israel. But now a man's table atones for him.'

The response of the Pharisees to the destruction of the temple is known to us only from rabbinic materials, which underwent revisions over many centuries. A story about Yohanan ben Zakkai and his disciple, Joshua ben Hananiah, gives us in a few words the main outline of the established Pharisaic-rabbinic view of the destruction:

> Once, as Rabban Yohanan ben Zakkai was coming forth from Jerusalem, Rabbi Joshua followed after him and beheld the temple in ruins.
> 'Woe unto us,' Rabbi Joshua cried, 'that this, the place where the iniquities of Israel were atoned for, is laid waste!'
> 'My son,' Rabban Yohanan said to him, 'be not grieved. We have another atonement as effective as this. And what is it? It is acts of lovingkindness, as it is said, <u>For I desire mercy and not sacrifice</u> [Hos. 6.6] (<u>Abot de Rabbi Nathan, ch. 4</u>).

How shall we relate the arcane rules about ritual purity to the public calamity faced by the heirs of the Pharisees at Yavneh? What connection between the ritual purity of the 'kingdom of priests' and the atonement of sins in the temple?

To Yohanan ben Zakkai, preserving the temple was not an end in itself. He taught that there was another means of reconciliation between God and Israel, so that the temple and its cult were not decisive. What really counted in the life of the Jewish people? Torah, piety. For the zealots and messianists of the day, the answer was power, politics, the right to live under one's own rulers.

What was the will of God? It was doing deeds of lovingkindness: 'I desire mercy, not sacrifice' (Hos. 6.6) meant to Yohanan, 'We have a means of atonement as effective as the temple, and it is doing deeds of lovingkindness.' Just as willingly as men would contribute bricks and mortar for the rebuilding of a sanctuary, so they ought to contribute renunciation, self-sacrifice, love, for the building of a sacred community. Earlier, Pharisaism had held that the temple should be everywhere, even in the home and hearth. Now Yohanan taught that sacrifice greater than the temple's must characterize the life of the community. If one were to do something for God in a time when the temple was no more, the offering must be the gift of selfless compassion. The holy altar must be the streets and market-places of the world, as, formerly, the purity of the temple had to be observed in the streets and marked-places of Jerusalem. The earlier history of the Pharisaic sect thus had laid the groundwork for Yohanan ben Zakkai's response to Joshua ben Hananiah. It was a natural conclusion for one nurtured in a movement based upon the priesthood of all Israel.

The Pharisees determined to elevate the life of the people, even at home and in the streets, to what the Torah had commanded: <u>You shall be a kingdom of priests and a holy</u>

people. A kingdom in which everyone was a priest, a people all of whom were holy -- a community which would live as if it were always in the temple sanctuary of Jerusalem. Therefore, the purity laws, so complicated and inconvenient, were extended to the life of every Jew in his own home. The temple altar in Jerusalem would be replicated at the table of all Israel. To be sure, only a small minority of the Jewish people, to begin with, obeyed the law as taught by the Pharisaic party. Therefore, the group had to reconsider the importance of political life, through which the law might everywhere be effected. The party which had abandoned politics for piety now had to recover access to the instruments of power for the sake of piety. It was the way towards realization of what was essentially not a political aspiration.

For the history of Judaism, the sole significant force to emerge from the catastrophe of 70 was the Pharisees. As we noted, that is not to suggest their influence from 70 to 135 was considerable. It almost certainly was negligible, because the very fact of the war of 132-5 suggests that others, not Pharisees, held predominance in the life of the Jewish people. Whatever we may think of the Pharisaic and larger rabbinic movement of this period, we cannot suppose it bore primary responsibility for the eschatological and messianic aspirations which seem to have produced the new war. The question before us is, How did the Pharisaic stress on the 'priesthood of all Israel', on constituting the temple in the everyday life of the people, develop in response to the task of the new age? For our present purpose, we shall take a single instance of the appropriation and revision of the temple's symbolic structure to exemplify a much larger phenomenon. That instance is the matter of 'leprosy'. Scripture held that a leper was unclean and therefore prohibited from entering the temple. Now, as we shall see, leprosy was given a social interpretation and assigned a place in the moral life of the community.

Leprosy is said to be caused by slander or pride. The connection with slander is based upon the case of Miriam, the connection with pride on that of Uzziah:

> [Take heed in an attack of leprosy to be very careful to do according to all that the levitical priests shall direct you...] Remember what God did to Miriam' (Deut. 24.9).
> What has one thing to do with the other?
> But it teaches that she was punished only on account of gossip.

>   And is it not an argument a fortiori? If this
> happened to Miriam, who did not speak in such a way in
> Moses' presence, one who speaks ill of his fellow in his
> very presence, how much the more so!
>   R. Simeon b. Eleazar says, 'Also leprosy comes on
> account of arrogance, for so we find concerning Uzziah,
> about whom Scripture says: "But when he was strong, he
> grew proud, to his destruction. For he was false to the
> Lord his God and entered the temple of the Lord to burn
> incense on the altar of incense. But Azariah the priest
> went in after him, with eighty priests of the Lord who
> were men of valor; and they withstood King Uzziah and said
> to him, 'It is not for you, Uzziah, to burn incense to the
> Lord, but for the priests the sons of Aaron, who are
> consecrated, to burn incense. Go out of the sanctuary,
> for you have done wrong, and it will bring you no honour
> from the Lord God.' Then when he became angry with the
> priests, leprosy broke out on his forehead...'" (II Chron.
> 26.16-19).
>   (Sifre Mesora^C Parashah 5.9 [Tos. Neg. 6.7; Sifre
> Deut. 275])

The rabbinic view that leprosy is caused by gossip or slander ('evil speech') depends upon the interpretation of Miriam's behavior. In Numbers 12.1-15, Miriam and Aaron are guilty of criticizing Moses because of his wife and saying that they are capable of prophecy just as much as he: 'Has the Lord indeed spoken only through Moses? Has he not spoken through us also?' So Moses' authority is called into question, and the divine response is to declare Moses' prophecy of a higher order than theirs. Then Miriam is turned into a leper. The issue of 'gossip' therefore is hardly obvious. To the rabbinic eisegetes, the rebellion against Moses is of no consequence, the criticism of his marriage is central. Then this criticism is interpreted as slander, lashon hara^C, and the rest follows.

Simeon b. Eleazar has a better case, for II Chronicles 26:16-21 says clearly that Uzziah was made a leper because of his intervening in the cult, and he did so because of pride. Both views of the origin of leprosy take for granted the established notion that the punishment of impurity signifies the commission of an antecedent crime; and the punishment will exactly fit the crime. Later on this latter idea will generate efforts to show why the punishment is fitting to the crime. Then all the other biblical references to leprosy will be tied to specific sins. In the first stage, towards the middle of the second century, of rabbinic thought on the subject, the attempt to spell out this correspondence produces only Judah b. Ilai's and Eliezer b. R. Yose's explanations for the association of croup with the mouth. The innovation of earlier rabbinic Judaism is the view of impurity -- leprosy -- not as a

metaphor for sin in general, but as a sign that a specific sin
has been committed. This then will generate the effort to show
the reasonable relationship between a particular form of
punishment, on the one side, and a specific sin on the other,
an approach to be richly elaborated later on.

This mode of thought is part of a larger rabbinic view
that suffering comes primarily in consequence of human fail-
ings. 'Measure for measure' characterizes divine justice. The
employment of purity laws in this connection therefore constitutes part of the rabbinic accounting for and justification of
the fate of the Jewish people after the destruction of the
second temple, and in particular, the disaster of the Bar-
Kokhba War. Just as the people were told by the rabbis that
they had sinned but could achieve regeneration through atonement and good behavior, so in the specific and very ordinary
instances of disease or early death one might try to show that
a particular sin lay at the origin of the suffering. The
purity rules provide an explanation for individual suffering
because the impurity -- leprosy, menstruation -- afflicts the
private person. So through their interpretation of the purity
laws, the generalized allegation of the rabbis after 70 that
Israel suffered on account of sin, after 135 is made precise
and concrete in the life of the private person. The emphasis
on the individual and his personal impurity is consistent with
the stress of the priestly prophet, Ezekiel, that the individual bears the burden of his own guilt. The person who sins
will die, but his family will not. Ezekiel's view of purity is
part of the larger priestly ideology. But the stress on the
individual -- in connection with either sin or uncleanness --
seems to have been at first Ezekiel's peculiar contribution,
for priestly law commonly views sacrifices as collective.
Ezekiel introduced his notion of individual retribution as a
novelty, given him by revelation and contradicting the common
opinion.

I think this broader theological task provides the context
in which to understand the sayings before us. If the rabbis of
the second century occur most commonly, it is because after the
disaster of the Bar-Kokhba War the problem of theodicy and the
application of the peculiarly rabbinic solution proved most
pressing for ordinary folk, who suffered in the general debacle
far more severely than was the case after 70. But the general
outlines of their answer, linking suffering to sin, had of
course been well-established for many generations.

The rabbinic theodicy of individual suffering occurs
within a still larger conception, beginning with Pharisaism
before 70 and carried forward by rabbinic Judaism afterwards.
As I stressed earlier, the Pharisees before 70 extended the
temple's sanctity to the affairs of ordinary folk, requiring
the people eat their meals in a state of purity appropriate for
the sanctuary and preserve their food from impurity originally
pertinent only to the cult and priesthood. After 70 the
rabbinical continuators of Pharisaism treated sacrifice itself
as something to be done in everyday life, comparing deeds of
lovingkindness to the sacrifices by which sins were atoned
for. So it was an established trait of Pharisaism and later
rabbinism to apply cultic symbols to extra-cultic, communal
matters, and thus to regard the temple's sanctity as extending
to the streets of the villages. This was done after 70 by
assigning ethical equivalents to temple rites, on the one side,
and by comparing study of Torah to the act of sacrifice and the
rabbi to the temple priest, on the other. It is in this
context that the interpretation of the purity rules was undertaken. By locating ethical lapses as the cause of impurity,
beginning with the view that leprosy is a sign that one is
guilty of having gossipped or been arrogant, the second-century
rabbis simply carried forward the established trait of rabbinism and its antecedent Pharisaism. Just as earlier, cultic
purity was extended to the home, and, later on, study of Torah
was substituted for cultic sacrifice and deeds of lovingkindness for sin-offering, so it now was natural to take over
the purity rules and to endow them with ethical, therefore with
everyday, communal significance, instead of leaving them wholly
within the cult. It was a continuation of an earlier tendency
to ethicize, spiritualize, and moralize the cult by treating
the holy people -- the community of Israel -- as equivalent to
the holy sanctuary. This tendency to be sure had already been
present in a vague and general way in the biblical treatment of
purity as a metaphor for righteousness and impurity for sin.
But it was not greatly elaborated and extended to the minutiae
of daily life, as was normal for rabbinism in many other ways.

What is noteworthy therefore is the extensive rabbinic use
of the symbols of impurity in connection with social ills.
Sermons against gossiping or selfishness may readily be constructed without inclusion of the claim that it is the leper in
particular who has gossiped or acted selfishly. The cultic
metaphor, 'unclean,' and its specification in terms of leprosy

or bodily discharges seem curiously inappropriate or unnatural to the specific social vices against which the rabbis inveighed. They are used by the rabbis because the community of Israel now is regarded as the temple. What kept people out of the sanctuary in olden times therefore is going even now to exclude them from the life of the community. The thrust of the rabbis' sermons is to remove from the community people guilty of gossiping or arrogance and the like; this very act of removal is offered by them as the explanation for their relating gossiping to leprosy, as we observed.

The rabbis' larger tendency to preserve, but to take over within the rabbinical system, the symbols of the temple is herein illustrated. Just as the rabbi is the new priest, study of Torah is the new cult, deeds of lovingkindness the new sacrifice, so the community formed on the basis of the rabbinic Torah is going to be protected from social uncleanness just as the old temple was protected from cultic uncleanness. This accounts not only for the preservation, but for the considerable elaboration and extension, of the cultic symbols of uncleanness. These usages after 70 were no more pertinent to, or part of the ordinary life of, the Jewish community in the land of Israel than they were before that time to Alexandrian Jewry. Two motives lie behind the rabbinic tendency to claim that impurity signifies antecedent sin: first, to extend the generalized theodicy to the specific situation of ordinary folk, and second, to exploit the temple's imagery for the rabbinic community. The second motive in general sets the context for what is done in a concrete way in the first.

Fully to appreciate the meaning of the destruction of the temple, we turn finally to the major anthropological statement on the subject of purity on which we have centred our attention. Professor Mary Douglas, studying pollution and uncleanness, produces results of consequence to the much larger issue of the temple and its place in the imagination of society. She shows what is at issue and allows us to interpret the full weight and significance of the temple -- and its destruction -- in the structure of being created by Israelite faith. She states, 'The more deeply we go...the more obvious it becomes that we are studying symbolic systems...'(34). This constitutes the main result of the inquiry before us. Ideas of purity and impurity were inseparable from, and expressive of, the larger conceptions of reality of the communities that held them. Because of that fact, the ideas adduced to explain or

interpret purity are going to carry implications for the larger
system of which they are a part. And that fact is admirably
explained within Douglas' larger theory:

> Now is the time to identify pollution. Granted that all
> spiritual powers are part of the social system. They
> express it and provide institutions for manipulating it.
> This means that the power in the universe is ultimately
> hitched to society, since so many changes of fortune are
> set off by persons in one kind of social position or
> another. But there are other dangers to be reckoned with,
> which persons may set off knowingly or unknowingly, which
> are not part of the psyche and which are not to be bought
> or learned by initiation and training. These are pollu-
> tion powers which inhere in the structure of ideas itself
> and which punish a symbolic breaking of that which should
> be joined or joining of that which should be separate. It
> follows from this that pollution is a type of danger which
> is not likely to occur except where the lines of struc-
> ture, cosmic or social, are clearly defined (113).

The full weight and meaning of the loss of the temple of
Jerusalem cannot be more forcefully stated.

Bibliography

Baron, S.W. A Social and Religious History of the Jews II:
    Ancient Times, II, New York: Columbia University Press,
    1952, 89-122, 368-77.

Douglas, M. Purity and Danger, London/New York: Routledge &
    Kegan Paul/Praeger 1966.

Neusner, J. A History of the Jews in Babylonia, I-V, Leiden:
    Brill, 1965-1970.

Idem, Development of a Legend: Studies on the Traditions
    Concerning Yohanan ben Zakkai, Leiden: Brill, 1970.

Idem, A Life of Yohanan ben Zakkai, SPB 6, [2]1970.

Idem, Eliezer ben Hyrcanus: The Tradition and the Man, I-II,
    Leiden: Brill, 1973.

Idem, From Politics to Piety: The Emergence of Pharisaic
    Judaism, New York: KTAV, 1977.

Idem, The Idea of Purity in Ancient Judaism: The Haskell
    Lectures, 1972-1973, Leiden: Brill, 1973.

Idem, A History of the Mishnaic Laws of Purities, I-XXII, SJLA
    6, 1974-1977.

Idem, First-Century Judaism in Crisis: Yohanan ben Zakkai and
    the Renaissance of Torah, Nashville: Abingdon Press 1975.

Yadin, Y. The Finds from the Bar Kokhba Period in the Cave of
    Letters, Jerusalem: Israel Exploration Society 1963.

Idem, Bar-Kokhba: The Rediscovery of the Legendary Hero of the
    Last Jewish Revolt Against Imperial Rome, London/New
    York: Weidenfeld & Nicolson/Random House 1971.

Chapter Six

THE FORMATION OF RABBINIC JUDAISM
METHODOLOGICAL ISSUES AND SUBSTANTIVE THESES

I

THE NATURE OF THE SOURCES

Rabbinic Judaism[1] took shape in the century from 70 to 170, making use of the antecedent heritage of the Old Testament as well as of the 'traditions of the fathers' associated with Pharisaism and of certain convictions and procedures of scribism. An amalgam of Pharisaism, scribism, and yet its own distinctive interests shaped in the crucible of the destruction of the Jerusalem Temple, Rabbinic Judaism left behind an immense literary corpus. The use of this literature for historical and religious-historical purposes, in particular for the examination of the history of the major ideas and mythic motifs of Rabbinic Judaism, is exceedingly complex. Since the present paper is addressed to scholars well aware of equivalent difficulties in the use of evidence pertinent to other philosophico-religious groups in ancient times, it is best to lay out, at the outset, the methodological alternatives under consideration and debate at present time. Then, having argued in favor of one available alternative, I shall present the primary results attained thereby. These results, as the title makes clear, pertain solely to the earliest stages of Rabbinic Judaism. But they should serve to illustrate what is to be expected from the nascent methodological approaches undertaken by this writer in the past decade.

---

[1]The term is defined below, part III. This paper is intended to summarize my research, cited in notes 3-5, on the nature of the sources pertinent to earlier Rabbinic Judaism and the way in which those sources are to be used for the historical enterprise. In the cited works, the sources are translated and fully analyzed from various perspectives. Merely citing an unanalyzed pericope in the present paper would serve no useful purpose, since without full discussion of the relationship of said pericope to all other evidence, the meaning and historical usefulness of the item are hardly going to be self-evident. That is why I refer the reader to the complete compendia of pertinent materials and their analysis. Here are given only the results of much more extensive work.

II

TWO APPROACHES TO THE USE OF SOURCES OF RABBINISM:

TRADITIONAL AND CRITICAL

The established, traditional and Orthodox conceptions on the use of the rabbinical literature for historical purposes are admirably illustrated in a current and important work by Ephraim Urbach.[2] Through the analysis and criticism of that work, I propose to indicate how and why these conceptions fail to accord with contemporary and correct criticism and to spell out the real problems and their methodological solutions. The established approach is called 'traditional' because it stands wholly within the presuppositions of the texts it proposes to use for historical purposes and because, for obvious reasons, it is staunchly espoused and defended within Orthodox Jewish circles, particularly in the State of Israel, where credulous traditionalism is deemed historical, and truly critical efforts are dismissed unread.

Ephraim E. Urbach, professor of Talmud at the Hebrew University and author of numerous articles and books on the Talmud and later rabbinic literature, in 'The Sages' presents a compendious and in mnay ways definitive work intended "to describe the concepts and beliefs of tl.e Tannaim and Amoraim and to elucidate them against the background of their actual life and environment". When published in Hebrew, in 1969, the work enjoyed immediate success, going into a second edition within two years. Urbach is an imposing figure in Israeli scholarly and religious-political circles, serving as president of the Israel Academy of Sciences and Humanities and running for the presidency of the State of Israel as candidate of the right-wing and 'religious' political parties. Within Orthodox Judaism Urbach derives from the German stream, which proposes to combine piety with academic learning. The work before us has been accurately described by M.D. Heer (Encyclopaedia Judaica 16, 1971, 4): "He [Urbach] outlines the views of the rabbis on the important theological issues such as creation, providence, and the nature of man. In this work Urbach synthe-sizes the voluminous literature on these subjects and presents the views of the Talmudic authorities". The topics are as

---

[2]The Sages. Their Concepts and Beliefs. By Ephraim E. Urbach. Translated from the Hebrew by Israel Abrahams. Jerusalem: The Magnes Press. The Hebrew University, 1975. Two volumes. I. Text, pp. xxii and 692; II. Notes, p. 383.

follows: belief in one God; the presence of God in the world;
"nearness and distance -- Omnipresent and heaven;" the power of
God; magic and miracle; the power of the divine name; the
celestial retinue; creation; man; providence; written law and
oral law; the commandments; acceptance of the yoke of the
kingdom of heaven; sin, reward, punishment, suffering, etc.;
the people of Israel and its sages, a chapter which encompasses
the election of Israel, the status of the sages in the days of
the Hasmoneans, Hillel, the regime of the sage after the
destruction of the Temple, and so on; and redemption. The
second volume contains footnotes, a fairly brief and highly
selective bibliography, and alas, a merely perfunctory index.
The several chapters, like the work as a whole, are organized
systematically, consisting of sayings and stories relevant to
the theme under discussion, together with Urbach's episodic
observations and comments on them.

In the context of earlier work on Talmudic theology and
religion, Urbach's contribution is, as I said, definitive, a
distinct improvement in every way. Compared to a similar,
earlier compendium of Talmudic sayings on theological subjects,
A. Hyman's Osar divré hakhamin ufitgamehem (Tel Aviv 1934), a
collection of sayings laid out alphabetically, according to
catchword, Urbach's volumes have the advantage of supplying not
merely sayings but cogent discussions of the various sayings
and a more fluent, coherent presentation of them in essay
form. Solomon Schechter's Some Aspects of Rabbinic Theology
(New York 1909, based on essays in the Jewish Quarterly Review
printed in 1894-1896) covers exactly what it says, some aspects, by contrast to the much more ambitious dimension of the
present work. The comparison to George Foot Moore's Judaism in
the First Centuries of the Christian Era: The Age of the
Tannaim (Cambridge 1927-1930) is somewhat more complex. Moore
certainly has the advantage of elegant presentation. Urbach's
prose, in I. Abraham's English translation, comes through as
turgid and stodgy, while Moore's is the opposite. Morton Smith
comments on Moore's work, "Although it too much neglects the
mystical, magical, and apocalyptic sides of Judaism, its
apology for tannaitic teaching as a reasonable, humane, and
pious working out of biblical tradition is conclusive..."
(Enclyclopaedia Judaica 12, 1971, 293-294; compare Harvard
Library Bulletin 15, 1967, pp. 169-179). By contrast to Moore,
Urbach introduces sayings of Amoraim into the discussion of
each category, and, since both Urbach and Moore aim to present

a large selection of sayings on the several topics, Urbach's
work is on the face of it a more comprehensive collection.

Urbach's comments on his predecessors (I, pp. 5-18)
underline the theological bias present in most, though not all,
former studies. Wilhelm Bousset and Hugo Gressmann, Die
Religion des Judentums im späthellenistischen Zeitalter (Leip-
zig 1926; repr. [Tubingen 1966]) is wanting because rabbinic
sources are used sparingly and not wholly accurately and
because it relies on "external sources", meaning apocryphal
literature and Hellenistic Jewish writings. Urbach's own
criticism of Moore, that "he did not always go deeply enough
into the essence of the problems that he discussed", certainly
cannot be leveled against Urbach himself. His further reserva-
tion is that Moore "failed to give an account of the origin of
the beliefs and concepts, of their struggles and evolution, of
their entire chequered course till their crystallization, of
the immense dynamism and vitality of the spiritual life of the
Second Temple period, of the tension in the relations between
the parties and sects and between the various sections of the
Sages themselves". This view underlines the historical ambi-
tion of Urbach's approach and emphasizes his view of his own
contribution, cited at the outset: to elucidate the concepts
and beliefs of the Tannaim and Amoraim against the background
of their actual life and environment. Since that is Urbach's
fundamental claim, the work must be considered not only in the
context of what has gone before, in which, as I said, it
emerges as a substantial step forward, but also in the setting
of its own definition and understanding of the historical task,
its own theory of how Talmudic materials are to be used for
historical knowledge. In this regard it is not satisfactory.

There are some fairly obvious problems, on which we need
not dwell at length. Urbach's selection of sources for analysis is both narrowly canonical and somewhat confusing. We
often hear from Philo, but seldom from the Essene Library of
Qumran, still more rarely from the diverse works assembled by
R.H. Charles as the Apocrypha and Pseudepigrapha of the Old
Testament (Oxford 1913), and the like. If we seek to describe
the Talmudic rabbis, surely we cannot ask Philo to testify to
their opinions. If we listen to Philo, surely we ought to hear
-- at least for the purpose of comparison and contrast -- from
books written by Palestinian Jews of various kinds. The
Targumim are allowed no place at all because they are deemed
'late'. (The work of historians of traditions, e.g., Joseph

Heinemann, and of comparative Midrash, e.g., Renée Bloch and
Geza Vermes, plays no role at all in this history!) But
documents which came to redaction much later than the several
Targumim (by any estimate of the date of the latter) make rich
and constant contributions to the discussion. Within a given
chapter, the portrayal of the sources will move rapidly from
biblical to Tannaitic to Amoraic sources, as though the line of
development were single, unitary, and harmonious, and as though
there were no intervening developments which shaped later
conceptions. Differentiations among the stages of Tannaitic
and Amoraic sayings tend to be episodic. Commonly, slight
sustained effort is made to treat them in their several sequences, let alone to differentiate among schools and circles
within a given period. Urbach takes with utmost seriousness
his title, The sages, their concepts and beliefs, and his
history, topic by topic, reveals remarkably little variation,
development, or even movement. It would not be fair to Urbach
to suggest that all he has done is publish his card-files. But
I think his skill at organization and arrangement of materials
tends to outrun his interest in differentiation and comparison
within and among them, let alone in the larger, sequential
history of major ideas and their growth and coherent development over the centuries. One looks in vain for Urbach's effort
to justify treating 'the sages' as essentially a coherent and
timeless group.

Let us turn, rather, to the more fundamental difficulties
presented by the work, because, as I said, it is to be received
as the definitive and (probably) final product of a long-
established approach to the study of Talmudic religion and
history. Urbach has certainly brought to their ultimate
realization the methods and concepts of his predecessors.

First, let us ask, does the world-view of the Talmudic
sages emerge in a way which the ancient sages themselves would
have recognized? From the viewpoint of their organization and
description of reality, their world-view, it is certain that
the sages would have organized their card-files quite differently. We know that is the case because we do not have, among
the chapters before us, a single one which focuses upon the
theme of one of the orders, let alone tractates, within which
the rabbis divided and presented their various statements on
reality, e.g., Seeds, the material basis of life; Seasons, the
organization and differentiation of time; Women, the status of
the individual; Damages, the conduct of civil life including

government; Holy Things, the material service of God; and Purities, the immaterial base of divine reality in this world. The matter concerns not merely the superficial problem of organizing vast quantities of data. The Talmudic rabbis left a large and exceedingly complex, well-integrated legacy of law. Clearly, it is through that legacy that they intended to make their fundamental statements upon the organization and meaning of reality. An account of their concepts and beliefs which ignores nearly the whole of the halakhah surely is slightly awry.

In fairness to Urbach, I must stress that he shows himself well-aware of the centrality of halakhah in the expression of the world-view of the Talmudic rabbis. He correctly criticizes his predecessors for neglecting the subject and observes, "The Halakha does not openly concern itself with beliefs and concepts; it determines, in practice, the way in which one should walk... Nevertheless beliefs and concepts lie at the core of many Halakhot; only their detection requires exhaustive study of the history of the Halakha combined with care to avoid fanciful conjectures and unfounded explanations". Urbach occasionally does introduce halakhic materials. But, as is clear, the fundamental structure of his account of Talmudic theology is formed in accord not with the equivalent structure of the Talmud -- the halakhah -- but with the topics and organizing rubrics treated by all nineteenth- and twentieth-century Protestant historical studies of theology: God, ethics, revelation, and the like. That those studies are never far from mind is illustrated by Urbach's extensive discussion of whether Talmudic ethics was theonomous or autonomous (I, pp. 320ff.), an issue important only from the viewpoint of nineteenth-century Jewish ethical thought and its response to Kant. But Urbach's discussion on that matter is completely persuasive, stating what is certainly the last word on the subject. He can hardly be blamed for criticizing widely-held and wrong opinions.

Second, has Urbach taken account of methodological issues important in the study of the literary and historical character of the sources? In particular, does he deal with the fundamental questions of how these paricular sources are to be used for historical purposes? The answer is a qualified negative. On many specific points, he contributes sporadic philological observations, interesting opinions and judgments as to the lateness of one saying as against the antiquity of another, subjective opinions on what is more representative or reliable than something else. If these opinions are not systematic and if they reveal no uniform criterion, sustainedly applied to all sources, they nonetheless derive from a mind of immense learning and cognitive experience. Not all judgment must be critical, and not all expression of personal taste systematic. The dogmatic opinions of a man of such self-evident mastery of the tradition, one who, in addition, clearly is an exemplar of the tradition for his own setting, are important evidence for the study and interpretation of the tradition itself, particularly in its modern phase.

Yet we must ask, if a saying is assigned to an ancient authority, how do we know that he really said it? If a story is told, how do we know that the events the story purports to describe actually took place? And if not, just what are we to make of said story and saying for historical purposes? Further, if we have a saying attributed to a first-century authority in a document generally believed to have been redacted five hundred or a thousand years later, how do we know that the attribution of the saying is valid, and that the saying informs us of the state of opinion in the first century, not only in the sixth or eleventh in which it was written down and obviously believed true and authoritative? Do we still hold, as an axiom of historical scholarship, 'ain muqdam ume'uhar (chronology does not apply) in the Talmud?! And again, do not the sayings assigned to a first-century authority, redacted in documents deriving from the early third century, possess greater credibility than those first appearing in documents redacted in the fifth, tenth, or even fifteenth centuries? Should we not, on the face of it, distinguish between more and less reliable materials? The well-known tendency of medieval writers to put their opinions into the mouths of the ancients, as in the case of the Zohar, surely warns us to be cautious about using documents redacted, even formulated, five hundred or a thousand or more years after the events of which they speak.

There is yet a further, equally simple problem. The corpus of evidence is simply huge. Selectivity characterizes even the most thorough and compendious accounts, and I cannot imagine one more comprehensive than Urbach's. But should we not devise means for the filtering downward of some fundamental, widely- and well-attested opinions, out of the mass of evidence, rather than capriciously selecting what we like

and find interesting? We have few really comprehensive accounts of the history of a single idea or concept. Urbach
himself has produced some of the better studies which we do
have. It seems somewhat premature to describe so vast a world
in the absence of a far more substantial corpus of Vorstudien
of specific ideas and the men who held them than is available.
Inevitably, one must characterize the treatment of one topic
after another as unhistorical and superficial, and this is
despite the author's impressive efforts to do history and to do
it thoroughly and in depth.

After all, Urbach has done this great work without the
advantage of studies of the history of the traditions assigned
over the centuries to one authority or another. He has at hand
scarcely any critical work comparing various versions of a
story appearing in successive compilations. He has no possi-
bility of recourse to comprehensive inquiries into the Talmud's
forms and literary traits, redactional tendencies, even definitive accounts of the date of the redaction of most of the
literature used for historical purposes. He cannot consult
works on the thought of any of the individual Amoraim or on the
traits of schools and circles among them, for there is none of
critical substance. Most collections which pass as biographies
even of Tannaim effect no differentiation among layers and
strata of the stories and sayings, let alone attempting to
describe the history of the traditions on the basis of which
historical biography is to be recovered. The laws assigned,
even in 'Mishnah-Tosefta', to a given Tanna have not been
investigated as to their underlying presuppositions and unifying convictions, even their gross thematic agendum. If Urbach
speaks of "the rabbis" and differentiates only episodically
among the layers and divisions of sayings, in accord either
with differing opinions on a given question or with the historical development of evidently uniformly-held opinions, he is
hardly to be criticized. The episodic contributions he himself
makes in large measure constitute such history of ideas as
presently is in hand. And, as I said, even that history is
remarkable for the pre-critical methods and uncritical presuppositions upon which it is based.

Nor have I alluded to the intractable problems of in-
ternal, philosophico-theological analysis of ideas and their
inner structures, once their evident historical, or sequential,
development, among various circles and schools of a given
generation and over a period of hundreds of years, has been

elucidated. That quite separate investigation, analysis of the
logic and meaning of the concepts and beliefs of the sages,
requires definition in its own terms, not in accord with the
limited and simple criteria of working historians. If Urbach
does not attempt it, no one else has entirely succeeded either. In this regard, Urbach's cavalier dismissal of the work
of Marmorstein, Heschel, and Kadushin, among others, is not
heartening. While they may not have 'persuaded' Urbach of the
correctness of their theses, while they may have been wrong in
some of their conclusions, and while their methods may have
been unrefined, they at least have attempted the task which
Urbach refuses even to undertake. One of the less fortunate
aspects of Urbach's book, which makes for unpleasant reading,
is the way in which he treats the work of other scholars. In
the case of the above named, this is not only disgraceful, it
also is disastrous for Urbach's own undertaking. And since the
whole opinion on works of considerable scholarship is the
single word 'worthless' or 'unpersuasive', it may be observed
that there is a certain subjectivity which seems to preclude
Urbach's reasoned discussion of what he likes and does not
like, in the work of many others and to prevent any sort of
rational exchange of ideas.

Urbach's work, as I said, in the balance majestically and
magnificently brings to their full realization the methods and
suppositions of the past hundred years. I cannot imagine that
anyone again will want, from these perspectives, to approach
the task of describing all of "the concepts and beliefs of the
Tannaim and Amoraim", of elucidating all of them "against the
background of their actual life and environment". So far as
the work can be done in accord with established methods, here
it has been done very competently indeed. Accordingly, we may
well forgive the learned author for the sustained homiletical
character of his inquiry and its blatantly apologetic purposes: "The aim of our work is to give an epitome of the
beliefs and concepts of the Sages as the history of a struggle
to instill religious and ethical ideals into the everyday life
of the community and the individual, while preserving at the
same time the integrity and unity of the nation and directing
its way in this world as a preparation for another world that
is wholly perfect... Their eyes and their hearts were turned
Heavenward, yet one type was not to be found among them...
namely the mystic who seeks to liberate himself from his ego
and in doing so is preoccupied with himself alone. They saw

their mission in work here in the world below. There were
Sages who inclined to extremism in their thought and deeds, and
there were those who preached the way of compromise, which they
did not, however, determine on the basis of convenience. Some
were severe and exacting, while others demonstrated an extreme
love of humanity and altruism. The vast majority of them
recognized the complexities of life with its travail and joy,
its happiness and tragedy, and this life served them also as a
touchstone for their beliefs and concepts". All of this may
well be so, but it remains to be demonstrated as historical
fact in the way in which contemporary critical historians
generally demonstrate matters of fact. It requires analysis
and argument in the undogmatic and unapologetic spirit characteristic of contemporary studies in the history of ideas and of
religions. But in the context in which these words of Urbach
are written, among the people who will read them, this statement of purpose puts forth a noble ideal, one which might well
be emulated by the 'sages' -- exemplars and politicians of
Orthodox Judaism -- to whom, I believe, Urbach speaks most
directly and persuasively, and by whom (alone) his results
certainly will be taken as historical fact. The publishing
success of the book and the well-merited recognition accorded
its learned author are hopeful signs that the ideal of the
sages of old indeed has not been lost upon their most recent
avatars. It is by no means a reduction of learning to its
sociological and political relevance to say that, if it were
only for his advocacy of the humane and constructive position
just now quoted, Urbach has made a truly formidable contribution to the contemporary theological life of Orthodox Judaism.

To respond to a work of such importance as Urbach's, it
will not suffice to outline problems of method which await
solution. Having stressed, for example, the importance of
beginning the inquiry into the world-view of the Talmudic
rabbis with the study of the law, in particular of the earliest
stratum, faithfully represented by 'Mishnah-Tosefta', I have
now to propose the sorts of work to be done. Since I have
raised the question of how we know what is assigned to a person
was really said by him, and since by implication I have suggested that we cannot affirmatively answer that question, what
sort of inquiry do I conceive to be possible, and upon what
historical-epistemological basis? Let me here present very
briefly an alternative conception of how to define and approach

the formidable task accomplished by Urbach, in accord with the
prevailing methods and within established suppositions about
the detailed and concrete historicity of Talmudic evidences:
the description of the world-view of 'our sages'.

The problems that lie ahead and the line of research
leading to their solution are now to be specified. Let us
begin with the matter generally regarded as settled: the
meaning of the texts. While philological research by Semitists
and archaeological discoveries self-evidently will clarify the
meanings of words and the identification of objects mentioned
in the rabbinical literature, there is yet another task, the
fresh exegesis of the whole of rabbinical literature within the
discipline of contemporary hermeneutical conceptions. The
established exegesis takes for granted an axiom which is simply
false: that all texts are to be interpreted in the light of
all other texts. Talmudic discussion of Mishnah and its
meanings invariably shape the received interpretation of
Mishnah, for example. If 'Tosefta' -- itself a commentary --
supplies a conception of Mishnah's principle or rule, then
'Tosefta' places the imprint of its interpretation upon the
meaning of Mishnah.

Now no one would imagine that the original meaning of
Tanakh (the Hebrew Scriptures) is to be uncovered in the pages
of Midrash or in the medieval commentaries to the Scriptures.
On the contrary, everyone understands that Tanakh has been
subjected to a long history of interpretation, and that that
history, while interesting, is germane to the original meaning
of Tanakh only when, on objective and critical grounds, we are
able to affirm it by historical criteria. By contrast, discussion of Mishnaic pericopae in Talmud and medieval commentaries
and codes invariably exhausts the analysis of the meaning of
Mishnaic pericopae. It is to the credit of H. Albeck that his
excellent commentary to Mishnah makes the effort at many points
deliberately to exclude considerations introduced only later
on. This is done not merely to facilitate a simple and popular
interpretation, though Albeck admirably succeeds in doing just
that, but also to present what Albeck considers to be the
primary and original meaning of the law. It is no criticism of
Albeck, limited as he was by his form, a commentary of the most
abbreviated sort, to say that the discussion of the primary
meaning of Mishnah has to begin.

What is meant is simply, What did these words mean to the
people who made them up, in the late first and second century?

What issues can have been in their minds? True, much is to be
learned from the answers to these questions supplied by the
exegetes from the third to the twentieth century. But since,
in the main, the supposition of the established exegetical
tradition is non-historical and therefore uninterested in what
pericopae meant at the outset, the established tradition,
without reevaluation, will not serve any longer. That is not
to suggest it cannot be drawn upon: the contrary is the case.
I know no other road into the heart of a pericope. At the same
time, the established agendum -- the set of issues, problems,
and questions deemed worth consideration -- is to be drastically reshaped, even while much that we have received will be
reaffirmed, if on grounds quite different from those which
motivated the great exegetes.

The classical exegetes faced the task of showing the
profound interrelationships, in logic and meaning, of one law
to the next, of developing and expanding the subtleties and
complexities of law, in the supposition that in hand is a
timeless and harmonious, wholly integrated and unitary structure of law and logic. In other words, the established exegetical tradition properly and correctly ignores questions of
beginning and development, regarding these questions as irrele-
vent to the true meaning of the law under the aspect of eter-
nity. And that is indeed the case -- except when we claim to
speak about specific, historical personalities, at some one
time, who spoke the language of their own day and addressed the
issues of their own epoch. Urbach claims to tell us not about
'Talmudic Judaism' in general -- organized, as is clear, around
various specific topics -- but to describe the history and
development of 'Talmudic Judaism'. Yet, if that is the case,
then the sources adduced in evidence have to be examined with
the question in mind, What did the person who made up or
formulated this saying mean to tell us? And the answer to that
question is not to be located either by repeating the essentially eisegetical results already in hand or by pretending
that everything is obvious.

We have to distinguish between the primary issue, present
to begin with in a pericope, and secondary problems or considerations only later on attached to the pericope. How do we
confidently distinguish between the primary message of a
pericope and the secondary eisegesis found in the great commentaries? We have to ask, What does the narrator, legislator,
or redactor propose to tell us in a particular, distinct

pericope? That is to say, through the routine form-analytical
and literary-critical techniques already available, we have to
isolate the smallest units of tradition, and, removing them
from their redactional as well as their exegetical-eisegetical
framework, ask about their meaning and original intent. Modes
of emphasis and stress, for example, are readily discerned.
Important materials will commonly be placed at the beginning of
a pericope, or underlined through balanced, contrary allegations. But stylistic considerations and formal traits are
helpful primarily in isolating pericopae and establishing their
primary units for analysis. What is decisive is the discern-
ment of what the narrator includes or omits, what seems to be
his obvious concerns and what he ignores.

Once the importance of a fresh exegesis of rabbinical
texts is established, the next problem is to select the documents on which the work should begin. Here Urbach's work
illustrates the fateful error of assuming that rabbinical
literature is essentially timeless, so that there is "neither
early nor late in Torah". Applied to the present work, it
results in the notion that whatever is attributed to anyone was
really said by the person to whom the saying is attributed,
therefore tells us about the period in which he lived -- and
this without regard to the date at which the document in which
said saying occurs was redacted, as I have stressed. Thus side
by side in Urbach's compilation are sayings in Mishnah and in
late Amoraic and even medieval compilations of materials. In a
fresh approach to the problem of the history of Talmudic
Judaism, we should, I believe, establish guidelines by which we
evaluate materials first occurring in late compilations.
Mishnah-Tosefta assuredly comes to redaction by ca. 200 A.D.
On the face of it, Mishnah-Tosefta therefore constitutes a more
reliable testimony to the mind of second-century rabbis than
does Yalqut Shime^{c}oni for our work with the analysis of the
main ideas attributed to authorities in Mishnah-Tosefta. These
have clearly to be worked out, and the materials occurring in
later compilations, of Amoraic and medieval origin, are to be
tested for conceptual and even thematic congruence against the
materials occurring in earlier documents.

The question remains. If it is assumed that Mishnah-
Tosefta testifies to the time in which the document was finally
redacted, then how shall we know what layers of thought come
before the time of the redaction of the document itself? How
shall we know, furthermore, whether a person to whom a saying

is attributed really said it? To deal with the latter question, I do not believe we have any way of verifying whether a
person to whom a saying is attributed actually said it. Our
history of Talmudic Judaism will unfold by periods, may even
produce significant differentiation among named authorities
within the several periods, but it will, so far as I can see,
not supply a definitive answer to the question of whether
^{C}Aqiba really said what he is claimed to have said. While
that question -- whether we have _ipsissima verba_ of a particular historical figure -- is deemed terribly pressing in the
study of the founder of Christianity, the importance of the
question is for theological, not historical reasons. We do not
know everything we might like to know; that does not mean what
we do know is not worth knowing. Yet the other matter -- how
we can find out whether anything in Mishnah-Tosefta antedates
the redaction of Mishnah-Tosefta -- requires more considerable
attention. Here we must begin with a working hypothesis and
test that hypothesis against the results attained in its
application.

The simplest possible hypothesis is that the attributions
of sayings to named authorities may be relied upon in assigning
those sayings to the period, broadly defined, in which said
authorities flourished. We do not and cannot know, for example, whether ^{C}Aqiba actually said what is attributed to
him. Are we able to establish criteria by which we may conclude that what is assigned to Aqiba likely belongs in the
period in which he lived, e.g., to his school or associates (or
even to the man himself)? This position can indeed be tested.
We have laws which interrelate in theme and conception and
which also bear attributions to successive authorities, e.g.,
to a Yavnean, to an Ushan, and to an authority of the time of
Rabbi (70-110, 140-170, 170-200, respectively). If we are able
to demonstrate that what is assigned to a Yavnean is conceptu-
ally earlier than, and not dependent upon, what is assigned to
an Ushan, then, on the face of it, the former indeed is an
earlier tradition, the latter a later one. The unfolding of
the rabbis' ideas on legal and other questions may be shown to
take place through sequences of logic, with what is assigned to
later masters often depending upon and generated by what is
assigned to the earlier ones. When we find a correlation
between such logical (not merely thematic) sequences and
temporal ones, that is, if what is assigned to a later master
does depend in theme, conception, principle, and inner logic

upon what is attributed to an earlier master, then we have
history: we know what comes earlier, what comes later. We are
able therefore to describe ideas probably characteristic of
authorities between the disaster of 70 and the Bar Kokhba
debacle, and from that time to the period of Rabbi, and in the
time of Rabbi. Doubtless work on Amoraic materials will yield
the same series of disciplined sequences of correlated attributions and logical developments, showing the general reliability
of the attributions by periods and making possible a description of ideals held in a given period by various authorities.
On that basis, indeed, we can describe the ideas really characteristic of one period in the historical unfolding of Talmudic
Judaism and relate them to ideas characteristic of earlier and
later periods. That sort of historical inquiry is virtually
not attempted by Urbach, simply because he takes for granted,
as I said, that what is assigned to a given authority really
was stated by that authority. Having no problems, he obviously
is unable to propose solutions and then to test them.

A further descriptive historical task is to be undertaken. When we concentrate attention on the most reliable
witnesses to the mind of the earlier rabbis, those of the first
and second century, we find ourselves engaged in the analysis
primarily of legal texts. Mishnah-Tosefta and related literature focus attention on halakhic problems. Are there underlying unities of conception or definitions of fundamental
principles to be discerned within the halakhah? No one familiar with the literature and its classical exegesis is in doubt
that there are. These are to be spelled out with some care,
also correlated and compared to conceptions revealed in writings of other Jews, not solely rabbinic Jews, as well as
Christians and 'pagans'. When, for example, we describe
primary concerns and perennial issues inherent in laws attributed to Ushans, we find that, in much acute detail, rather
fundamental issues of physics are worked out, e.g., the nature
of mixtures, which will not have surprised Stoic, natural
philosophers (History of the Mishnaic Law of Purities. XII.
Tohorot. Commentary [Leiden 1976], pp. 206-209). Again, an
enduring interest of Yavnean pericopae is in the relationship
between intention and action, an issue both of interest to Paul
and those who told stories about Jesus, on the one side, and of
concern to philosophers of disaster and rebuilding in the
earlier destruction, for instance, Jeremiah. The thought of
Yavneh in any event has to be brought into relationship with

the context in which the rabbis did their work, the aftermath
of the loss of the Temple, just as the work of the Ushans,
following the much greater this-worldly catastrophe brought on
by Bar Kokhba, must always be seen against the background of
crisis.   Indeed, the formation of earlier rabbinic Judaism,
from its primitive beginnings after 70 to its full and complete
expression by the end of Ushan times in 170, is the product of
an age of many painful events, events deemed at the time to
bear the most profound theological weight.   Much of the
halakhah both can and should be interpreted in this particular
context, and many of its issues, not to be reduced to economic
or social concerns, express profound thought on the inner
meanings of the age itself.   It follows that once the exegetical work is complete (if provisionally) and the historical
sequences of individual units of law fairly well established,
the larger issues emergent in underlying unities of conception
and definitions of fundamental principles are to be uncovered,
so that the legal materials may produce a history of major
ideas and themes, not merely sets of two or three logical-
temporal sequences of minor details.

     That is how we must answer the question, if Mishnah was
redacted in ca. A.D. 200, then how do we know that anything in
Mishnah derives from before A.D. 200?   Traditionalists in
Jewish scholarly circles have different answers.   They posit
transmission in exact words said by a given authority through
oral means.   They further hold that what is not assigned to a
given authority goes "way way back".   But materials not given
in the name of a particular master share not only the literary,
but also the conceptual, traits of materials assigned to a
great many named masters, in particular in the period from 140
to 170.   The traditional view in this matter is simply wrong.

     In time, when the work outlined here is done, we shall see
the outlines of the much larger history of legal, therefore
religious, ideas, the unfolding of the world-view of the rabbis
who created rabbinic Judaism.   These outlines will emerge not
merely from discrete sayings, chosen more or less at random,
about topics of interest chiefly to us, e.g, was rabbinical
ethics theonomous or autonomous? what did 'the rabbis' believe
about life after death, the Messiah, eschaton? and so on.
Rather, the morphology of the rabbinic world-view will emerge
inductively, differentiated as to its historical stages and as
to the distinctive viewpoints and the conceptions held by
individual authorities or circles, within which that larger
world-view originated.

Second, a new approach to the description and interpretation of the world-view of the earlier rabbis should emerge.
This proceeds along critical-historical lines, taking account
of the problems of dating sayings, of the diversity of the
documents which purport to preserve opinions of the earlier
masters, and the like. That is important, to be sure. But
there are more important aspects of this work.

People do not seem to realize the immense dimensions of
the evidence in our hands. We have much more than just a few
sayings on this and that. We have a vast law-code, a huge
exegetical corpus in respect to the Hebrew Scriptures and their
translation, collections of stories about authorities, various
kinds of sayings assigned to them -- an extraordinarily large
mass of materials. Our approach, for the first time, must
encompass the totality of the evidence, cope with, take account
of, sources of exceptional density and richness. The law, as I
said, is the definitive source of the world-view of the earlier
rabbis. What is earliest and best attested is Mishnah-
Tosefta. Therefore, if we want to know what people were
thinking in the first and second centuries, we have to turn, to
begin with, to that document, which must serve as criterion in
the assessment of whatever first appears in the later compilations of rabbinical sayings and stories. Books on rabbinic
Judaism which focus upon non-legal sayings (without regard,
even, to the time at which the documents containing those
sayings were redacted) simply miss the point of rabbinic
Judaism.

But the legal sayings deal with picayune and inconsequential matters. The major problem is to derive, from arcane and
trivial details of laws of various sorts, the world-view which
forms the foundations of, and is expressed by, these detailed
rules. That work must be done in a systematic and comprehensive way. And, in consequence, the definition of the agendum
of scholarship is to be revised, not merely in terms of the
adaptation and systematic application of methods of literary-
critical, form-analytical, and redactional-critical, work
hitherto unknown in this field, nor in terms of the introduction of historical-critical considerations, hitherto neglected
or introduced in an episodic way and with dismal lack of
historical sophistication, -- not merely in these aspects, but
in terms of its very shape and structure.

Let us now ask, If we do take account of the entire corpus
of sayings attributed to a given authority, if we do preserve

the critical stance and perspective on their pertinence to the
person to whom they are assigned, then what sort of questions
are we able to answer? How shall we define, or redefine, the
historical agendum? The pages which follow are an effort to
exemplify answers to these questions.

III

DEFINITION OF RABBINIC JUDAISM

The central conception of rabbinic Judaism is the belief
that the ancient Scriptures constituted divine revelation, but
only part of it.[3] At Sinai, God had handed down a dual
revelation: the written part known to one and all, but also
the oral part preserved by the great scriptural heroes, passed
on by prophets to various ancestors in the obscure past,
finally and most openly handed down to the rabbis who created
the Palestinian and Babylonian Talmuds. The 'whole Torah' thus
consisted of both written and oral parts. The rabbis taught
that that 'whole Torah' was studied by David, augmented by
Ezekiel, legislated by Ezra, and embodied in the schools and by
the sages of every period in Israelite history from Moses to
the present. It is a singular, linear conception of a revelation, preserved only by the few, pertaining to the many, and in
time capable of bringing salvation to all.

The rabbinic conception of Torah further regards Moses as
'our rabbi', the first and prototypical figure of the ideal
Jew. It holds that whoever embodies the teachings of Moses
'our rabbi' thereby conforms to the will of God -- and not to
God's will alone, but also to his way. In heaven God and the
angels study Torah just as rabbis do on earth. God dons
phylacteries like a Jew. He prays in the rabbinic mode. He
carries out the acts of compassion called for by Judaic
ethics. He guides the affairs of the world according to the
rules of Torah, just as does the rabbi in his court. One
exegesis of the creation legend taught that God had looked into
the Torah and therefrom had created the world.

The symbol of Torah is multidimensional. It includes the
striking detail that whatever the most recent rabbi is destined

---

[3]The sources on which the following section is based
will be found in J. Neusner, <u>History of the Jews in Babylonia</u>
(Leiden, 1965-1970), II, 151-240; III, pp. 95-194; IV, pp.
279-402; and V, pp. 133-216. A summary of the matter is in
Id., <u>The Way of Torah. An Introduction to Judaism</u> (Belmont,
CA, 1983, third edition) pp. 3-98.

to discover through proper exegesis of the tradition is as much a part of the Torah revealed to Moses as is a sentence of Scripture itself. It therefore is possible to participate even in the giving of the law by appropriate, logical inquiry into the law. God himself, studying and living by Torah, is believed to subject himself to these same rules of logical inquiry. If an earthy court overruled the testimony, delivered through miracles, of the heavenly one, God would rejoice, crying out, "My sons have conquered me! My sons have conquered me!"

The final element in the rabbinic conception of Torah concerns salvation. It takes many forms. One salvific teaching holds that had Israel not sinned -- that is, disobeyed the Torah -- the Scriptures would have closed with the story of the conquest of Palestine. From that eschatological time forward, the sacred community would have lived in eternal peace under the divine law. Keeping the Torah was therefore the veritable guarantee of salvation. The opposite is said in many forms as well. Israel had sinned, therefore God had called the Assyrians, Babylonians, and Romans to destroy the Temple of Jerusalem; but in his mercy he would be equally faithful to restore the fortunes of the people when they, through their suffering and repentance, had expiated the result and the cause of their sin.

So in both negative and positive forms, the rabbinic idea of Torah tells of a necessary connection between the salvation of the people and of the world and the state of Torah among them (just as I stressed in Chapter Three). For example, if all Israel would properly keep a single Sabbath, the Messiah would come. Of special interest here is the rabbinic saying that the rule of the pagans depends upon the sin of Israel. If Israel would constitute a full and complete replication of 'Torah', that is, of heaven, then pagan rule would come to an end. It would end because all Israel then, like some few rabbis even now, would attain to the creative, theurgical powers inherent in Torah. Just as God had created the world through Torah, so saintly rabbis could now create a sacred community. When Israel makes itself worthy through its embodiment of Torah, that is, through its perfect replication of heaven, then the end will come.

Learning thus finds a central place in the rabbinic tradition because of the belief that God had revealed his will to mankind through the medium of a written revelation, given to

Moses at Mount Sinai, accompanied by oral traditions taught in
the rabbinical schools and preserved in the Talmuds and related
literature. The text without the oral traditions might have
led elsewhere than into the academy, for the biblicism of other
groups yielded something quite different from Jewish religious
intellectualism. But belief in the text was coupled with the
belief that oral traditions were also revealed. In the books
composed in the rabbinical academies, as much as in the Hebrew
Bible itself, was contained God's will for man.

The act of study, memorization, and commentary upon the
sacred books is holy. The study of sacred texts therefore
assumes a central position in Judaism. Other traditions had
their religious virtuosi whose virtuosity consisted in knowledge of a literary tradition; but few held, as does Judaism,
that everyone must become such a virtuoso.

Traditional processes of learning are discrete and exegetical. Creativity is expressed not through abstract disserta-
tion, but rather through commentary upon the sacred writings,
or, more likely in later times, commentary upon earlier commentaries. One might also prepare a code of the law, but such
a code represented little more than an assemblage of authoritative opinions of earlier times, with a decision being offered
upon those few questions the centuries had left unanswered.

The chief glory of the commentary is his hiddush, 'novelty'. The hiddush constitutes a scholastic disquisition upon a
supposed contradiction between two earlier authorities, chosen
from any period, with no concern for how they might in fact
relate historically, and upon a supposed harmonization of their
'contradiction'. Or a new distinction might be read into an
ancient law, upon which basis ever more questions might be
raised and solved. The focus of interest quite naturally lies
upon law, rather than theology, history, philosophy, or other
sacred sciences. But within the law it rests upon legal
theory, and interest in the practical consequences of the law
is decidedly subordinated.

The devotion of the Jews to study of the Torah, as here
defined, is held by them to be their chief glory. This senti-
ment is repeated in song and prayer, and shapes the values of
the common society. The important Jew is the learned man. The
child many times is blessed, starting at birth, "May he grow in
Torah, commandments, good deeds".

The central ritual of the rabbinic tradition, therefore,
is study. Study as a natural action entails learning of

traditions and executing them -- in this context, in school or in court. Study becomes a ritual action when it is endowed with values extrinsic to its ordinary character, when set into a mythic context. When a disciple memorizes his master's traditions and actions, he participates in the rabbinic view of Torah as the organizing principle of reality. His study is thereby endowed with the sanctity that ordinarily pertains to prayer or other cultic matters. Study loses its referent in intellectual attainment. The act of study itself becomes holy, so that its original purpose, which was mastery of particular information, ceases to matter much. What matters is piety, piety expressed through the rites of studying. Repeating the words of the oral revelation, even without comprehending them, might produce reward, just as imitating the master matters, even without really being able to explain the reasons for his actions.

The separation of the value, or sanctity, of the act of study from the natural, cognitive result of learning therefore transforms studying from a natural to a ritual action. That separation is accomplished in part by the rabbis' conception of Torah, and in part by the powerful impact of the academic environment itself.

A striking illustration of the distinction between mere learning and learning as part of ritual life derives from the comment of Mar Zutra, a fifth-century A.D. Babylonian rabbi, on Isaiah 14:5, "The Lord has broken the staff of the wicked, the scepter of rulers". He said, "These are disciples of the sages who teach public laws to boorish judges". The fact that the uncultivated judge would know the law did not matter, for he still was what he had been, a boor, not a disciple of the sages. Mere knowledge of the laws does not transform an ordinary person, however powerful, into a sage. Learning carried with it more than naturalistic valence, as further seen in the saying of Amemar, a contemporary of Mar Zutra: "A sage is superior to a prophet, as Scripture says, 'And a prophet has a heart of wisdom'" (Psalm 90:12). What characterized the prophet was, Amemar said, sagacity. Since the prophet was supposed to reveal the divine will, it was not inconsequential that his revelation depended not upon gifts of the spirit but upon learning.

The rabbi functioned in the Jewish community as judge and administrator. But he lived in a society in some ways quite separate from that of Jewry as a whole. The rabbinical academy

was, first, a law school. Some of its graduates served as
judges and administrators of the law. The rabbinical school
was by no means a center for merely legal study. It was, like
the Christian monastery, the locus for a peculiar kind of
religious living. Only one of its functions concerned those
parts of the Torah to be applied in everyday life through the
judiciary.

The school, or Yeshiva (literally, 'session') was a
council of Judaism, a holy community. In it men (not women)
learned to live a holy life, to become saints. When they left,
sages continued to live by the discipline of the school. They
invested great efforts in teaching that discipline by example
and precept to ordinary folk. Through the school classical
Judaism transformed the Jewish people into its vision of the
true replica of Mosaic revelation.

The schools, like other holy communities, imposed their
own particular rituals, intended, in the first instance, for
the disciples and masters. Later, it was hoped, all Jews would
conform to those rituals and so join the circle of master and
disciples.

As with study, the schools' discipline transformed other
ordinary, natural actions, gestures, and functions into rituals
-- the rituals of 'being a rabbi'. Everyone ate. Rabbis did
so in a 'rabbinic' manner. That is to say, what others regarded as matters of mere etiquette, formalities and conventions intended to render eating aesthetically agreeable, rabbis
regarded as matters of 'Torah', something to be learned. It
was 'Torah' to do things one way, and it was equally 'ignor-
ance' to do them another (though not heresy, for theology was
no issue).

The master of Torah, whether disciple or teacher, would
demonstrate his mastery not merely through what he said in the
discussion of legal traditions or what he did in court. He
would do so by how he sat at the table, by what ritual formulas
he recited before eating one or another kind of fruit or
vegetable, by how he washed his hands. Everyone had to relieve
himself. The sage would do so according to 'Torah'. The
personality traits of men might vary. Those expected of, and
inculcated into, a sage were of a single fabric.

We must keep in mind the fundamental difference between
the way of Torah and ways to salvation explored by other holy
men and sacred communities. The rabbi at no point would admit
that his particular rites were imposed upon him alone, apart

from all Israel. He ardently 'spread Torah' among the Jews at
large. He believed he had to, because Torah was revealed to
all Israel at Sinai and required of all Israel afterward. If
he was right that Moses was 'our rabbi' and even God kept the
commandments as he did, then he had to ask of everyone what he
demanded of himself: conformity to the halakhah, the way of
Torah. His task was facilitated by the widespread belief that
Moses had indeed revealed the Torah and that some sort of
interpretation quite naturally was required to apply it to
everyday affairs. The written part of Torah generally shaped
the life of ordinary pious folk. What the rabbi had to accomplish was to persuade the outsider that the written part of the
Torah was partial and incomplete, requiring further elaboration
through the oral traditions he alone possessed and embodied.

IV
THE ORIGINS OF RABBINIC JUDAISM

While the rabbinic conception of Torah naturally is
believed, by people within rabbinic Judaism, to originate with
Moses at Sinai and to constitute nothing other than a statement
of historical facts, the beginnings of the rabbinic structure
are to be located in the aftermath of the destruction of the
Second Temple in 70 C.E.[4] At that time, remanants of various
groups in the Judaism of the period before 70 gathered at
Yavneh, and, under the leadership of Yohanan ben Zakkai, began
to construct the ruins of the old age into a new synthesis.

Before the destruction, there was a common 'Judaism' in
the Land of Israel, and it bore no relationship whatsoever to
what we now understand as rabbinic Judaism. The common religion of the country consisted of three main elements, first,
the Hebrew Scriptures, second, the Temple, and third, the
common and accepted practices of the ordinary folk -- their
calendar, their mode of living, their everyday practices and
rites, based on these first two. In addition we know of a
number of peculiar groups, or sects, which took a distinctive
position on one or another aspect of the inherited religious
culture. Among these sects, the best known are the Pharisees,
the Sadducees, and the Essenes; this third group, described, as
we saw in Chapter Four, in the writings of Josephus at the end

---

[4]This section summarizes the results of J. Neusner, A
Life of Yohanan ben Zakkai (2nd ed., Leiden, 1970) and Id.,
Development of a Legend. Studies on the Traditions concerning
Yohanan ben Zakkai (Leiden, 1970).

of the first century, exhibits traits in common with the group
known to us from the so-called Dead Sea Scrolls but cannot have
been identical to it in every respect.

When the Temple was destroyed, it is clear, the foundations of the country's religious-cultural life were destroyed.
The reason is that the Temple had constituted one of the
primary, unifying elements in that common life. The structure
not only of political life and of society, but also of the
imaginative life of the country, depended upon the Temple and
its worship and cult. It was there that people believed they
served God. On the Temple the lines of structure -- both
cosmic and social -- converged. The Temple, moreover, served
as the basis for those many elements of autonomous self-
government and political life left in the Jews' hands by the
Romans. Consequently, the destruction of the Temple meant not
merely a significant alteration in the cultic or ritual life of
the Jewish people, but also a profound and far-reaching crisis
in their inner and spiritual existence.

The reconstuction of a viable cultural-religious existence
is the outcome of the next half-century, for between ca. 70 and
ca. 120, we know in retrospect, a number of elements of the
religious-cultural structure of the period before 70 were put
together into a new synthesis, the synthesis we now call
rabbinic Judaism. It was in response to the disaster of the
destruction that rabbinic Judaism took shape, and its success
was in its capacity to claim things had not changed at all --
hence the assertion that even at the start, Moses was 'our
rabbi' -- while making the very destruction of the Temple
itself into the verification and vindication of the new structure. Rabbinic Judaism claimed that it was possible to serve
God not only through sacrifice, but also through study of
Torah. There is a priest in charge of the life of the community -- but a new priest, the rabbi. The old sin-offerings
still maybe carried out, through deeds of loving kindness. Not
only so, but when the whole Jewish people will fully carry out
the teachings of the Torah, then the Temple itself will be
rebuilt. To be sure, the Temple will be reconstructed along
lines laid out in the Torah -- that is, in the whole Torah of
Moses, the Torah taught by the rabbis. And, like the prophets
and historians in the time of the First Destruction, the rabbis
further claimed that it was because the people had sinned, that
is, had not kept the Torah, that the Temple had been destroyed. So the disaster itself was made to vindicate the
rabbinic teaching and to verify its truth.

Now let us stand back from this synthesis and ask, how was it put together? What are its primary elements? What trends or movements before 70 are represented by these elements?

Two primary components in the Yavneh synthesis are to be discerned, first, the emphases of Pharisaism before 70, second, the values of the scribal profession before that time. The former lay stress upon universal keeping of the law, so that every Jew is obligated to do what only the elite -- the priests -- are normally expected to accomplish. Pre-70 Pharisaism thus contributed the stress on the universal keeping of the law. The second component derives from the scribes, whose professional ideal stressed the study of Torah and the centrality of the learned man in the religious system.

The unpredictable, final element in the synthesis of Pharisaic stress on widespread law, including ritual-law observance, and scribal emphasis on learning, is what makes rabbinic Judaism distinctive. That is the conviction that the community now stands in the place of the Temple. The ruins of the cult, after all, did not mark the end of the collective life of Israel. What survived was the people. It was the genius of rabbinic Judaism to recognize that the people might reconstitute the condition of sanctification of the Temple, in its own collective life. Therefore the people had to be made holy, as the Temple had been holy, and the people's social life had to be sanctified as the surrogate for what had been lost. This position is spelled out in the Mishnah. The rabbinic ideal further maintained that the rabbi served as the new priest, the study of Torah substituted for the Temple sacrifice, and deeds of loving kindness were the social surrogate for the sin-offering, that is, personal sacrifice instead of animal sacrifice. This position is worked out in the two Talmuds.

V

PHARISAISM AFTER 70

Pre-70 Pharisaism is clearly defined by the Gospels' Pharisaic pericopes and the rabbinic traditions, about the Pharisees.[5] Both stress the same concerns; first, eating

---

[5]This section summarizes the results of J. Neusner, The Rabbinic Traditions about the Pharisees before 70 (Leiden, 1970). I. The Masters. II. The Houses. III. Conclusions.

secular food in a state of ritual purity; second, careful
tithing and giving of agricultural offerings to the priests,
and obedience to the biblical rules and taboos concerning
raising crops; third, to a lesser degree, some special laws on
keeping the Sabbaths and festivals; and, finally, still less
commonly, rules on family affairs. Therefore, late Pharisaism
-- that which flourished in the last decades of the Temple's
existence and which is revealed in the Gospels and in rabbinic
traditions -- is a cult-centered piety, which proposes to
replicate the cult in the home, and thus to effect the Temple's
purity laws at the table of the ordinary Jew, and quite literally to turn Israel into a "kingdom of priests and a holy
nation". The symbolic structure of Pharisaism depends upon
that of the Temple; the ideal is the same as that of the
priesthood. The Pharisee was a layman pretending to be priest
and making his private home into a model of the Temple. The
laws about purity and careful tithing were dietary laws,
governing what and how a person should eat. If a person kept
those laws, then, when he ate at home, he was like God at the
Temple's altar table, on which was arrayed food similarly
guarded from impurity and produced in accord with Levitical
revelation. By contrast, the rabbi was like God because he
studied the Torah on earth, as did God and Moses 'our rabbi' in
the heavenly academy.

The best corpus of traditions supplied by the post-70
rabbis concerns the Houses, or disciples, of Shammai and
Hillel, circa A.D. 10-70, approximately sixty-five of whose
pericopes are attested by early Yavnean comments or continua-
tions or other discussions indicating knowledge of pericopes in
pretty much their present state. When we compare the pericopes
of Eliezer b. Hyrcanus, attested at Yavneh, with those of the
Houses, evidently deriving from the same period, we find that
Eliezer stands well within the framework of pre-70 Pharisaism.[6] The subject matter of Eliezer's rulings attested at
Yavneh covers much the same ground as the Houses' rulings but
introduces new issues as well. The two bodies of material
compare as follows("same" = Eliezer rules on or in the same
pericope):

---

[6]This table summarizes the results of a comparison of
the traditions attributed to Eliezer b. Hyrcanus, among the
earliest authorities of Yavneh, and those assigned to the
Houses of Shammai and Hillel. The sources are in J. Neusner,
Eliezer ben Hyrcanus. The Tradition and the Man (Leiden,
1973). I. *The Tradition*. II. *The Man*.

	HOUSES		ELIEZER

A. Temple Law, Jerusalem, Pilgrimage, and Priestly Dues

	HOUSES		ELIEZER
1.	Burning unclean with clean meat	1.	Same
2.	Laying on of hands	2.	---
3.	Bitter-water ritual	3.	....(But Eliezer rules on on other aspects of the ritual; M. Sot. 1:1)
4.	Israelites eat first-born animals with priests	4.	---
5.	Children make pilgrimage	5.	---
6.	---	6.	Cattle given to the Temple are not sacrificed but sold
7.	---	7.	Liability for lost redemption lamb set aside for firstling of an ass
8.	---	8.	One may not dedicate all one's property to Temple
9. - 10.	---	9. - 10.	Preparing sin-offering water, two rulings
11.	---	11.	Whole-offering parts confused with sin-offering parts are burned together
12.	---	12.	Blood from blemished offerings mixed with blood from unblemished offerings is sprinkled
13.	---	13.	Wrong intention renders meal offering invalid

B. Agricultural Tithes, Offerings, and Taboos

	HOUSES		ELIEZER
1.	Unclean heave offering mixed with clean (Eliezer b. Hyrcanus)	1.	Same
2.	Giving heave offering of grapes and the remainder is eventually made into raisins (Eliezer b. Hyrcanus)	2.	Same
3.	Removing old produce at Nisan (Joshua b. Hananiah)	3.	---
4.	Peah from olives, carobs -- how given (Gamaliel II)	4.	---
5.	Forgotten-sheaf rules (Eliezer b. Azariah; Joshua b. Hananiah)	5.	
6.	Seventh-year-produce rules (Tarfon)	6.	
7.	Second-tithe money in Jerusalem (Tarfon; Ben Zoma; Ben Azzai; Aqiva)	7.	---
8.	Heave-offering vetches (Aqiva)	8.	---
9.	Fleece offering (Aqiva)	9.	---
10.	Date of New Year for trees (Aqiva)	10.	---
11.	Olive presses in walls of Jerusalem (Aqiva)	11.	---
12.	Fourth-year-fruit rules (Aqiva)	12.	---

13.	Mixed seeds in vineyard (Aqiva)	13.	---
14.	Heave offering from black and white figs (Ilai)	14.	Same
15.	---	15.	Clean heave offering for unclean
16.	---	16.	Cakes of thank offering of Nazirite exempt from dough offering
17.	---	17.	Orlah laws abroad
18.	---	18.	Status of etrog
19.	---	19.	Seventh-year oil may be used for anointing hide
20.	---	20.	Dough offering on 15 Nisan
21.	...(but cf. M. Shev. 4:2B)	21.	First-fruits in garden are guarded, therefore liable
22.	---	22.	Fruit from abroad is free of liability
23.	---	23.	Making olives and grapes into oil and wine

C. Sabbath Law

1.	Eruv in public domain (Hananiah, nephew of Joshua)	1.	---
2.	Eruv for separate kinds of food (Hananiah, nephew of Joshua)	2.	---
3.	Eruv for alley (Eliezer b. Hyrcanus + Aqiva + disciple of Ishmael)	3.	Same
4.	Gentile/Sadducee in alley re eruv (Gamaliel II = Meir + Judah)	4.	...(but see no. 7)
5.	Work started before Sabbath (Aqiva)	5.	
6.	---	6.	No eruv if field has wall
7.	...(but see no. 4)	7.	Failure of partner to participate in eruv does not restrict others
8.	---	8.	Woman may wear tiara on Sabbath
9.	---	9.	Acquiring a share in the eruv

D. Festival Law

1.	How much does one drink to be liable on the Day of Atonement (Eliezer b. Hyrcanus)?	1.	Same
2.	Large cakes re Passover (Gamaliel II)	2.	---
3.	Pick pulse on festival (Gamaliel II)	3.	---
4.	Other festival rules (Gamaliel II)	4.	---
5.	Size of Sukkah (Eleazar b. R. Saddoq)	5.	---
6.	---	6.	Hart's tongue on Passover
7.- 10.	---	7. - 10.	Rulings on rite of Atonement

11. ...(Eliezer attests Houses' dispute; M. Bes. 1:1)	11.	Egg born on festival
12. ---	12.	New millstone on festival week

E. Liturgy

1. Order of blessing: oil versus myrtle (Gamaliel II)	1.	---
2. Proper position of saying Shema (Eleazar b. Azariah; Ishmael; Tarfon)	2.	---
3. How far recite Hallel at Seder (Tarfon; Aqiva)	3.	---
4. Tefillin in privy (Aqiva)	4.	---
5. Where shake lulav (Aqiva, re Gamaliel; Joshua)	5.	---
6. Limit re sisit (Jonathan b. Batyra)	6.	---
7. Circumcision of child born circumcised (Eleazar b. R. Saddoq)	7.	---
8. ---	8.	New Year liturgy (Lev. 23:24)

F. Uncleanness Laws

1. Quarter qab on bones in 'tent' (Joshua b. Hananiah)	1.	---
2. Woman kneading in 'tent' (Aqiva; Joshua b. Hananiah)	2.	---
3. If man shook tree -- preparation for uncleanness by reason of water (Joshua b. Hananiah)	3.	---
4. Uncleanness of liquids -- Yosi b. Yo'ezer (Eliezer b. Hyrcanus + Aqiva)	4.	Same
5. Uncleanness of scroll wrappers (Gamaliel II)	5.	---
6. When do olives receive uncleanness in harvest (Gamaliel II)	6.	---
7. Mustard strainer (Eleazar b. R. Saddoq)	7.	---
8. Itch inside itch (cleanness rite) (Aqiva)	8.	---
9. Insusceptibility of sheet (Aqiva)	9.	---
10. Searching grave area (Aqiva)	10.	---
11. Issue of semen in third day (Aqiva)	11.	---
12. Uncleanness of fish (Aqiva)	12.	---
13. ---	13.	Partitions in 'tent'
14. ---	14.	Shoe on the last in incomplete, therefore clean
15. ---	15.	Even though door is open, house is clean -- re 'tents'
16. ---	16.	Jars tightly covered with bit of corpse inside
17.	17.	Dirt from grave area
18. ---	18.	Leprosy sign deliberately removed

19.   ---   19. Ritual status of honey-
                                          comb

G. Civil Law, Torts, and Damages; Criminal Law
  1. Damaged bailment (Aqiva)   1.   ---
  2.   ---   2. Woman hanged ± naked

H. Family Law and Inheritances
  1. Vow not to have intercourse   1. Same (may not be our
      (Eliezer)   Eliezer)
  2. Husband's inheritance when   2. Same
      wife dies as a minor
      (Eliezer b. Hyrcanus)
  3. Signs of adulthood (Eliezer   3. Same
      b. Hyrcanus)
  4. Levirate rules re brothers   4. Same
      married to sisters (Eliezer
      b. Hyrcanus; Eleazar b.
      Azariah; Abba Saul)
  5. Levirate rules re co-wives   5.   ---
      (Tarfon; Eleazar b.
      Azariah; Aqiva; Joshua
      b. Hananiah)
  6. Test rags for each act of   6.   ---
      intercourse (Joshua b.
      Hananiah)
  7. Santifies property and   7. Same
      intends to divorce wife
      (Joshua b. Hananiah +
      Eliezer b. Hyrcanus)
  8. Wife remarries on testimony   8.   ---
      of one witness (Aqiva;
      Gamaliel II)
  9. Grounds for divorce (Aqiva)   9.   ---
 10. Dividing estate where order 10.   ---
      of deaths is unclean
      (Aqiva)
 11. Blood of woman who has   11. Same
      given birth and not
      immersed (Eliezer)
 12. ...(but see no. 2)   12. Deed of a female minor
                                        is null
 13.   ---   13. Levir refused by minor
 14. ...(but see no. 9)   14. Conditional divorce valid
 15.   ---   15. Minor who has exercised
                                        right of refusal still
                                        controls usufruct of
                                        melog (= no. 12)

I. Miscellany
  1. Taboo against drinking   1.   ---
      gentile wine (Gamaliel II)
  2. Eliezer b. Hyrcanus re   2. Same
      overturning couch before
      festival (b.M.Q. 20a) is
      given by Eleazar b. R.
      Simeon as Houses dispute
      (Tos. M.Q. 2:9)

Eliezer Alone
  1. Releasing vows made easy
  2. Gambler may not testify
  3. Samaritan bread permitted to Israelites
  4. Repent before death

5. Many sinful acts of a single type are punished by an
    equivalent number of sin offerings
6. Spinning blue wool for fringe
7. - 9. Nazir who contracts uncleanness on last day of his
    period -- various rulings

    The themes of Eliezer's rulings are much the same as those
of the Houses, and the proportions seem about right, with one
exception. In this stratum, Eliezer is strikingly silent on
liturgical matters. This would accord with his ruling that a
fixed liturgy is not to be followed; if so, Eliezer would not
issue many rulings on the subject.

    But the substance in detail of Eliezer's rulings strik-
ingly differs from that of the Houses. Eliezer paid attention
to dedications to the Temple; the pericopes of the Houses
attested at Yavneh ignore the subject. He has important
rulings on the preparation of sin-offering water. The Houses
do not rule on the subject. He solves through logic various
problems of mixtures of diverse holy materials and how they are
to be disposed of. The Houses do not enter those problems at
all. He deals with the problem of intention in the cult. The
Houses do not. His rulings on the Temple thus concern strikingly fundamental matters. The tendency of those rulings is to
figure out the logic and consistent order to be imposed on the
Temple cult and its conduct.

    While some of the rules on agricultural taboos concern
both the Houses and Eliezer, others involve Eliezer alone.
These tend to represent striking innovations in antecedent
laws. Two themes seem important; first, the status of the
produce of foreign countries; second, and of fundamental
importance, the easing of the distinctions in produce subject
to heave offering. As to Sabbath law, for both the Houses and
Eliezer, the _eruv_ (Sabbath limit) appears as a predominate
concern. In respect to festival law, Eliezer has important new
rulings on the rite of the Day of Atonement -- appropriate for
his agendum for the Temple, which concentrates on the conduct
of the cult.

    The subject matter of the uncleanness rules is pretty much
the same, but the specific rulings of Eliezer are original.
Again, this tendency is to solve problems through abstract
reasoning rather than through a simple edict or citation of
established practice. This would account for the difference
between the discrete rules attributed to the Houses on when and
whether various objects are susceptible to uncleanness, in

contrast with Eliezer's effort on the same themes to give reasons applying to more than the single case at hand.

Civil and criminal law is virtually ignored by both the Houses and Eliezer. The interest in family law and inheritances is much the same; vows, inheritance, Levirate rules, and divorces concern both parties. But Eliezer's generalization about the nullity of the deed of a female minor and the rule, susceptible to generalization and expansion, about the conditional divorce are unknown to the Houses and constitute far-reaching theoretical innovations.

Entirely new legal themes involve releasing vows, rules of testimony, the law of the Nazirite who has become unclean, and the general principle about liability for various similar sinful acts. These do not yield completely new agenda of legislative legal interests. But they are, individually, quite novel topics on which the Yavnean pericope of the Houses are silent.

VI

YOHANAN BEN ZAKKAI AS A PHARISEE

Clearly, Eliezer was a post-70 continuator of pre-70 Pharisaism. But what evidence do we have that Yohanan b. Zakkai was a Pharisee in pre-70 times?[7] If we examine his legal rulings, we find strikingly few that are pertinent to the predominant agenda of pre-70 Pharisaism:

1. Sifre Num. 123: Heifer sacrifice carried out in white garments.
2. Sifre Shemini 7:12: Loaf unclean in the second degree makes another unclean in the third.
3. Sifra Emor 16:9: <u>Lulav</u> taken as a memorial to the Temple.
4. Sifra Emor 16:9: New produce is prohibited on the entire Day of Waving.
5. M. (=Mishnah) Shabbat 16:7: One may cover a scorpion on the Sabbath.
6. M. Shabbat 22:3: One may open a jar to eat dried figs, but one may not pierce the plug of a jar on the Sabbath.
7. M. Sheqalim 1:4: priests have to pay the <u>sheqel</u>.
8. M. Sukkah 2:5: Food must be eaten in the <u>Sukkah</u> even for a random meal.

---

[7]The source is given above, n. 5.

9. M. Rosh HaShanah 1:1:   The shofar may be sounded on the Sabbath.

10. M. Rosh HaShanah 4:4:   Witnesses may testify about the new moon throughout the day.

11. M. Ketuvot 13:1:   A woman swears at the end with respect to maintenance.

12. M. Ketuvot 13:2:   A person who maintains another man's wife has no claim to recompense.

13. M. Sanhedrin 5:2:   Evidence should be carefully tested.

14. M. Eduyyot 8:3,7:   Courts cannot tell the priests whom to marry.

15. M. Kelim 2:2:   Broken sides of large jugs are not susceptible to uncleanness (not attributed to Yohanan).

16. M. Kelim 17:16:   A beam of a balance (etc.) is susceptible to uncleanness (not attributed to Yohanan).

17. M. Yadaim 4:3:   Ammon and Moab give poorman's tithe in the seventh year.

18. M. Yadaim 4:6:   Scriptures render the hands unclean (not attributed to Yohanan).

The Mishnaic evidence deals, therefore, with the following:

> Temple and priesthood: Nos. 1, 7, 14.
> Agricultural rules: Nos. 4, 17.
> Festival law: Nos. 5, 6.
> Liturgy: Nos. 3, 8, 9, 10.
> Uncleanness laws: Nos. 2, 15, 18.
> Civil law, torts, damages, criminal law: Nos. 11, 12, 13.
> Family law and inheritances: None.

Pre-70 Pharisees and Eliezer tend to rule primarily on agricultural law, Sabbath and festival rules, and uncleanness. Yohanan's traditions are scattered; most of those on the festivals have to do with the problems posed by the destruction of the Temple and adoption of its rites in the synagogue. The law in numbers 11, 12, 17, and 18 is not accredited to Yohanan; he simply approves what others have done. In all, Yohanan's legal agenda hardly correspond to those of the pre-70 Houses -- about which he himself knows nothing -- and seem, on the whole, to focus upon the consequence for the liturgy and priesthood of the Temple's destruction, rather than upon any other matter. The greater number of his other rulings has to do with Sabbath and festival laws. To be sure, the whole thing adds up to very

little. But while, on the basis of the extant laws, one may
reasonably claim Eliezer was a Pharisee, on the same basis one
cannot claim the same for Yohanan. At best, one may say he
might have been a Pharisee. The external evidence does not
help; Luke-Acts knows Gamaliel; Josephus knows Simeon b.
Gamaliel; but no external source knows about Yohanan, despite
the decisive role in events of the day claimed for him by the
later storytellers.

VII
ELIEZER'S PHARISAISM FOR THE POST-TEMPLE PERIOD

Eliezer legislated, in theory if not in practice, primarily for people subject to Pharisaic discipline and mainly about
matters important to Pharisaic piety, so his program for the
post-Temple period concerned Pharisaism and little else. We
simply do not know what, if anything, he might have had to say
to non-Pharisaic Jews at Yavneh and in other parts of the
country. Perhaps saying, at that time, to repent before death
would have seemed more important than it does now; but it
hardly constitutes much of a program for a country which has
just lost its autonomous government and capital and for a
people suddenly without a sanctuary or a cult.

In the aftermath of the destruction, as I shall now suggest, Eliezer intended to liberalize the application of the
Pharisaic discipline. I see no necessary connection between
his intent and recent disaster. Perhaps he simply thought
that, by making it easier for large numbers of Jews to take on
the Pharisaic way of living, he might win over people who
formerly were not Pharisees. Since, moreover, the Pharisaic
laws enabled Jews outside of the Temple to participate in its
cult in their own homes and so to share in its sanctity, he may
have posited the Pharisaic way as a means of preserving both
the sanctity and the symbolic presence of the cult during the
interim in which they were no more. Hence, it may have seemed
wise to formulate the Pharisaic laws in as lenient a way as
possible. But if this was Eliezer's intent -- and we certainly
cannot show that it was -- I doubt his motive was purely propa-
gandistic. He gives no evidence that his interest was to win
as many Jews as possible to the Pharisaic way and by subterfuge
to make it easier for them to undertake the sect's discipline.

The main outlines in his policy for the present age are
clear. From the Jews outside of Palestine, obedience to

neither the laws of tithing nor the laws of ritual purity nor
the agricultural taboos would be required. For the Pharisees
among them, the conditions of life in exile were made considerably easier. But this was done by effectively destroying the
entire form of their earlier piety. We have no evidence of
what, if anything, was offered in its stead. For Pharisees in
Palestine, the application of the primarily sectarian laws was
to be done in a more lenient way than earlier. Giving heave
offering was simplified. One no longer would have to distinguish between clean and unclean produce of the same species in
the same state but might give heave offering from the one for
the other. Presumably, other distinctions formerly operative
in the giving of heave offering would likewise be obscured.
The laws of the seventh year similarly would be applied less
rigidly than earlier, if the case of the hide annointed by
seventh-year oil signifies a broader policy. Hence, greater
benefit from the produce of the seventh year would be enjoyed
by the pietists. It may be that the more difficult conditions
of economic life required some such lenient ruling, but we have
not a shred of evidence that economic considerations figured in
Eliezer's enactments. The Pharisaic custom of providing an
eruv, or Sabbath limit, to permit carrying on the Sabbath was
extended, so that, first, a fence would be sufficient to
establish a single courtyard, however large; second, a person
might simply buy a share in an eruv from a storekeeper; third,
any sort of food, not merely bread, might be used; and fourth,
dissenters or forgetful people would not be subject to pressure
from their neighbors.

This last point suggests that Eliezer hoped to improve
relationships between Pharisees and other Jews, on the one
side, and between Jews and Samaritans, on the second. Eliezer
allowed Jews to eat with Samaritans. Hence, the xenophobia
characteristic of the recent war was rejected in favor of a
more irenic approach to relationship within the Jewish community, formerly characterized by heated sectarian and civil
strife, and between Jewry and its neighbors, earlier marked by
Jewish hostility toward closely kindred groups.

The Sabbath rules were set aside in favor of other,
equally important religious duties. The tendency to erect ever
higher walls around the Sabbath was thus countered by Eliezer's
view that the Sabbath was to be no more important than other
religious requirements such as circumcision or the Passover.
(This corresponds to the Gospels' view that the "son of man is

Lord of the Sabbath".) Its sanctity was separate and distinct
from, and no greater than, that of the coincident festival.
Eliezer may have planned also to liberalize the rules governing
work on the intermediate days of a festival.

Vows were to be virtually excluded from the pious life.
To be sure, temperamental people would continue to make them.
But Eliezer would render the nullification of a vow a routine
and simple matter. One might, on any pretext whatever, simply
express regret that he had vowed, and the matter was done
with. The dedication of one's property to the Temple -- which
now would mean its destruction -- was limited. An oath to give
the whole of one's property to the sanctuary was null. Presumably anyone in sufficient command of his senses to refrain
from giving the whole lot would be unlikely to make such a gift
to begin with. Likewise, a Nazir, subject to his earlier vow,
would not be forced by last-minute accidents into a perpetual
renewal of the binding rules. His liability was limited to a
few days rather than to the repetition of the whole spell of
Naziriteship.

Consistent with his leniency in the giving of tithes and
heave offerings, Eliezer may have intended to limit the effect
of the uncleanness rules by ruling that uncleanness pertains to
no liquids, except (presumably) those specified in Scriptures.
Here, matters are less certain; we have a number of conflicting
details which seem not wholly in accord with one another or
with this basic principle. Certainly, Eliezer wanted to make
it easy to neutralize the prohibiting effects of holy materials
which have fallen into secular produce or of impaired materials
of the cult mixed with acceptable materials. The rules of
neutralizing heave offering which has fallen into secular
produce are enforced in a lenient way. Mixtures of bowls of
blood or of blemished and unblemished sacrificial parts will be
readily rendered fit for use on the pretext that one may easily
remove the prohibited substance.

Eliezer evidently proposed for the cult to be ruled in
accord with an orderly logic, which would settle all manner of
details. What may have seemed illogical or inconsistent was to
be rationalized. I do not see what practical consequences for
the Yavnean situation were to be anticipated. Eliezer continued the earlier Pharisaic tendency to apply to the Red-
Heifer ceremony a less strict rule as to purity and other
questions than was regarded by the Sadducees as proper. But
this is not original to him and therefore has nothing to do
with his Yavnean program.

One ethical issue seems important. Eliezer held that, faced with a choice of taking affirmative action to prevent a possible violation of the law or of doing nothing at all, a person should assume responsibility and therefore take action. It would not be proper to disclaim responsibility and to stand aside. The contrary view was that one needs do nothing at all, so long as his own hands are not sullied.

In general, therefore, the tendency of Eliezer's own rulings seems to have been in a single direction, and that was toward the rationalization and the liberalization of the application of Pharisaic law. We cannot, to be sure, take for granted that all or even the very best-attested traditions derive from Eliezer and have been formulated in his exact language. Nor is our interpretation of each detail necessarily the only possible way of seeing things. But if this view of Eliezer's own contribution is in the main valid, then it follows that what is asserted by the later tradition is absolutely correct: Eliezer really said nothing he had not heard from his masters. In an exact sense, he was profoundly 'conservative'. By attempting to reform details and to ease the strictness of the Pharisaic law, he hoped to conserve the Pharisaic way of piety substantially unchanged and unimpaired, essentially intact. This must mean that for Eliezer the destruction of the Temple did not mark a significant turning in the history of Judaism. Just as the destruction of the first Temple was followed, in a brief period, by the construction of the second, so he certainly supposed the same would now happen. He would see to it that the third Temple would be different from the second only in the more logical way in which its cult would be carried on, on the one side, and in the slightly simpler requirements of the application of the cult's purity rules to daily life and of the enforcement of the priestly taxes, on the other.

In Eliezer's time, Rome ended its former experiments with the government of the Jews and established direct rule. We know nothing about Eliezer's attitude toward Rome and the new regime in Palestine. Gamaliel had to negotiate with it; Eliezer evidently did not. This must mean that in Yavneh he did not enter into direct relationships with the Roman regime; but we do not know whether other masters of the day, except for Gamaliel, had any more direct contact with the Romans than he evidently did. The larger problems faced by the Jews deprived of their cult and its celebrations, including the observance in

the Temple and in Jerusalem of the pilgrim festivals, not to
mention the bringing of first fruits and of the second tithes
or equivalent funds to the city for consumption -- none of
these seems to have elicited his attention. He does not
legislate about the observance of Sukkot after the destruction,
as did Yohanan b. Zakkai, although we have two rulings pertinent to the festival. He has nothing to say about the New
Year, or the use of the shofar on the Sabbath that coincides
with the New Year, as did Yohanan; also omitted are the use of
new produce and the waving of the omer. The various Temple-
oriented festival celebrations subject to Yohanan's taqqanot
(ordinances) are ignored in Eliezer's legislation. This is
striking, for Eliezer, as an early Yavnean master, ought to
have had more to say about the sacred rites now no longer
possible to effect than we can discern in respect to these
lively issues.

Eliezer certainly did not anticipate that the Temple would
never be rebuilt. He had no program for any considerable time
before the reconstruction. Perhaps it was hoped that the
Romans would not delay in permitting the buildings to be
restored. No one in his time could foresee the disastrous Bar
Kokhba war or the definitive prohibition of the Jews from
Jerusalem in its aftermath.

VIII
RABBINISM AT YAVNEH

Eliezer's legislation, therefore, suggests he assumed life
would soon go on pretty much as it had in the past. Issues
important to pre-70 Pharisees predominate in his laws; issues
absent in the rabbinic traditions about the Pharisees are --
except the cult -- mostly absent in his as well. Eliezer
therefore comes at the end of the old Pharisaism. He does not
inaugurate the new rabbinism, traces of which are quite absent
in his historically usable traditions. Indeed, on the basis of
his laws and sayings, we can hardly define what his rabbinism
might consist of. The centrality of the oral Torah, the view
of the rabbi as the new priest and of study of Torah as the new
cult, the definition of piety as the imitation of Moses 'our
rabbi' and the conception of God as a rabbi, the organization
of the Jewish community under rabbinic rule and by rabbinic
law, and the goal of turning all Israel into a vast academy for
the study of the (rabbinic) Torah -- none of these motifs
characteristic of later rabbinism occurs at all.

Since by the end of the Yavnean period the main outlines of rabbinism were clear, we may postulate that the transition from Pharisaism to rabbinism, or the union of the two, took place in the time of Eliezer himself. But he does not seem to have been among those who generated the new viewpoints; he appears as a reformer of the old ones. His solution to the problem of the cessation of the cult was not to replace the old piety with a new one but, rather, to preserve and refine the rules governing the old in the certain expectation of its restoration in a better form than ever. Others, who were his contemporaries and successors, developed the rabbinic idea of the (interim) substitution of study for sacrifice, the rabbi for the priest, and the oral Torah of Moses 'our rabbi' for the piety of the old cult.

Eliezer has not been anachronistically 'rabbinized'. To be sure, the transmitters and compilers of traditions later on assumed everyone before them -- back to Moses -- was a rabbi. But they did not regularly attribute to Eliezer sayings to link him specifically to the rabbinic system of symbols; and this suggests that, just as with the laws a limited agendum defined topics appropriate for attribution to Eliezer, so, with theological matters, ideas originally not within Eliezer's agendum were not commonly added afterward.

If so, we may take seriously the attribution of rabbinic ideas to others of his contemporaries. Where do we first find them? Clearly, Yohanan b. Zakkai -- whom we could not conclusively show to have been a Pharisee -- stands well within the structure of rabbinic symbols and beliefs. It is in his sayings, admittedly first occurring in late compilations, that we find the claim of replacing the cult with something -- anything -- just as good. He is alleged to have told Joshua that deeds of loving kindness achieve atonement just as satisfactorily as did the cult. He is further made to say that man was created in order to study the Torah. When Israel does the will of its father in heaven -- which is contained in the Torah and taught by the rabbi -- then no nation or race can rule over it. The cult is hardly central to his teachings and seldom occurs in his laws. The altar, to be sure, serves to make peace between Israel and the father in heaven, but is not so important ("how much the more so") as a man who makes peace among men or is a master of Torah. Yohanan's taqqanot are even better testimony, for they take account of the end of the cult and provide for the period of its cessation. The Temple rites

may be carried on ("as a memorial") outside of the old sanctuary. The old priesthood is subjected to the governance of
the rabbi. The priest had to pay the sheqel and ideally should
marry anyone the rabbi declares to be a fit wife. Eliezer says
nothing of the sort; what Yohanan has to say about the situation after 70 is either without parallel in Eliezer's sayings
or contradictory by their tendency.

To be sure, we are scarcely able to claim that rabbinism
begins with Yohanan or that Pharisaism ends with Eliezer. But
Yohanan's tradition certainly reveals the main themes of later
rabbinism, although these themes are more reliably attributed
to later Yavneans and still more adequately spelled out in
their sayings. And Eliezer's laws and theological sayings are
strikingly silent about what later on would be the primary
concern of the rabbinic authorities, the oral Torah in all its
social and political ramifications, and are remarkably narrow
in their focus upon the concerns of pre-70 Pharisaism. Further
investigation may show that the list of M. Avot 2:1 of
Yohanan's disciples represents a composite of the five components of the Yavnean group: Eliezer clearly was a Pharisee;
Yosi was a priest; Simeon b. Nathaniel was an am ha'ares, not
observant of the purity laws; Eleazar b. Arakh was a mystic;
and Joshua b. Hananiah should represent rabbinism. But this
remains to be studied.

IX

RABBINISM AND SCRIBISM

If Eliezer stands for the old Pharisaism, who stands for
the pre-70 scribes? The scribes form a distinct group -- not
merely a profession -- in the Gospels' accounts of Jesus's
opposition. Scribes and Pharisees are by no means regarded as
one and the same group. To be sure, what scribes say and do
not say is not made clear. One cannot derive from the synoptic
record a clear picture of scribal doctrine or symbolism, if
any, although one certainly finds an account of the Pharisaic
law on ritual uncleanness and tithing. Since materials now
found in the synoptics were available in Palestine between 70
and 90, however, they may be presumed accurately to portray the
situation of that time, because their picture had to be credi-
ble to Christians of the period. (Even the Fourth Gospel
contains traditions that go back to Palestine before 70, but we
concentrate attention on the picture presented by the synoptics.) If so, we have in the synoptics a portrait of two

groups at Yavneh in close relationship with one another, but
not entirely unified.

Now, having seen in Eliezer an important representative of
the old Pharisaism, we find no difficulty in accounting for the
Pharisaic component of the Yavnean synthesis. It likewise
seems reasonable to locate in the scribes the antecedents of
the ideological or symbolic part of the rabbinic component at
Yavneh. Admittedly, our information on scribism in the rabbinic literature is indistinguishable from the later sayings
produced by rabbinism. But if we consider that scribism goes
back to much more ancient times than does Pharisaism, and that
its main outlines are clearly represented, for instance, by Ben
Sira, we may reasonably suppose that what the scribe regarded
as the center of piety was study, interpretation, and application of the Torah. To be sure, what was studied and how it was
interpreted are not to be identified with the literature and
interpretation of later rabbinism. But the scribal piety and
the rabbinic piety are expressed through an identical symbol,
study of Torah. Unless rabbinism begins as the innovation of
the early Yavneans -- and this seems to me unlikely -- it
therefore should represent at Yavneh the continuation of pre-70
scribism.

But pre-70 scribism continued with an important difference, for Yavnean and later rabbinism said what cannot be
located in pre-70 scribal documents: the Temple cult is to be
replaced by study of Torah, the priest by the rabbi (=scribe);
and the center of piety was shifted away from cult and sacrifice entirely. So Yavnean scribism made important changes in
pre-70 scribal ideas. It responded to the new situation in a
more appropriate way than did the Yavnean Pharisaism represented by Eliezer. Eliezer could conceive of no piety outside
of that focused upon the Temple. But Yavnean and later scrib-
ism-rabbinism was able to construct an expression of piety
which did not depend upon the Temple at all. While Eliezer
appears as a reformer of old Pharisaism, the proponents of
rabbinism do not seem to have reformed the old scribism. What
they did was to carry the scribal ideal to its logical conclusion. If study of Torah was central and knowledge of Torah
important, then the scribe had authority even in respect to the
Temple and the cult; indeed, his knowledge was more important
than what the priest knew. This view, known in the sayings of
Yohanan b. Zakkai, who certainly held that the priest in
Yavnean times was subordinate to the rabbi, is not a matter

only of theoretical consequence. Yohanan also held that he
might dispose of Temple practices and take them over for the
Yavnean center -- and for other places as well -- and so both
preserve them ("as a memorial") and remove from the Temple and
the priests a monopoly over the sacred calendar, festivals, and
rites. This meant that Jews everywhere might fully observe the
pilgrim-festivals. Earlier scribism in its symbolic structure
thus contained within itself the potentiality to supersede the
cult. It did not do so earlier because it had no reason to and
because it probably could not. The latter rabbinism, faced
with the occasion and the necessity, realized that potentiality. By contrast, earlier Pharisaism invested its best energies in the replication of the cult, not in its replacement.
After 70, it could do no more than plan for its restoration.

Scribism as an ideology, not merely a profession, begins
with the view that the law given by God to Moses was binding
and therefore has to be authoritatively interpreted and applied
to daily affairs. That view goes back to the fourth century
B.C., by which time Nehemiah's establishment of the Torah of
Moses as the constitution of Judea produced important effects
in ordinary life. From that time on, those who could apply the
completed (written) Torah constituted an important class or
profession. The writings of scribes stress the identification
of Torah with wisdom and the importance of learning. Ben
Sira's sage travels widely in search of wisdom and consorts
with men of power. Into the first century, the scribes continue as an identifiable estate high in the country's administration. Otherwise, the synoptics' view is incomprehen-
sible. Therefore, those who were professionally acquainted
with the Scriptures -- whether they were priests or not --
formed an independent class of biblical teachers, lawyers,
administrators, or scribes, alongside the priesthood. We do
not know what they actually did in the administration of the
country. Perhaps Yohanan b. Zakkai's reference to decrees of
Jerusalem authorities (M. Ketuvot 13:1ff.) alludes to the work
of scribes, who therefore were involved -- as the Pharisees
certainly were -- in the determination of family law and in the
settlement of trivial disputes.

The New Testament references support the supposition that
the scribes were a separate group, differentiated from Sadducees and Pharisees.[8] The scribes occur in association with

---

[8]E. Schürer, <u>History of the Jewish People in the Time of Jesus Christ</u> (Edinburgh, 1889), I, pt. 2, pp. 319ff.

the high priests in Matt. 2:4, 16:21, 20:18, 21:15, 27, 27:41;
Mark 8:31, 10:33, 11:18, 27, 14:1, 43, 53, 15:1, 31, etc; with
the Pharisees in Matt. 5:20, 12:38, 15:1, 23:2, 13ff.; Mark
2:16, 7:1, 5. But they are not the same as the one or the
other. The scribes are called "learned in the law" and jurists
(Matt. 22:35; Luke 7:30, 10:25, 11:45, 52, 14:3). They are
teachers of the law (Luke 5:17; Acts 5:34).

Mishnaic literature obviously will miss the distinction
between Pharisees and scribes, both of whom are regarded as
HKMYM, sages. But we have no reason to suppose all scribes
were Pharisees. Schürer points out, "Inasmuch ... as the
'scribes' were merely 'men learned in the law,' there must have
been also Sadducaean scribes. For it is not conceivable that
the Sadducees, who acknowledged the written law as bindng,
should have had among them none who made it their profession to
study it. In fact those passages of the New Testament, which
speak of scribes who were of the Pharisees (Mark 2:16, Luke
5:30, Acts 23:9) point also to the existence of Sadducaean
scribes". The scribes therefore represent a class of men
learned in Scriptures, perhaps lawyers in charge of the administration of justice. They therefore had to develop legal
theories, teach pupils, and apply the law. Naturally, such
people would come to the center of the administration of
government and law, so they could not have remained aloof from
Yavneh. Some of them may, to be sure, have come because they
were Pharisees. But others, whatever their original ritual
practices, would have come because Yavneh represented the place
in which they might carry on their profession.

Josephus -- himself a new adherent of the Pharisees --
does not confuse the scribes with the Pharisees. In none of
his allusions to the Pharisees does he also refer to the
scribes (grammateis) or call Pharisees scribes. In Life
197-198, he refers to a delegation of Jerusalemites to Galilee. Two were from the lower ranks of society and adherents of
the Pharisees, the third was also a Pharisee, but a priest; the
fourth was descended from high priests. These were all able to
assert that they were not ignorant of the customs of the
fathers. To be sure, the Pharisees are referred to as knowl-
edgeable in the Torah; and they have "traditions from the
fathers" in addition to these that Moses had revealed. But
they are not called scribes. They were (War 1:107-114) exact
exponents of the laws. But again they are not called scribes.
The long 'philosophical school' account in Antiquities 18:11-17

describes the Pharisees as virtuous and says that "all prayers
and sacred rites of divine worship are performed according to
their exposition" -- but they too are not scribes.

When Josephus does refer to Scribes, he does not refer to
Pharisees. For example, in War 1:648ff. (= Antiquities 17:152)
he refers to two sophistai who ordered their disciples to pull
down the eagle that Herod had set up in the Temple. They are
Judah son of Sepphoraeus and Matthias son of Margalus, men who
gave lectures on the laws, attended by a large, youthful
audience. If these are scribes, they are not said also to be
Pharisees, who do not occur in the account. We find also
hierogrammateis and patrion exegetai nomon -- but not in the
context of the passages about the Pharisees. While, therefore,
the Pharisees and the scribes have in common knowledge of the
country's laws, the two are treated separately. Josephus does
not regard the scribes as wholly within the Pharisaic group'
he presents the scribe as a kind of authority or professional
teacher of law. Josephus's further references to grammateis
(singular or plural) are as follows:

Apion 1:290: The sacred scribe Phritobeuates;

Antiquities 6:120: It was reported to the king by the
scribes that the host were sinning against God; 7:110: He
made Seisa scribe; 7:293 = 7:110; 7:219: Joab took the
chiefs of the tribes ad scribes and took the census;
7:264: David appointed six thousand Levites as judges of
the people and as scribes; 9:164: When the scribe and
priest of the treasury had emptied the chest; 10:55: When
the money was brought, he gave superintendence of the
temple ... to the governor of the city [and] Sapha the
scribe, etc.; 10:94f.: Baruch, scribe of Jeremiah;
10:149: the scribe of Saccias; 11:22, 26, 29: Semelios
the scribe, etc.; 11:128: On the scribes of the sanctuary
you will impose no tribute; 12:142: The scribes of the
Temple; 11:248, 250, 272, 287: scribes of the Persian
kings; 16:219: the scribe of Diophantus had imitated his
manner of writing; 20:208f.: the sicarii kidnapped the
secretary of the captain;

War 1:479: village clerks; 5:532:0 Aristeus, the secretary of the council.[9]

It is clear that Josephus does not associate scribes with
Pharisees; no scribe is a Pharisee; and no Pharisee is described as a scribe. The two are separate and distinct. One
is a sect, the other is a profession.

---

[9]H. Thackeray, Josephus Lexicon (Paris 1932), Fasc. 2,
pp. 117-118.

Since later rabbinism found pre-70 scribism highly congenial to its ideal, it is by no means farfetched to trace the
beginnings of Yavnean rabbinism to the presence of representatives of the pre-70 scribal class, to whom the ideal of study
of Torah, rather than the piety of the cult and the replication
of that cultic piety in one's own home, was central. At
Yavneh, therefore, were incorporated these two important
strands of pre-70 times -- the one the piety of a sect, the
other the professional ideal of a class. Among them, as we
have seen, Eliezer's teachings made for pre-70 Pharisaism an
important place in the Yavnean synthesis.

X
INSTITUTIONALIZED RABBINISM

Thus far, our definition of rabbinism has focused upon its
central symbols and ideals. These seem to continue symbols and
ideas known, in a general way, from 'scribism' -- if not known
in detail from individual scribes, who, as I have stressed,
formed a profession, not a sect. But what of the later, and
essential, singularly characteristic traits of rabbinism: its
formation as a well-organized and well-disciplined movement,
its development of important institutions for the government of
the Jewish communities of Palestine and Babylonia, its aspiration to make use of autonomous political instruments for the
transformation of all Jews into rabbis? Of this, we have no
knowledge at all in the earliest stratum of the Yavnean period. Clearly, Yohanan b. Zakkai worked out the relationship
between the synagogue and the Temple. But the nature of the
'gathering' at Yavneh -- whether it was some sort of 'academy',
or a nascent political institution, or merely an inchoate
assembly of various sorts of sectarians, professionals, pre-70
authorities, and whatever -- we simply do not know. Eliezer's
historical record is strikingly silent on this very point.
From his materials, we have no evidence on either how he
enforced or applied the law outside of his own household or
disciple-circle or how anyone else did. We have no hint about
the evolution of an institution one might regard as a nascent
political authority -- a government -- in any terms. Eliezer's
laws omit reference even to the legal theory behind such an
authority. And they are strikingly silent about the whole
range of laws to be applied in civil life. Whence such laws
reached the Yavneans we do not know. They cannot have come
from Eliezer, and, given the nature of the rabbinic traditions

about pre-70 Pharisaism, they also do not derive from other
Pharisees.

So in all the 'rabbinism' possibly present in Yohanan's
corpus and remarkably absent in Eliezer's is simply the symbolic and ideological element represent by the study of Torah
as the central expression of piety. The political institutions
and social expressions of rabbinism make no appearance in the
earliest years of the Yavnean period. They emerge, for the
first time, in the development of the government under the
patriarchate and its associated rabbinical functionaries,
beginning with Gamaliel II -- circa A.D. 90 -- and fully
articulated, in the aftermath of the Bar Kokhba debacle, by
Simeon b. Gamaliel II, circa A.D. 150. At that point, the
rabbinical ideal produced serious effects for the political and
social realities of Judaism.

XI
PERSONAL POST-SCRIPT

In this chapter we have reviewed all together the results
of several quite separate researches: (1) method in the
history of ideas based upon the rabbinic canon; (2) the rabbinic traditions about the Pharisees before 70; (3) Eliezer ben
Hyrcanus as a Pharisee after 70; (4) Yohanan ben Zakkai as a
scribe; and (5) Yavnean-scribism. All of these are then drawn
together into a single account. In Medawar's categories, the
results fall into the category of the imaginative, the possible, proposal, conjecture, and what might be true. I do not
think we yet know what was in fact the case. My work --
radical and sedulously ignored in its day -- in fact was deeply
conservative, shaped by the established consensus except in
some few ways. I was the one who opened the way, who raised
possibilities never before imagined, who considered propositions never earlier found possible or proposed. I asked, What
if these writings do not tell us what people really said and
did? What then do they tell us? And how are we to use them to
find out what was going on, if not in the time to which the
writings refer, then in the time in which the writings were
closed and deemed authoritative? These were, and remain, the
right questions, and I was the first to ask them. The answers,
in that context, are less important. For they will change, as
our minds open to still fresher possibilities. But the questions, once asked, frame the standing inquiry for quite some
time.

Part Three

LITERARY STUDY OF FORMATIVE JUDAISM

Chapter Seven

THE BABLYONIAN TALMUD AS A DOCUMENT
OF RELIGION AND OF LITERATURE

After the Tanakh ('Scripture,' or 'Old Testament'), the
Talmud is the single most influential document in the history
of Judaism. This is for both religious and cultural reasons.
The Talmud, viewed as part of the Revelation of the Torah (the
Pentateuch) to Moses on Mount Sinai, has from the time of its
redaction been treated as the authoritative interpretation of
Scripture and as a corpus of revealed Law in its own right.
The cultural traits inculcated by the Talmud, moreover, defined
the shape of the civilizations of the Jewish people in many
different lands. These traits -- respect for reason, belief in
the orderly and logical character of the good life, reverence
for rational discourse and a high sense of the potentiality of
the human intellect -- derive in particular from the study of
the Talmud. They include, as well, moral and ethical teachings
about love of neighbor, respect for law and order and the
conviction that the good life consists in studying Torah,
keeping the Commandments, both those now seen as ritual and
those perceived as moral, and doing deeds of lovingkindness,
acts of grace beyond the measure of the Law. The Talmud thus
defined for the Jews the way in which the good life would be
conducted. The Talmud constitutes the principal, formative
element in the life of the Jewish people.

But, in point of fact, we err when we treat the Talmud as
a single document. It is true that, when most people refer to
'the Talmud,' they think of the Babylonian Talmud, a compilation, produced in Babylonia in the 6th and 7th centuries A.D.,
consisting of the Mishnah, a Palestinian law-code of the late
2nd century A.D., and the Gemara, or commentary of the Mishnah,
accumulated in the following three or four centuries. But
there is another Talmud, the one produced in the Land of Israel
(in Palestine: the Jerusalem, or Palestinian, Talmud) towards
the end of the 5th century A.D., also consisting of that same
Mishnah, but with its own Gemara, the Mishnah-commentary
produced in the Land of Israel from the 3rd to the end of the
5th century. The Mishnah is a sizeable autonomous document
which originally existed on its own. Around it gathered not

only the Gemaras but also another body of law and theology
known as the Tosefta, or supplement (to the Mishnah), independent of the Gemaras and in fact cited in them. At the same
time as this literature (Mishnah, Tosefta, Palestinian Talmud,
Babylonian Talmud) was being written, the same authorities, in
the same religio-legal institutions, were also producing
sizeable corpora of exegesis and interpretation of the Tanakh.
These are put together into collections of interpretations of
various books of the Pentateuch, e.g., Genesis Rabbah and
Leviticus Rabbah. Attributed to the authorities of the Mishnah, moreover, are interpretations of the legal passages of
Exodus, Leviticus, Numbers, and Deuteronomy, known as Mekhilta
for Exodus, Sifra for Leviticus, and Sifre for Numbers and
Deuteronomy. And when we turn to the sorts of materials put
together in the Gemaras of the Babylonian and Palestinian
Talmuds, furthermore, we discover not a single, unitary and
harmonious discussion, but a fairly wide variety of types of
materials, each serving its own purpose. It follows that
before us is a considerable corpus of literature. Calling the
whole 'Talmud' or even 'talmudic literature' is misleading.
And even if we do, the Talmud is only one document produced by
the Judaic authorities of late Antiquity, and we cannot be sure
that, from their perspective, it was their central and most
important creation.

     These authorities are called rabbis. The form of Judaism
that bears their imprint and definition in known as rabbinic
(or talmudic) Judaism. Previously there were other kinds of
Judaism, but rabbinic Judaism has grown until, today, it
predominates among nearly all those Jews who draw upon the
Revelation of Moses and view the world from within the religious system based on that Revelation. As an example of an
earlier form of Judaism, if the priests of the Temple of
Jerusalem before 70 were asked to describe their central
religious act, it surely would have been the sacrifice of
animals to the Lord in the Temple. If the Messianic teachers
of the Essene community, whose library was discovered at
Qumran, by the Dead Sea, could tell us what activity was most
important in their kind of Judaism, it probably would have been
the communal meal, eaten in a state of cultic purity in accordance with the purity-taboos of Leviticus, and the study of the
meaning of Scripture in, and to, the life of their commune.
Obviously, to those Jews who believed that Jesus was the
Messiah promised of old but who also saw themselves as Jews,

the Church of Peter in Jerusalem, at the heart of Judaism, will
have been yet another quite distinctive symbol. To the rabbis
-- of ancient times as of today -- the central symbol of
Judaism is Torah, the most important activity is the study of
Torah, the principal authority is the learned man, the rabbi,
and the ancient Scriptures are read as the record of the
masters of Torah, from Moses, whom they called 'our rabbi,'
onwards. Clearly, calling Moses 'our rabbi' indicates a
considerable rewriting of the history of biblical Israel and
tells us that the Talmud stands in the very centre of a massive
reformation of Judaism, past, present, and future.

I

THE MISHNAH

    To gain a clearer picture of the complex literature
produced by the rabbis of late Antiquity, let us isolate the
single component of that literature viewed by the ancient
rabbis as most important. It is undoubtedly the Mishnah, which
the rabbinic account of the history of rabbinic or talmudic
literature assigns to Judah the Patriarch, ruler of the Jewish
community of Palestine in the late 2nd and early 3rd century.
Mishnah stands out because it is called part of the Torah
revealed by God to Moses at Sinai. That is an extraordinary
claim. For one thing, how can Mishnah be attributed to Judah
the Patriarch and also be received as 'Torah revealed to Moses
on Sinai'? We must wonder about the conception of revelation
contained within this contradictory statement, and, in due
course, we shall plumb its meaning. What is stated above, in
Chapter Two, is apropos here as well.
    Mishnah, a corpus of sayings divided into six principal
sections, which themselves are subdivided into sixty-three
tractates in all, contains its own theological verification.
The opening chapter of the tractate called the 'Sayings of the
Fathers' (Pirqe aboth) explicitly links the authorities of
Mishnah itself upwards to Sinai:

> Moses received Torah [not: the Torah, the written Torah]
> on Sinai and handed it on to Joshua, and Joshua to elders,
> and elders to prophets, and prophets handed it on to the
> men of the great assembly.

The men of the great assembly, supposed to have lived in the
4th century B.C., then are succeeded by such non-biblical

paragons as Simeon the Righteous, Antigonus, Yose ben Yo^{C}ezer
and Yose ben Yohanan, Joshua ben Perahiah and Nittai the
Arbelite, Judah ben Tabbai and Simeon ben Shatah, Shema^{C}iah
and Abtalion, and, finally, Hillel and Shammai. With Hillel
and Shammai, we find ourselves at the threshold of the 1st
century A.D. The disciples, or 'Houses,' of Shammai and Hillel
stand at the beginning of the numerous and important names to
which Mishnah attributes the bulk of its materials, so that by
beginning with Moses and coming down to Shammai and Hillel, the
apologists of Mishnah lay claim to origination of their document not only in ancient times, but on Sinai. Mishnah is part
of the Revelation to Moses on Sinai, but clearly a part that
was not written down -- since the Scriptures do not contain
anything like Mishnah -- and hence is deemed to have been
formulated and transmitted orally.

According to this account, therefore, Mishnah is part of
the Torah revealed to Moses on Sinai, and hence must be understood as a major document in the history of Judaism. Together
with its commentaries and appended materials (Gemara), it
constitutes the true beginning of Judaism, since Judaism has
been defined -- from ancient times to the present -- as Scripture interpreted by the talmudic rabbis.

How then does Mishnah and its related documents define and
explain the meaning of Torah? By Torah is meant both a book
and an activity. The book is the written Scripture, the
Tanakh. The activity is the unwritten Revelation of God to
Moses 'our rabbi' on Mount Sinai, which produces, in time, the
Mishnah. Thus 'Torah' refers to 'the whole Torah of Moses our
rabbi,' a Torah in two parts, distinguished by the forms of the
formulations and transmission. The one part is written down.
The other part is memorized. The two together constitute
Torah, and it is by combining both that one learns Torah,
principally through memorization and critical inquiry into what
is memorized (that is, the paramount mode of the second half of
Torah). Accordingly, for talmudic Judaism, literary texts
constitute the data of religion, and interpreting them defines
the quest for, and experience of, the sacred. It follows that,
to the ancient rabbis and their continuators, one seeks God
through the worship effected in a particular kind of learning
of a distinctive sort of literature.

The reader will be helped at this point if we clarify the
meaning of Torah, which already has been used in more than one
sense, and which, in the history of Judaism, bears a variety of

meanings. As I said above, in the beginning, Torah meant
teaching or instruction, but very soon after the creation of
the Torah-literature, about 450 BCE, Torah becomes 'the Torah,'
the Pentateuch or the Five Books of Moses, Genesis, Exodus,
Leviticus, Numbers and Deuteronomy. In Judaism today, the
Torah as a physical object, a scroll, contains these five
books. They constitute the sancta, sacred objects, of the
synagogue worship, being kept in the place of honor and carried
in procession, then handled and proclaimed, at the very centre
of the divine service. But when the concept of the whole
Scripture came into being, towards the end of the 1st century
A.D., then 'Torah' came to refer to the whole of the written
Scripture known, as we pointed out, as the 'Old Testament.'
Now, in using the word Torah to mean Divine Revelation, rabbinic Judaism reverted to the most ancient usage and claimed on
behalf even of its holy documents and teachings the status of
torah, Divine Revelation. To speak explicitly of Mishnah:
when Mishnah is referred to as part of Torah, it is claimed
that, when Moses received Torah from God on Mount Sinai, he
received Torah in two parts, one in writing, the other to be
memorized. This much is clear, of course. It will follow that
(1) Mishnah as a distinct document, and (2) Mishnah as part of
Torah must be kept separate. Mishnah as a distinct document
existed before Mishnah was assigned a place in the Torah of
Moses. The Talmud, attached as it is to Mishnah, likewise
joined in that Torah of Moses because it is deemed to be part
of the Oral Torah, and much that came into being later on
likewise was deemed to be holy, therefore to be Torah. So,
while Mishnah came to closure c. A.D. 200, and the Talmud of
Palestine c. A.D. 450, and that of Babylonia c. A.D. 500 (all
these dates are merely guesses and stand upon very little firm
evidence), the whole found its way into the Torah of Moses on
Sinai. It is this curious fact that we must now try to appreciate.

     To the talmudic rabbis Torah -- Revelation -- remained
open, an uncompleted canon, as late as the early 3rd century
A.D., if not later. Mishnah was regarded as part of it by
people who personally knew the authorities of Mishnah. Samuel
and Rab, who could have known Judah the Patriarch himself, know
Mishnah as Torah. No wonder, then, that they could deem
Torah-learning to be the chief locus of the open way toward the
sacred, for it is through the processes of qabbalah and
massoret -- handing down, 'traditioning' -- that they claim on

behalf of Mishnah its status as part of Mosaic Revelation: Torah-learning is a mode of attaining Revelation of Moses on Sinai, and transcendence by rabbis is defined as receiving Divine Revelation. Mishnah itself is called Mosaic and assigned to Sinai by people who stand within decades of the work that brought Mishnah into being, an amazing fact. Accordingly, so far as the talmudic rabbis are concerned, Torah is, as I said, an unfilled basket, a canon still open and uncompleted. Because Judah, Meir, Simeon, Yose and Simeon ben Gamaliel of the mid-2nd century are the main authorities of Mishnah, it means that the 3rd and 4th-century rabbis cannot have supposed the processes or revelation had closed a thousand or more years earlier. Not for them the route of pseudepigraphy, assigning their great ideas to Adam or Enoch or the sons of Jacob. Nor do they even take the trouble to put the language of Mishnah into the forms and syntax of the biblical tongue, as do the masters of the Essene community at Qumran. They do not imitate the forms of the sacred literature of old nor hide themselves in the cloak of pseudepigraphic anonymity. For to them the sacred and Revelation are as available as to Moses. Nothing said to Moses may not also be said to them.

Mishnah is a work formulated in the processes of redaction. That is, the particular linguistic formulation of Mishnah took place among the men who combined and collected its materials into a well composed and orderly document. These materials dated from the previous two or three centuries, but the forms that were imposed on them in earlier times were not totally obliterated by men wholly in command of themselves and confident of their own superior judgement of how things should be put together and worded. Mishnah is set out in highly stereotyped sentences. The range of such sentences is very limited. We can list their paramount forms on the fingers of one hand. The patterned sentences, e.g, 'If X is so, then Y is the rule, and if X is not so, the Y is not the rule,' will run on in groups of threes or fives. When the pattern shifts, so does the topic under discussion. The patterns are so worked out and put together that it is exceedingly easy to memorize Mishnah. Just as the authorities of Mishnah, speaking in their own names, do not take the trouble to put their ideas into the mouths of Adam, Enoch, or their own heroes, e.g. Moses and David, and just as they do not bother to copy the formulary patterns of Scripture, so they take decisive action to wipe out the traces of the literary and aesthetic forms in which intellectual materials, then nearly three centuries old, had come down into their own hands.

What the redactors and formulators of Mishnah do, they do only in Mishnah. The companion compilation, Tosefta, does not reveal equivalent traits of formulation aimed at facilitating memorization, Nor, in the later rabbinic documents, do we find equivalent linguistic structures encompassing whole chapters and even larger units of redaction, though, to be sure, brief formulae seem to have been memorized throughout. Mishnah is unique. It alone was made into literature for memorization, and on its behalf alone was the claim laid down, 'Moses received Torah on Sinai, and handed it on to Joshua, and Joshua to the sages, and sages to the prophets,' and so on down to the named authorities who stand within the pages of Mishnah itself, including, as we have seen, such recent figures as Shammai and Hillel.

Exactly how do the framers of Mishnah facilitate memorization? Let me state first what they do not do. They do not give us rhyme-schemes. Although probably meant to be sung, the text does not follow disciplined rhythms. Its principal forms consist of arrangements of words in certain syntactical patterns, not of the repetition of the same words, then with some stunning variation at the start or end of a thought. It is the presence of these recurrent syntactical patterns that makes it easy to memorize. They are deeply embedded within the structure of language, rather than expressed superficially. The mishnaic mnemonic is defined by the inner logic of word patterns: grammar and syntax. Even though Mishnah is to be handed on orally and not in writing, it expresses a mode of thought attuned to highly abstract syntactical relationships, not concrete and material ones. Rabbis who memorize Mishnah are capable of amazingly abstract perceptions, for their ears and minds perceive regularities of grammatical arrangements running through a whole range of diverse words. What is memorized is a recurrent notion expressed in diverse examples but framed in a single, repeated rhetorical pattern. The diverse cases are united by a principle that is contained within all of them. But that principle is seldom made explicit. Rather, it is embedded in the deep structure of thought and language and has to be discovered there by the mind of the person who memorizes and studies the several cases.

Mishnaic rhetoric creates a world of discourse distinct from the concrete realities of a given time, place and

society. The exceedingly limited repertoire of grammatical
patterns imposed upon all ideas on all matters gives symbolic
expression to the notion that beneath the accidents of life are
comprehensive, unchanging and enduring relationships. It is
through how things are said, therefore, as much as what is
said, that Mishnah proposes to express its message. Mishnah is
made out of meaningful statements, the form of which is meant
to convey deep meaning. The framers of Mishnah expect to be
understood by keen ears and active minds. They therefore
convey what is fundamental at the level of grammar, indepen-
dently of specific meanings of words and cases. They manifest
confidence that the listeners will put many things together and
draw the important conclusions for themselves. Mishnah assumes
an active intellect capable of perceiving implications and of
vivid participation. Apart from the message memorized, Mishnah
demands the perception of the unarticulated message contained
within the medium of syntax and grammar. And the hearer is
assumed to be capable of putting the two together to create
still deeper insight. The cogent syntactical pattern underlying statements about different things expresses a substantive
cogency among those diverse and divergent cases.

There are, then, these two striking traits of mind re-
flected within Mishnah: first, the perception of order and
balance, and, second, the view of the mind's centrality in the
construction of order and balance. The mind imposes wholeness
upon discrete cases. Mind perceives meaning and pattern,
because, to begin with, it is mind -- the will, understanding
and intention of man (rarely do women participate actively) --
that imparts meaning to the world. To give one concrete
example: to the rabbis of the 2nd century CE, it is human
intention, not material reality or the automatic working of
mindless laws, that defines what is unclean or clean. In one
area of the law of purities after another, the conclusion is
reached that what man thinks is determinative of what can be
made unclean and definitive of the processes of contamination.
for instance, Scripture states (Lev. XI:34, 37) that if a dead
creeping thing falls on dry food, the food is unaffected, but
if it is wet, it is made unclean. The late 1st- and 2nd-cen-
tury rabbis add, however, that food that is wet accidentally is
not affected by the source of uncleanness. It is still clean
and insusceptible. Only whan a man deliberately draws water
and intentionally applies it to grain, for example, does the
grain becomes susceptible to uncleanness. It follows that, if

you have two stacks of grain, one on which rain has fallen,
another which a man has watered, and if a dead creeping thing
falls on both, only the latter is unclean. The two sorts of
grain are identical, except for man's intention. That is one
among literally hundreds of examples of the same viewpoint.

The claim for Mishnah, laid down, as we have seen, in
Abot, Mishnah's first and most compelling apologetic, is that
the authority of Mishnah rests upon its status as received
tradition of God. This tradition, handed on through memory, is
essential to the whole Torah. In a world in which writing was
routine, memorization was special. What happens when we know
something by heart, which does not happen when we read it or
look for it in a scroll or a book, is this: when we walk in
the street and when we sit at home, when we sleep and when we
wake, we carry with us, in our everyday perceptions, that
memorized saying. The process of formulation through formalization and the coequal process of memorizing patterned cases to
sustain the perception of the underlying principle, uniting the
cases just as the pattern unites their language, extends the
limits of language to the outer boundaries of experience, the
accidents of everyday life itself. Wise sayings are routine in
all cultures; but the reduction of all truth, particularly to
wise sayings, is not.

To impose upon these sayings an underlying and single
structure of grammar corresponding to the inner structure of
reality is to transform the structure of language into a
statement of ontology. Once our minds are trained to perceive
principle among cases and pattern within grammatical relationships, we further discern, in the concrete events of daily
life, both principle and underlying autonomous pattern. The
form of Mishnah is meant to correspond to the formalization
perceived within, not merely that imposed upon, the conduct of
concrete affairs. The matter obviously is not solely ethical,
though the ethical component is self-evident. It also has to
do with the natural world and the things that break its routine. In Mishnah, all things are a matter of relationship,
circumstance, fixed and recurrent interplay. 'If X, then Y, if
not X, then not Y' -- that is the datum by which minds are
shaped.

The way to shape and educate minds is to impart into the
ear, thence into the mind, perpetual awareness that what
happens recurs, and what recurs is pattern and order, and,
through them, wholeness. How better to fill the mind than with

formalized sentences, generative of meaning for themselves and
of significance beyond themselves? In such sentences meaning
rests upon the perception of <u>relationship</u>. Pattern is to be
discovered in the multiplicity of events and happenings, none
of which themselves state or articulate pattern. Mind, trained
to memorize through what is implicit and beneath the surface,
is to be accustomed and taught in such a way as to discern
pattern. Order <u>is</u>, because order is discovered, first in
language, then in life. As the cult, in all its precise and
obsessive attention to fixed detail, demonstrated that from the
orderly center flowed lines of meaning to the periphery, so the
very language of Mishnah, in its precise and obsessive concen-
tration on innate and fixed relationship, demonstrated order
deep within the disorderly world of language, nature, and man.

While rabbinic Judaism is commonly described as a highly
'traditional' kind of religion, and while Mishnah, with its
stress on memorization and obedience to the Law, is treated as
a document of tradition, Mishnah is hardly traditional; as we
shall see, the Gemara preserves for its part an equally independent frame of mind vis-a-vis Mishnah itself. The Talmud as
a whole is anything but traditional, in the commonplace sense
of tradition as something handed on, that bears authority over
us simply because it has come down to us from old. The foundation of Mishnah's world view is the claim that revelation
continues to occur and is embodied in the work of men of the
recent past. It, therefore, is the <u>contemporaneity</u> of Mishnah
-- a contemporaneity effected through the detachment of its
cases from specific time and place and even particular linguistic context -- that is its principal trait. The later history
of Mishnah, its capacity to generate two large Talmuds as
commentaries, its unfathomed implications that led later
generations to produce their commentaries on Mishnah and on <u>its</u>
commentaries, their responses to specific questions or Torah-
law, and their efforts to codify the law -- these testify to
the permanent contemporaneity of Mishnah.

Accordingly, we must ask, why is it that Mishnah, while
being accepted as Torah, escapes being fossilized as tradition? In my view, the chief reason is to be found in the
intentions of Mishnah's own framers, who do not present their
ideas as ancient tradition but in their own names as living
Torah. They therefore keep open the path of continuing recep-
tivity to revelation through continuing use of the mind. I
think it is done deliberately.

By stating Mishnah in terms essentially neutral to sages'
own society (though, to be sure, drawing upon the data of their
context), Rabbi Judah the Patriarch sees to it that his part of
the Torah will pass easily to other places and other ages.
Through patterned language, Mishnah transcends the limitations
of its own society and time. There is, however, a second side
to matters. What makes Mishnah useful is not only its compre-
hensibility, but also its incomprehensibility. It is a deeply
ambiguous document, full of problems of interpretation. Easy
to memorize, it is exceptionally difficult to understand.
Mishnah not merely permits exegesis. It demands it. That
accounts for its Talmuds. We can memorize a pericope of
Mishnah in ten minutes. But it takes a lifetime to draw forth
and understand the meaning. Mishnah contains within itself,
even in its language, a powerful statement of the structure of
reality. But that statement is so subtle that, for eighteen
centuries, disciples of Mishnah, the Talmuds and the consequent
literature of exegesis, have worked on spelling out the meaning
(not solely the concrete application) of that statement.

It is not accident at all that the most influential works
of Jewish intellectual creativity, such as the Zohar, the
13th-century corpus of mystical lore laid down in the names of
2nd-century authorities, and Maimonides's legal code, and the
Shulhan Aruch of Joseph Caro, link themselves specifically to
Mishnah. Zohar claims for itself the same authorities as those
of Mishnah, as if to say: 'This is the other part of Mishnah's
Torah.' And Maimonides's work, the Mishneh Torah, is in the
model of, but an improvement upon, the language and structure
of Mishnah itself. Nor should we forget that still a third
religious genius of Judaism, Joseph Caro, heard the Mishnah
personified speak to him and wrote down what the Mishnah had to
tell him. These are diverse testimonies to the ineluctable
demand, imposed by Mishnah itself, for further exegesis. The
first, pesudepigraphic, the second, an imitation of the language and form, and the third, a curious personification of the
document -- all look backwards, not forwards. For each is a
way taken earlier in response to the written Torah. The Zohar
takes the model -- as to its authority -- of the pseudepigrapha
of the 'Old Testament.' Maimonides, like the sages of the
Essene community at Qumran, takes the model of the inherited
linguistic choices of the holy book. Joseph Caro, of course,
in his hearing the personification of Mishnah talking, will
have been at home among those who talk of Torah or wisdom

personified. So, in all, from A.D. 200 onward, the Mishnah
stood firm as the foundation of Judaism, the focus of exegesis
-- hence the two Talmuds -- and the model for exegesis of
Scripture, undertaken later on in the Rabbah-Midrash-collec-
tions as well.

II
BABYLONIAN TALMUD: MISHNAH AND TOSEFTA

Having seen how and why Mishnah not merely requires, but
actually generates, commentaries, we now turn to the most
important one, which is the Babylonian Gemara. What we shall
see, first of all, is that Mishnah as Mishnah -- an autonomous
part of Torah -- is submerged into the processes of amplification and discussion of individual units of thought -- pericopae
-- of Mishnah. The document thus loses its independent character. The commentary, with its atomistic and line-by-line
exegesis of the text, obliterates the character of the text as
a document with its own literary, legal and theological
traits. The second interesting trait of the Gemara (not evident in the particular selection we shall examine) is its
critical stance towards Mishnah. Just as Mishnah takes up its
independent position vis-a-vis the written Torah, not imitating
the language of the written Torah and not adducing, as proof of
the correctness of Mishnah's propositions, texts of the written
Torah, so the Gemara, while commenting on Mishnah, establishes
its own viewpoint. What strikes the Gemara as interesting in
Mishnah is the absence of proof-texts, leading from Scripture
to the propositions of Mishnah. It therefore chooses, wherever
possible, to provide proof-texts, which Mishnah, for its part,
deems unnecessary. Mishnah claims to be an independent unit of
Torah, half of the whole Torah of Moses our rabbi, and, by its
exegetical interest, Gemara subverts that claim by setting
Mishnah forth as essentially secondary to, and dependent upon,
the proof -- the truths -- of the written Torah.

The best way to come to an assessment of the character of
Gemara is to examine a sample of its immense literature, to see
how it is put together and conducts its inquiry. Because
Judaism takes the conduct of every detail of life with utmost
seriousness, we shall consider how the Talmud considers a
matter of ritual law, rather than a more practical, ethical or
moral issue. This passage allows us to see the solemn character accorded to small matters of religious life, how one says a

blessing over wine, for example. It shows, in a concrete way, how talmudic discourse treats various injunctions that constitute the practice of Judaism. To be sure, it is easy enough to consider what follows as an instance of hair-splitting or nit-picking, and, viewed from some perspectives, a discussion such as this is nothing more than that. But if we consider that, to the rabbis of the Talmud, the good life is orderly, logical and rational, and that to them no detail of everyday life is exempt from the criticism of applied reason, we cannot be surprised that nits too must be picked and hairs split. We, therefore, take up a brief unit of Mishnah-tractate Berahkot, which deals with diverse blessings, and shall consider, in sequence, first, a pericope of Mishnah, second, the corresponding supplement of _Tosefta_, and, third, the Babylonian Talmud's treatment of that same Mishnah. This will allow us to see how one small part of the Babylonian Talmud works, the modes of argument and of practical logic that generate the bulk of that immense work. Before us is the opening pericope of the eighth chapter of _Berakhot_:

> A.   These are the things which are between the House of Shammai and the House of Hillel in [regard to] the meal:
> B.   The House of Shammai say, 'One blesses [says the blessing for] the day, and afterwards one says the blessing over the wine.'
> C.   And the House of Hillel say, 'One says the blessing over the wine, and afterwards one blesses the day.'

The chapter begins with a superscription, A, which announces the subject and identifies the authorities whose opinions are to be given. No one can suppose that the only laws 'in regard to the meal' derived from the Houses, or that no one thereafter raised issues or formulated opinions on the same subject. Nor are these the only points about meals on which the Houses differed. The _Gemara_ lists others. What we have are elements of a much larger tradition, which have been chosen for redaction and preservation. What we do not have, by and large, are the items omitted or passed over by those editors responsible for the documents in our hands. To some measure, these omitted materials are preserved in other compilations of rabbinical traditions, or occur as single items, not in collections, in the _Gemara_; they will be signified as deriving from the authorities of the 1st and 2nd centuries, called Tannaim ('repeaters' -- the Aramaic root, TNY, is equivalent to the Hebrew SHNY, thus Mishnah teachers), masters whose opinions

were formulated and included in the Mishnah, or in the stratum
of materials from which the Mishnah was finally selected.

The first difference, B, concerns the order of blessing
the wine and saying the Sanctification of the Sabbath day. The
House of Shammai say the Sanctification comes first, then the
blessing for the wine. The House of Hillel rule contrariwise.
The Mishnah explains nothing about these requirements and their
meaning. We are supposed to know that 'say' means reciting the
Sanctification, 'wine' means saying a blessing over the wine.

Since we have already noticed that Mishnah is formulated
so as to facilitate memorization, we can hardly be surprised to
observe an obvious mnemonic at B-C. The opinions of the Houses
are verbally identical except for the order of the operative
words, day/wine as against wine/day. The remainder of the
chapter exhibits similar mnemonic devices. If we give the
Hebrew letters in their English equivalents, we have for B-C
the following:

    MBRK ^{C}L HYWM W'HR KK MBRK ^{C}L HYYN

    MBRK ^{C}L HYYN W'HR KK MBRK ^{C}L HYWM

These words preserve a fixed order and balance from one
House-saying to the next, as is obvious above.

As we have seen, although the Mishnah is the primary
component of the Talmud, there is a second, almost equally
important collection of tradition, also attributed to 1st- and
2nd-century masters: the Tosefta, the supplement of the
Mishnah. Indeed, the <u>Gemara</u> centers more on the analysis of
the Tosefta than on the Mishnah. The Mishnah supplies the form
and structure for the Talmud as a whole. But our chapter cites
the Tosefta and that document provides the focus of interest.

The passage of Tosefta which serves our unit of Mishnah is
as follows (<u>Tosefta Berakhot</u> 5:25):

A.   [The] things which are between the House of Shammai
and the House of Hillel in [regard to] the meal:
B.   The House of Shammai say, 'One blesses over the day,
and afterwards he blesses over the wine, <u>for the day
causes the wine to come, and the day is already sanctified, but the wine has not yet come.</u>'
C.   And in the House of Hillel say, 'One blesses over the
wine, and afterwards he blesses over the day, <u>for the wine
causes the Sanctification of the day to be said.</u>
   '<u>Another explanation: The blessing over the wine is
continual [always required when wine is used], and the
blessing over the day is not continual [but is said only
on certain days].</u>'
D.   <u>And the Law is according to the words of the House of
Hillel</u>.

The underlined words belong to the Tosefta. The Tosefta supplies reasons for the rulings of the Mishnah. The opinion of the House of Shammai is explained by B. You have to have the wine in order to say the Sanctification of the Sabbath. On an ordinary day, not the Sabbath, the man is not required to have wine before the meal. Therefore, the 'day,' that is, the Sanctification, supplies the occasion for the wine to be brought. The day is already sanctified, for at sunset one no longer works. The Sabbath day has already begun. The Evening Prayer for the Sabbath has been said before the meal. So the Sanctification is said first. Then comes the recitation of the blessing over the wine. The House of Hillel, C, argue that what is essential is the blessing of the wine. Without wine you do not say the Sanctification of the day at all. Therefore, you bless over the wine first, then the day. The House of Hillel are given a second reason for their ruling. The man must always bless wine before he drinks it, on any day of the week. Therefore, the requirement of blessing the wine is continual or perpetual. He first carries out a continuing obligation, then the one that is not continuing, for the former takes precedence under all circumstances. The final decision is then given by D. The Law, as is mostly the case, will be observed according to the opinion of the House of Hillel.

The _Gemara_ will combine the two sets of traditions and discuss their contents. But it takes for granted that the whole is a seamless fabric of Law. It is not going to perceive that the relationships between the traditions and the ways in which they are formulated pose problems for literary analysis. We now receive the Mishnah and compare the Tosefta's materials pertinent to it. The Tosefta's additions to the Mishnah's language are underlined.

Mishnah (8:I)
A. These are the things which are between the House of Shammai and the House of Hillel in [regard to] the meal:

Mishnah (8:I)
B. The House of Shammai say, 'One blesses the day, and afterwards one blesses over the wine.'

Tosefta (5:25)
[The] things which are between the House of Shammai and the House of Hillel [as regards the meal]:

Tosefta (5:25)
The House of Shammai say, 'One blesses the day, and afterwards one blesses over the wine, for the day causes the wine to come, and the day is already sanctified, but the wine has not yet come.'

Mishnah (8:I)	Tosefta (V:25)
And the House of Hillel say, 'One blesses the wine, and afterwards one blesses over the day.'	And the House of Hillel say, 'One blesses the wine, and afterwards one blesses over the day, <u>for the wine cause the Sanctification of the day to be said.</u> <u>'Another matter: The blessing of the wine is continual, and the blessing of the day is not continual.'</u> <u>And the Law is according to the words of the House of Hillel.</u>

The relationships between the mishnaic and the toseftan versions of the Houses' disputes are fairly clear. The Tosefta tends to expand the Mishnah's terse laws. Mishnah VIII:1/ Tosefta 5:25 -- the expansion takes the form of an addition to the Mishnah.

III

BABYLONIAN TALMUD: GEMARA

This brings us to the Babylonian Talmud's treatment of our Mishnah pericope. For reasons of space, we consider only the first part of the Talmud (Babylonian Talmud <u>Berakhot</u> 51B) to our Mishnah. The Talmud is written in two languages, Hebrew and Aramaic. The use of the one rather than the other is by no means accidental. Normally, though not always, the sayings attributed to the Tannaim and statements of normative law will be in Hebrew. The comments and analyses of the Amoraim and stories will be in Aramaic. The editors' own remarks will be in Aramaic. To signify the differences, Hebrew will be in regular type, Aramaic, in italics.

To begin with, we must know that the presupposition of the Talmud is that nothing will be stated that is obvious; redundancy, it goes without saying, will not occur. But the Talmud also objects to the inclusion of well known facts. This is regarded as bad style. The reference to the 'echo which has gone forth' alludes to a story about the House of Shammai's and the House of Hillel's debating for three years, until heaven intervened with the Divine Announcement, delivered by an echo, that both Houses possess the words of the living God, but the Law follows the House of Hillel. Supernatural intervention into legal matters is commonplace. The Talmud was created in a

world that took for granted that heaven cared about, therefore
influenced or interfered in, the affairs of men, particularly
the affairs of the people of Israel, and especially those of
the rabbis, who were believed to study Torah on earth exactly
as it was studied by Moses 'our rabbi' in the Heavenly Academy. Words in Aramaic are underlined in the abstract to
follow.

>Gemara (51B)
>A.   Our rabbis have taught:
>B.   The things which are between the House of Shammai and
>the House of Hillel in [regard to] a meal:
>   The House of Shammai say, 'One blesses over the day
>and afterwards blesses over the wine, for the day causes
>the wine to come, and the day has already been sanctified,
>while the wine has not yet come.'
>   And the House of Hillel say, 'One blesses over the
>wine and afterwards blesses over the day, for the wine
>casuses the Sanctification to be said.
>   'Another matter: The blessing over the wine is
>perpetual, and the blessing over the day is not perpet-
>ual. Between that which is perpetual and that which is
>not perpetual, that which is perpetual takes precedence.'
>   And the Law is in accordance with the words of the
>House of Hillel.

The Gemara opens with a simple citation of the Tosefta we have
already studied. It then proceeds to analyze the passage.

>C.   What is the purpose of 'Another matter'?

The first peculiarity is simply the second 'reason'
assigned to the Hillelites. Why should we require two reasons
for their position, while we have only one for the Shammaites?

>   If you should say that there [in regard to the
>opinion of the House of Shammai] two [reasons are given],
>and here [in regard to the opinion of the House of Hillel]
>one, here too [in respect to the House of Hillel], there
>are two [reasons, the second being;] 'The blessing of the
>wine is perpetual and the blessing of the day is not
>perpetual. That which is perpetual takes precedence over
>that which is not perpetual.'

The Gemara reads into the Shammaite saying to separate
reasons, and so explains that in order to balance those two
reasons, the Hillelites likewise are given two.

>D.   'And the Law is in accord with the opinion of the
>House of Hillel.'

The statement of the final decision is cited from Tosefta, but this poses a new problem. For the Law normally will follow the Hillelites. Why say so?

> This is obvious [that the Law is in accord with the House of Hillel] for the echo has gone forth [and pronounced from Heaven the decision that the Law follows the opinion of the House of Hillel].

Now the question is spelled out. In rabbinic lore, it was believed that, a few years after the destruction of the Temple in A.D. 70, a heavenly echo had announced that the Law follows the House of Hillel.

> E. If you like, I can argue that [this was stated] before the echo.
> F. And if you like, I can argue that it was after the echo, and [the passage is formulated in accord with the] opinion of [52A] R. Joshua, who stated, 'They do not pay attention to an echo [from heaven].'

Two answers are given. The first is that the final decision was formulated before the echo had been heard; the second, that it came afterwards but accords with the view of those who nonetheless deny supernatural intervention into the formulation of the Law, for instance, Joshua ben Hananiah, who lived at that time and was alleged to have rejected the testimony of supernatural signs.

Let us review the whole pericope.

The Talmud opens with a citation, A, of the Tosefta's parallel to the Mishnah. Our chapter consistently supplements the Mishnah with the Tosefta, primarily in order to analyze the latter. The Tosefta is cited with the introduction of A, a fixed formula that indicates that a tannaitic source (that is, a source attributed to 1st- or 2nd-century authorities) is quoted. Other such formulae include We have learned, the formula for introducing a citation to the Mishnah; It has been taught, introducing a teaching attributed to the authority of Tannaim, though not necessarily to a specific mishnaic teacher. These Aramaic formulae function like footnotes, providing information on the source of, or type of authority behind, materials cited in the text.

In B, the Tosefta we have already examined is simply stated. Then, C undertakes the analysis of the passage. The explanation and elucidation are ignored; it is assumed that these are clear. What C wants to know is why the House of

Hillel give two reasons for their opinion. The 'two reasons'
of the Shammaites are (1) the wine is brought on account of the
Sabbath, and (2) it is already the Sabbath, yet the wine is
still lacking. The Hillelites' reason then is cited without
comment.

The analysis of the toseftan passage is continued by D.
The statement that the Law follows the House of Hillel is
regarded as obvious, since normally that is so.

A simple, 'historical' answer is provided by E: D was
included before the echo had delivered its message; F then
gives a somewhat more substantial response: some rabbis
opposed accepting supernatural signs of the determination of
the Law by heaven. Chief among these is Joshua ben Hananiah
(c. A.D. 90), who, when presented by Eliezer ben Hyrcanus with
supernatural evidence on behalf of the latter's position,
proclaimed, "The Torah -- is not in heaven" (Deut. 31:12).
Thus D is credited to Joshua, who would not accept the heavenly
decision and, therefore, had to provide earthly counsel based
on reason.

IV

THE PALESTINIAN TALMUD

We now consider the equivalent treatment of the Palestinian Talmud for the same unit of Mishnah.

Mishnah (8:I)
        The House of Shammai say, 'One blesses the day and
afterwards one blesses over the wine.'
        And the House of Hillel say, 'One blesses over the
wine and afterwards one blesses the day.'
A.   What is the reason of the House of Shammai?
        The Sanctification of the day causes the wine to be
brought, and the man is already liable for the Sanctification of the day before the wine comes.
        What is the reason of the House of Hillel?
        The wine causes the Sanctification of the day to be
said.
        Another matter: Wine is perpetual, and the Sanctifi-
cation is not perpetual. [What is always required takes
precedence over what is required only occasionally.]

The Gemara first cites the available toseftan explanations
for the positions of the two Houses. All that is added is the
introduction, 'What is the reason ... '

B.   R. Yose [c. A.D. 150] said, '[It follows] from the
opinions of them both that with respect to wine and

> Havdalah, [the prayer marking the end of the Sabbath day
> and the beginning of the week of labour], wine comes
> first.'

Now, Yose begins the analysis of the two opinions. He
wants to prove that both Houses agree the wine takes precedence
over Havdalah. That is, you bless the wine, then you say
Havdalah.

> 'Is it not the reason of the House of Shammai that
> the Sanctification of the day causes the wine to be
> brought, and here, since Havdalah does not cause wine to
> be brought, the wine takes precedence?'
> 'Is it not the reason of the House of Hillel that the
> wine is perpetual and the Sanctification is not perpetual,
> and since the wine is perpetual, and the Havdalah is not
> perpetual, the wine comes first?' Similarly, since the
> Hillelites say what is perpetual takes precedence over
> what is episodic, they will agree the wine takes prece-
> dence over Havdalah. So both Houses will agree on this
> point.'
> C. R. Mana [3rd century] said, 'From the opinions of
> both of them [it follows] that with respect to wine and
> Havdalah, Havdalah comes first.'

Since the Shammaites hold that the reason wine comes after
the Sanctification is that the Sanctification is the cause,
then, when the prayer is not the reason for saying a blessing
over wine, as in the case of Havdalah, the wine will normally
take precedence over the prayer.

Now Mana wants to turn things upside down. The opinions
of both Houses are such that they will agree Havdalah takes
precedence over wine -- the opposite of Yose's claim!

> 'Is it not the reason of the House of Shammai that
> one is already obligated [to say] the Sanctification of
> the day before the wine comes, and here, since he is
> already obligated for Havdalah before the wine comes,
> Havdalah comes first?'

The Shammaites' principle is that a person carries out the
obligation that already applies -- the Sanctification -- before
the obligation that does not yet apply. The reason the Sanctification comes before the wine is that, as soon as the sun
sets, you are obligated to say the Sanctification. But the
wine only comes later.

> 'Is it not the reason of the House of Hillel that the
> wine causes the Sanctification of the day to be said, and
> here, since the wine does not cause the Havdalah to be
> said, Havdalah comes first?'

The Hillelites are going to agree with Mana's proposition, for they say wine comes first when it is the pretext for some other prayer. But the wine is not the pretext for saying Havdalah.

> D.   R. Zeira [3rd century] said, 'From the opinions of both of them [it follows] that they say Havdalah without wine, but they say the Sanctifiation only with wine.'

Zeira draws from the foregoing the necessary consequence: you may say Havdalah without wine. But you may say the Sanctification only in connection with wine. The House of Hillel make this point clear: wine is not the pretext for saying Havdalah. Therefore, Havdalah may be said without wine. The House of Shammai say that the Sanctification of the day supplies the prextext for reciting the blessing over the wine. The Havdalah does not. So they will agree also. Zeira's point seems well founded.

> E.   This is the opinion of R. Zeira, for R. Zeira said, 'They may say Havdalah over beer but they go from place to place [in search of wine] for the Sanctification.'

Now Zeira's rule is applied. You must go in search of wine for sanctification. But Havdalah may be said over beer.

Let us now review the argument as a whole.

Once again, we observe that the Talmud's interest is to find the reasons for the Laws. These will be elucidated, then criticized according to logic and finally tested against the evidence supplied by related rules. Like the Babylonian Gemara, the Palestinian one draws heavily upon the Tosefta. Its inquiry into the Tosefta, however, tends to be more thorough and systematic than the one we have seen in the Babylonian version. The opinions of both sides are examined; questions addressed to the one will be brought to the other. Thus a perfect balance is maintained throughout. Then new issues will be raised and worked out.

The stage is set by A for what is to follow, rapidly reviewing the reasons given in the Tosefta, for the opinions of the respective Houses. Then B, C, and D draw conflicting inferences from the foregoing in respect to Havdalah.

Yose's view, B, is that both Houses agree that the wine comes before Havdalah. The Houses' principles are reviewed. As to the Shammaites: which one supplies the pretext for the other? Havdalah does not require wine, therefore the wine will

take precedence. As to the Hillelites: what is 'perpetual'?
The wine. The wine, therefore, is going to precede Havdalah.
So both Houses will agree that the order is wine, Havdalah.

Mana, in C, takes the opposite view. If the reason of the
House of Shammai is that the obligation to say the Sanctification is already present, then Havdalah, the obligation of which
likewise is already present, will come first. If the reason of
the House of Hillel is that wine comes first on the evening of
the Sabbath because the Santification may not be said without
it, then at the end of the Sabbath, Havdalah will come first,
for it may be said without wine. The dispute is made possible,
therefore, because both Houses give two reasons for their
opinions. Yose concentrates on one of the reasons for each of
the Houses, Mana on the other.

Zeira, D, then concludes that, in the opinion of both
Houses, Havdalah may be said without wine, but Santification
may not. Then E provides an abstract formulation of Zeira's
view.

V

THEOLOGY AND LITERATURE

The literary character of Talmud has emerged from an
examination of the development of a single unit of thought. It
remains briefly to state the fundamental theological conviction
of the Talmud. We saw the simple fact that the sages wanted
both rules and reasons for why things are done in one way and
not in some other. What does this quest imply? Let me spell
it out.

The supposition of the Talmud is that order is better than
chaos, reflection than whim, decision than accident, rationality than force. The Talmud's purpose is so to construct the
disciplines of everyday life and to pattern the relationships
among men that all things are made intelligible, well regulated
and trustworthy. Its view is that order and rationality are
not ours alone. We are made in God's image. And that part of
us that is like God is the thing separating human from beast:
consciousness. It is when we use our minds that we act like
God.

All reality comes under the discipline of the critical
intellect; all is therefore capable of sanctification. Torah,
represented by Mishnah, reveals the way things are, whether or
not that is how they actually may be at some particular time or
place. Reality surpasses particularities and derives from the

plan and will of the Creator of the world, foundation of all reality. God looked into the Torah and created the world, just as an architect follows his plan in making a building. The single whole Torah, in two forms, underlies the one seamless reality of the world. The search for the unity hidden by the pluralities of the trivial world -- the supposition that some one thing is revealed by many things -- these represent in intellectual form the theological and metaphysical conception of a single unique God, creator of heaven and earth, revealer of one whole Torah, guarantor of the unity and ultimate meaning of all human actions and events.

God supplies the model for our mind. Therefore, through reasoning in Torah we penetrate God's intent and plan. We attain revelation by learning Torah. The rabbis of the Talmud believe they study Torah as God does in heaven; their schools on earth replicate the Heavenly Academy. Just as God puts on tefillin (phylacteries), so do they. Just as God visits the sick, comforts the suffering and buries the dead, so do they. In studying Torah they seek the heavenly paradigm revealed by God in God's image and handed down from Moses and the prophets to their own teaching. If, therefore, the rabbis of Mishnah and Talmud learn and realize the divine teaching of Moses whom they call 'our rabbi,' it is because of the order they perceive in heaven: the rational construction of reality. Torah reveals the mind of God, the principles by which he shapes reality. Torah is revealed in the principles of reality. These were discovered even by the most modern-thinking men, the rabbis of the 2nd century who made Mishnah and knew they were making Mishnah, yet who called it part of the Torah God revealed to Moses on Sinai!

The modes of learning are holy because they lead from earth to heaven, which synagogue prayer, or fasting, or other, merely tolerated, holy rites cannot. Reason is the way, God's way; the holy person is the one who is able to think clearly and penetrate profoundly into the mysteries of Torah, and, especially, its so very trivial laws. In context, those trivialities contain revelation and serve to impart to the one who grasps them the fully realized experience of the sacred. The task, as I said at the outset, is to surpass ourselves: to undertake the reconstruction of reality through the interpretation of what is, in terms of what can and should be. The experience of sanctification both through the intellect and of the intellect is the mode of the transcendent laid open, once for all time, by the rabbis of the Talmud.

VI

THEOLOGY AND HISTORY

It remains to ask: what is the shape of this world of
meaning so carefully and precisely constructed by Talmud and
its accompanying Talmud? What the Talmud has to say about the
world is summarized in one word: 'holiness.' And the question
raised by the Talmud is how we achieve holiness, how we become
like God, in the ordinary and everyday world. We already have
noticed that central to the talmudic view of life is the
conception that the human being plays the crucial role in
imparting meaning and significance to ordinary and unimportant
things. The reason is that the intention and will of a person
transform what is ordinary into what is holy. To take one
unimportant example: if one has a pile of a hundred apples and
sets aside two of them for whatever purpose, those two apples
are not thereby made holy, sanctified or consecrated. But if,
when setting aside those two apples, <u>one has the intention of
setting them aside for the priest as the heave-offering</u> from
that pile of one hundred apples, then those two apples become
holy and cannot be eaten by ordinary folk or used for secular
purposes. Again and again, in diverse areas of Law, the
importance of the human will comes to the fore.

To Mishnah and the commentaries that flow from it, what
one wants costitutes a fundamental norm of reality, because
when Mishnah took shape all that was left for ancient Israel
was the unfettered will of the people, the hope of Israel to
endure. The most important fact about the Mishnah and the
Talmud is that they came into being after the destruction of
the Second Temple in 70, and after the devastation by the
Romans of the southern part of the Land of Israel, the territory of Judaea, a consequence of Bar Kokhba's disaster of 132.
The former brought out, in all their stark and urgent character, the issues of sin and punishment, atonement and reconciliation, originally encountered by the ancient Israelites in the
aftermath of the destruction of the First Temple in 586 B.C.
But now, it is clear, the biblical message required repetition
and amplification. For, in olden times (586), the people had
sinned and atoned, and God had forgiven them, they believed, by
restoring them to the Land and by allowing them to rebuild the
Temple. After 70 the question of why the disaster had come
about, and what sin punished thereby, necessarily arose, but
the question was now more difficult to answer. The reason is

that, having sinned, suffered, achieved atonement and found
reconciliation with God one time, the Israelites could not so
readily re-enter the trying process without some sense that the
old meanings yet endured, that the whole system had not, in
fact, collapsed in the ruins of the Temple. The disorder of a
formerly orderly world is best symbolized by the Temple, where
not a stone was left upon stone in the aftemath of its ruin.

The stress on exactness, precision and order revealed in
mishnaic language and literature, on the one side, and in
talmudic analysis and argument, on the other, has to be seen
against the background of the chaos of the 2nd century and
beyond. In a time when old meanings and ancient certainties
seemed no longer to explain and construct meaning, Mishnah's
stress on the reconstruction of a world of precision and order
constituted a firm response, an assertion that, amid chaos, the
order of language is yet available. It will then follow that
what effects the orderliness of the world is the will of the
human being, which, through careful speech and careful deed,
imposes regularity and trustworthiness upon ordinary life. The
everyday deeds and people living their mundane lives constitute
the last realm over which the Israelite ruled, lacking now a
government, a Temple, an administation of his own. It then
would be in that one remaining area of inner autonomy, the
commmonplace life at home and in the village, that the Israelite would construct the world of meaning. So Israel would
transcend the vagaries of history, with its disasters and its
disappointments. Here at home, through patterned language and
a life of infinite structure, they would find their way to a
world above history and beyond time. A much later folk-song
states the rabbinic view very clearly: the nations of the
world think that their kings are kings, but the Holy One,
blessed be He, is the King of kings of kings. The Israelites
would be ruled by that supreme monarch, and the effects of his
dominion would be seen in their every deed and gesture, whether
in the realm of morality or ritual, whether at home or with
Gentiles.

When we turn to the concrete details of mishnaic and
talmudic Law, we see the main lines of the delineation of the
divine realm of dominion, the definition of the reality subjected to God's rule. Mishnah itself, as we noticed above, is
divided into six parts. These six divisions describe for us
the aspect of life and of metaphysical reality to be sanctified
and consecreated to the Divinity through the will and right
intention of man. The six are Zera^{c}im, seeds; Mo^{c}ed,

seasons; <u>Nashim</u>, women (thus: family life, personal status);
<u>Neziqin</u>, torts; <u>Qodoshim</u>, holy things; and <u>Tohorot</u>, purities.
The issues of the Law, to state matters somewhat more broadly,
are in three parts: (1) agriculture and the passage of time;
(2) family, home, property relationships, civil and criminal
affairs; and (3) the cult and purity laws, principally affecting the cult but additionally concerning the table at home, to
be conducted in a state of cleanness as if it were the Lord's
altar in the now-devastated Temple. The first of the three
divisions makes clear that Mishnah proposes to subject to
Divine Law, and so to sanctify, the economy of the people,
which was chiefly agricultural, and the passage of time and the
seasons. It begins with these for the obvious reason that the
life of the Israelite society rested upon the foundation of
agriculture and took shape in the differentiation of days,
weeks, and months through the agricultural calendar. The
second division concerns practical matters of society, which
also have to be subjected to close regulation and sanctification: the status of the individual, the rights to property and
the transfer of property, the creation of the family, the
protection of man's property and the life from criminal tres-
pass, and the proper organization of social institutions of
government. The third division treats the service of the Lord
in the Temple, through the conduct of the cult, and the protection of the cult from unseen forces of danger and contamination
already described in Leviticus.

This last division of course makes the question urgent:
who kept this Law? For we realize that there was no Temple at
the time that Mishnah came into being, and vast areas of the
Law in fact lay in desuetude. Mishnah then describes a world
out of relationship with ordinary, everyday reality. Those
parts of its Law that can be kept were kept. But the study of
Mishnah and its accompanying Talmud encompasses the whole. And
what that means is that Mishnah and Talmud constitute principally a document describing a reality that is within, on the
one hand, or in time to come, on the other. People enter that
reality by learning and reflection, even though, in practical
fact, a negligible part of the whole may be brought into
concrete being. The whole realm of literature and Law, learning and deep human anguish and yearning, is meant to reconstruct that ancient, now ruined, realm of cult and priesthood,
to serve God through the continuing study of Revelation and
through the making of that study into the motive and definition
of the purpose and meaning of Israelite life.

Chapter Eight
PARSING THE RABBINIC CANON WITH THE HISTORY OF AN IDEA
THE MESSIAH

Each of the diverse systems produced by Jews in ancient times constituted a world-view and way of life for a circum-scribed social group.[1] While these various Judaic systems drew upon a common Scripture and referred to some of the same themes, they sufficiently differed from one another to be regarded as essentially distinct social-religious construc-tions. Each found full expression in a symbolic structure particular to itself. None might be forced to conform to a definition of a single normative and authoritative "Judaism," let alone measured against an "Orthodox Judaism." Those categories indeed prove anachronistic when applied to ancient times. It follows that, just as, for antiquity, we cannot speak of a single "Judaism" but only of "Judaisms," so we cannot imagine there was a "(the) Messianic idea of Judaism" everywhere present, always authoritative.

Indeed, the notion of a ubiquitous and systematic "messi-anism" in "Judaism" has been vastly overstated. Some Judaic systems present cogent doctrines concerning a messiah, part of a whole and systematic world view and way of life. Others do not -- Philo, the Mishnah, for instance. The conception or category, Judaism's Messianic doctrine, as a systematic con-struct, yields only confusion. What we find, rather, is a theme, common to a number of systems, worked out in ways distinctive to each. The shape of the messianic theme moreover expressed the larger points of insistence of the system by which the theme was adopted. Scripture to begin with provided a sizable repertoire of information, facts about the Messiah, when he would come, what he would do, and the like. In the diverse writings collected as the Old Testament Apocrypha and Pseudepigrapha, we find many more facts. But if we turn to the writings of particular social groups or individuals, we dis-

---

[1]The statements of fact in this paper are supported by full repertoire of texts in my Messiah in Context: Israel's History and Destiny in Formative Judaism (Philadelphia, 1984: Fortress). In this paper I wish to spell out the argument of that larger work.

cover not a random repertoire of information, but rather,
carefully selected and purposefully used facts. So these
points of reference to the Messiah form part of a larger
world-view brought to expression in the composite theological
literature of a given social group. That was the case for the
Israelite religious commune of Essenes at Qumran. Everyone
knows that it was the case for the Israelite religious communes
organized in the name of Christ. What each group did with the
messianic theme tells us about the larger, distinctive perspective of the group, rather than about "the Messianic idea of
Judaism," in general.

I

MESSIANIC THEMES IN RABBINIC JUDAISM

When we come to the writings by rabbis, from the end of
the second century to the end of the seventh, which, all
together, constitute the canon of the Judaism normative from
late antiquity to the present day ("Talmudic," "rabbinic,"
"normative," "classical"), we find a still more suggestive
fact. The messianic theme is carefully shaped in the founda-
tion-document of the rabbinic canon, the Mishnah, and serves
the larger purposes of that document. When, many centuries
later, the Babylonian Talmud reached closure, a great many more
facts about the Messiah were swept up and drawn into the great
encyclopaedia of the end. These facts, used also in other
Judaic systems of late antiquity, served to make a point
distinctive to the ultimate rabbinic system. And, as I shall
now suggest, that very point turns out to express, through the
messianic theme, what the framers of the Mishnah, for their
part, wished to say without reference to that theme at all.

Let me spell out this point. The rabbinic system took
over the fundamental convictions of the mishnaic world-view
about the importance of Israel's constructing for itself a life
beyond time. The rabbinic system then transformed the
Messiah-myth, in its totality, into an essentially ahistorical
force. If people wanted to reach the end of time, they had to
rise above time, that is, history, and stand off at the side of
great movements of political and military character. That is
the message of the Messiah-myth as it reaches full exposure in
the rabbinic system of the two Talmuds. It therefore is at its
foundation _precisely_ the message of teleology without eschatology expressed by the Mishnah and its associated documents. In

the Talmuds and their associated documents we see the restatement of the ontological convictions that informed the minds of
the second-century philosophers of the Mishnah: Israel must
turn away from time and change, submit to whatever happens, so
as to win for itself the only government worth having, that is,
God's rule, accomplished through God's anointed agent, the
Messiah.

To state matters in simple terms, salvation depended upon
sanctification, which therefore took precedence as the governing principle of the world view and way of life commanded by
the rabbis' Torah.   It follows, of course, that the rabbis who
stand behind the principles of messianic eschatology worked out
in the Talmuds in fact continued on an absolutely straight line
the fundamental convictions of the Mishnah.   That document they
claimed to continue and complete.   Superficially, that claim is
without justification, but at a deeper level it is quite proper.

II
FACTS ABOUT THE MESSIAH IN THE CANON OF RABBINIC JUDAISM

The summmary-tables in this section show the provenance of
diverse assertions, concerning the Messiah, on the one side,
and Israel's history and destiny, on the other, that add up to
the canonical corpus on formative Judaism's eschatological
teleology.   I list the topics in the rough order of the rabbinic documents in which they occur.   The important point,
however, is not documentary sequence.   We must not confuse the
evident precedence of one rabbinic compilation over another
with the historical order by which a given fact appeared before
some other.   That claim is undemonstrable and, further, it is
quite beside the point I wish to make.

Let me briefly explain the order and division of documents.   The Mishnah is assumed to have reached closure at ca.
A.D. 200, so it comes first.   The next group, Tosefta, Abot,
and Abot de R. Nathan, come to closure sometime after the
formation of the Mishnah; Abot serves as the Mishnah's first
apologetic.   The Tosefta constitutes a corpus of secondary
amplification of the Mishnah.   It is cited, normally verbatim,
in the Talmud of the Land of Israel, therefore presumably
reached a conclusion prior to the formation of the latter
document, which follows next in sequence (ca. A.D. 400).   The
group beyond, the four compilations of exegeses of the Pentateuchal books of Exodus, Leviticus, Numbers, and Deuteronomy,

bear the names only of authorities who appear, also, in the Mishnah, so are regarded as "Tannaitic," for one title accorded to the Mishnah's authorities. But the Mishnah itself turns out to be cited in the documents that deal with Leviticus, Numbers, and Deuteronomy, so these compositions also follow in time. We do not know when they were composed; setting them after the Talmud of the Land of Israel is only a guess. Genesis and Leviticus Rabbah, compilations of exegeses of the named biblical books, construct their units of discourse along the lines of exactly the same logoi as we find in the Talmud of the Land of Israel and are to be located in the same period, ca. A.D. 400. The next groups -- Lamentations Rabbah, Esther Rabbah I, Song of Songs Rabbah, Ruth Rabbah, and Pesiqta de R. Kahana, are assumed to have been composed in roughly the two hundred years after the Talmud of the Land of Israel. Among the canon of rabbinical writings, the Talmud of Babylonia then comes at the end, ca. A.D. 500-600. So before us is only the canonical order of the ideas at hand. By that I mean the ideas concerning the messiah found in various rabbinical compositions of late antiquity are laid out in the rough and approximate order in which they appear in the documents that preserve them.

The final group, Siddur (Prayerbook), Targum Onqelos, Targum Pseudo-Jonathan, and Fragmentary Targum, all to the Pentateuch, derive from a different life-setting from the items listed earlier. All of them serve the synagogue, rather than the master-disciple-circle ("school") and derive from it. We do not know the relationship between the rabbinical estate and the organization of the Prayerbook; among the Aramaic translations of Scripture, only Onqelos is assuredly rabbinic. Further discussion of the items at hand, specific references to the sources in which they appear, and justification for the procedure at hand, will be found in my Messiah in Context. Israel's History and Destiny in Formative Judaism (Philadelphia, 1984: Fortress Press).

I. The Messiah

1.	Messiah = anointed priest	a, b, c, d, e
2.	Messiah = son of David (Ruth, Boaz)	a, d, e, f, h, i, j, k, l
3.	This age vs. age of the Messiah	a, b, d, e, h
4.	Tribulations before Messiah	a, d, f, g, h
5.	Sages suffer before the end	a, f, h
6.	David's dominion is eternal	c, h, i
7.	David's son restores horn of Israel	c, h, i
8.	Messiah's coming and resurrection of dead	c, h, i
9.	David as a rabbi	c, h
10.	Messiah's name: Menahem	c
11.	Messiah from Bethlehem	c
12.	Messiah born when Temple destroyed	c
13.	Aqiba said Bar Kokhba was a Messiah	c
14.	When Israel repents, they will be saved (no messianic reference)	c, h
15.	Israel must be humble to bring Messiah. Bar Kokhba was arrogant and no messiah, so he lost	c, h
16.	Israel punished for neglect of Torah	c
17.	If Israel would do..., the Messiah would come	c, d, h
18.	Because Israel does..., the Messiah has not come	h
19.	Messiah: David-Hillel	e
20.	Messiah will gather exiles	e, h, i

a = Mishnah
b = Tosefta, Abot, and Abot de R. Nathan
c = Talmud of the Land of Israel
d = Mekhilta, Sifra, Sifre Num., Sifre Dt.
e = Gen. Rabbah and Lev. Rabbah
f = Lam. R., Est. R. I, Song R., Ruth R.
g = Pesiqta de R. Kahana
h = Talmud of Babylonia
i = Siddur
j = Targum Onqelos to the Pentateuch
k = Targum Pseudo-Jonathan to Pent.
l = Fragmentary Targum to the Pentateuch

21.	Israel will not require the Messiah as teacher	e
22.	Messiah records peoples' good deeds	e, h
23.	Unusual incidents prior to Messiah	f, h
24.	Messiah comes to worst generation	f, g, h
25.	Messiah will come when God chooses, do nothing in advance	f, h
26.	Reckoning the end	f, h, k, l
27.	Gentiles convert when Messiah comes	g
28.	Gentile rule ends	g, h
29.	God clothes Messiah	g
30.	Description of person of the Messiah	g, h
31.	God restores Jerusalem, Zion, Temple cult, through the Messiah	g, h, i, j
32.	6000 years, Messiah's age the middle 2,000	g, h
33.	Messiah came in Hezekiah's time. (Denied.)	h
34.	Messiah's name was Shiloh, etc.	h
35.	Length of Messiah's rule	h
36.	Messiah in Nisan	g, h
37.	Messiah in 7th year	h
38.	Messiah not coming on a Sabbath	h
39.	Prayer may bring the Messiah	h, i
40.	Messiah comes in 468	h
41.	Messiah will only replace pagan rulers	h
42.	Sinners punished by Messiah	h

---

a = Mishnah
b = Tosefta, Abot, and Abot de R. Nathan
c = Talmud of the Land of Israel
d = Mekhilta, Sifra, Sifre Num., Sifre Dt.
e = Gen. Rabbah and Lev. Rabbah
f = Lam. R., Est. R. I, Song R., Ruth R.
g = Pesiqta de R. Kahana
h = Talmud of Babylonia
i = Siddur
j = Targum Onqelos to the Pentateuch
k = Targum Pseudo-Jonathan to Pent.
l = Fragmentary Targum to the Pentateuch

43. Israel will be served by gentiles,   h, i, j
    Messiah will rule gentiles

44. Messiah comes when souls are all born   h

45. Messiah comes when patriarch + exilarch go   h

46. Messiah of house of Joseph killed   h

47. Messiah called "Holy One"   h

48. Messiah created before creation   h

49. Messiah comes only after Rome rules the   h
    whole world

50. King-Messiah is a captive in Rome, etc.   l

II. Israel's History and Destiny

1. Destruction in 70 marked decline in   a, b, h
   supernatural world and in life of the
   sages

2. Legal changes after 70   a, b, h

3. Periods of history marked by location   a, b, c
   of cult

4. This world/world to come, life/death   b, h

5. Why was Jerusalem destroyed   b, c, h

6. Tales about sages   b, c, h

7. Tales about priests, cult and super-   b, h
   natural events in cult

8. Rome's history is the counterpart to   c, h
   Israel's

9. Rome's deeds explicable in terms of   c, h
   Israel's logic

10. Age of idolatry vs. God's reign   c, h

---

a = Mishnah
b = Tosefta, Abot, and Abot de R. Nathan
c = Talmud of the Land of Israel
d = Mekhilta, Sifra, Sifre Num., Sifre Dt.
e = Gen. Rabbah and Lev. Rabbah
f = Lam. R., Est. R. I, Song R., Ruth R.
g = Pesiqta de R. Kahana
h = Talmud of Babylonia
i = Siddur
j = Targum Onqelos to the Pentateuch
k = Targum Pseudo-Jonathan to Pent.
l = Fragmentary Targum to the Pentateuch

11. Days distinguished by secular events,   c, h
    not only by natural one

12. When Israel learns lessons of its   c, h
    history, it commands its destiny

13. Israel saved by submission to God,   c, h
    not arrogance of its own deeds

14. Four kingdoms, four periods (four   e, f, h
    animals)

15. Just as punishment has come, so   f, g, h
    redemption will surely follow

16. Israel must accept pagan rule, pagans   e, h
    must not oppress Israel too much.
    Israel must not act on its own.

17. Iran (Persia) parallel to Rome   h

18. Various empires' history governed by   h
    their relationship to Israel

19. Nations wise to treat Israel well   h

20. Israelites are own worst enemy but   h
    control own destiny

21. Decline in merit of generations   h

22. God shares Israel's fate   h

23. Empires' history governed by study of   h
    Torah

24. Exile of Israel is so that proselytes   h
    might join them

25. Nations hate Israel because of the Torah   h

26. God loves Israel because it is humble   h
    (cf. #13)

---

a = Mishnah
b = Tosefta, Abot, and Abot de R. Nathan
c = Talmud of the Land of Israel
d = Mekhilta, Sifra, Sifre Num., Sifre Dt.
e = Gen. Rabbah and Lev. Rabbah
f = Lam. R., Est. R. I, Song R., Ruth R.
g = Pesiqta de R. Kahana
h = Talmud of Babylonia
i = Siddur
j = Targum Onqelos to the Pentateuch
k = Targum Pseudo-Jonathan to Pent.
l = Fragmentary Targum to the Pentateuch

III

MESSIANIC THEMES AND DIFFERENTIATION WITHIN
THE RABBINIC CANON

Tracing the principal expressions of the Messiah-myth across the canon of rabbinical writings tells us more about the canon than about the history of the Messiah-myth. We see which documents tend to group themselves around a given set of ideas, and which stand essentially distinct from the other. The Mishnah and its close associates, Abot, the Tosefta, and Abot de R. Nathan, fall together, on the one end of the spectrum, the Talmud of the Land of Israel and the Talmud of Babylonia, on the other. Closer to the former pole are the exegetical compilations serving the Pentateuch, specifically, Mekhilta, Sifra, Sifre Numbers, and Sifre Deuteronomy. The Rabbah-collections of the pre-Islamic period, Genesis Rabbah, Leviticus Rabbah, Lamentations, Song, Ruth, and Esther Rabbah I, fit somewhere closer to the Pentateuchal-exegetical compilations than they do to either of the two Talmuds, and Pesiqta de R. Kahana stands close to the Talmud of Babylonia.

The synagogue-based writings, both Siddur and Targum, form a group by themselves, treating the Messiah-myth in an entirely different way. Concretely, they evoke the theme in all its mythic manifestations -- David, Jerusalem, Temple, cult, and the restoration of all of these. But they scarcely follow up with discussion of a single one of the propositions important in the scholastic compositions, e.g., factual statements, on the one side, systemically consequential doctrines, on the other.

Overall, therefore, we may group the rabbinical canon in two parts, and the entire extant corpus of writing of Judaism in late antiquity into three: first, the Mishnah and its circle, on the one side, second, the two Talmuds and their associates, at the center, and third, quite outside of the circle of the schools, the synagogual compositions. Of these three, there can be no doubt about the most comprehensive document: the Talmud of Babylonia covers everything found in all the other writings. It is the great vacuum cleaner of ancient Judaism, sucking up the entire antecedent corpus. The achievement of its compilers, as is now clear, was to create encyclopaedic summaries of all the data at their disposal, then to attempt, with limited success to be sure, to harmonize the mass of contradiction and conflict which resulted.

What we now see clearly is how the Mishnah and its associated compositions relate to the Talmuds and their literary
fellows. The two components of the great rabbinical canon
stand essentially separate from one another, though related in
important ways. They are separate in that the Mishnah's circle
covers a very limited number of topics and does so in a quite
distinctive way. The Talmuds' circle covers the mishnaic
material, but encompasses a very much larger territory of its
own as well. The Mishnah's circle exhibits its own traits of
mind and method, presenting a system unto itself. The two
Talmuds fully cover the Mishnah's range, in their own way,
absorbing the Mishnah's entire repertoire of ideas, one by one,
but making of those ideas, taken up discretely, something quite
other than what they had been when viewed as a whole.

So the principal result of this survey is to uncover, for
the subject at hand, two concentric circles. These contain two
Judaisms, so to speak -- one small, the other huge, one quite
compact and internally coherent, the other, while not totally
formless, yet not entirely self-consistent. The Mishnah
presents us with a complete system. The two Talmuds offer us a
huge repertoire of facts, a fair number of which serve as major
elements in the system, but some which remain unintegrated and
discrete. As we have seen time and again, the Mishnah inte-
grates everything that comes its way or that it selects. The
Babylonian Talmud uses to its own advantage some of the components of the larger Messiah-myth, while preserving but
essentially neglecting others.

IV

THE MISHNAH'S MESSIAH

If I had to specify the <u>systemically</u>-characteristic, even
definitive, elements of the catalogues of facts at hand, I
should have no difficulty in pointing to what the Mishnah finds
critical, namely, the few topics to begin with appearing in the
Mishnah column of the catalogue (Nos. 1-5 on the Messiah-list,
fewer still on the other list). Indeed, what the Mishnah does
not utilize is more interesting than what it does. The Mishnah's framers choose for their system five facts, three of them
commonplaces and (once the subject comes up) unavoidable.
These are, first, that the Messiah comes from the house of
David; second, that there is a difference between the present
age and the age of the Messiah; and, third, that there will be

tribulations before the coming of the Messiah, for the people
in general, but especially for sages.

These commonplaces, deriving from Scripture and well known
to virtually every writer on the subject of the Messiah, are
joined by two others. First, there is no such thing as the
Messiah; there is only the taxonomic classification, messiah.
Into that classification fall two kinds of messiahs, both
cultic: that is, priests anointed for office as specified in
Mosaic law, and another kind. The former appear extensively
and play a significant part in specified tractates. The
Messiah in the other guise, the one familiar to everyone else,
appears only as part of the undifferentiated background of
accepted, but systemically-neutral, facts. The Messiah
receives no close attention; no problems take shape around
which a tractate, an intermediate unit of discourse, or even a
single pericope (even M. Sot. 9:15), might take shape. Obviously, the Mishnah's framers wished to reshape the issue into
terms they found interesting, hence their special concern for
the classification, Messiah-priest, on the one side, and their
special pleading about the special suffering of sages in the
awful times prior to the Messiah's coming. These facts about
the use and neglect of the Messiah-myth point to a single
conclusion. The philosophers of the Mishnah chose to talk
about other things. Hence they were addressing people other
than those eager to learn about the Messiah, when he would
come, and what he would do.

The same pattern repeats itself when we turn to the issue
of the meaning of the history of Israel, the message of
Israel's destiny. What the Mishnah's framers said about
history parallels what they reported about the Messiah: as
little as they possibly could. And what they did say expressed, in this detail, the larger polemic of their system as
a whole. They regarded the critical issue of Israelite reality
as sanctification, the operative dimension as timeless ontology. They therefore had no difficulty in singling out as
critical a particular historical event, namely, the destruction
of the Temple in 70. But that event proved critical, for the
Mishnah's framers, because of its two-fold impact, upon the
supernatural world, on the one side, and the moral life of
Israel, as lived by sages, on the other. That affirmation (M.
Sot. 9:15) runs parallel to (indeed, appears in the same
pericope with) the conviction that sages, in particular, would
suffer when the messianic age drew near. The event of 70
marked changes in the condition of the cult, and produced legal

revisions to compensate. Naturally, periods of Israelite
history -- to begin with bisected by the destruction of the
Temple -- would find further differentiation based on places
where the cult had been located. To be sure, the Tosefta's
repertoire of historical points of interest is somewhat longer,
but its additions, tales about sages, about priests and the
cult and supernatural events affecting them, and explanations
for Jerusalem's destruction, prove entirely congruent to the
Mishnah's lines of inquiry. Just as the Messiah-myth turns out
to have been shaped by, and cut down to fit the interests of,
the larger system of which it would form part, so the issues of
Israel's historical life were defined by the encompassing
system of the Mishnah. The topics discussed, the ways in which
they are worked out -- these constitute mere expressions of
that larger, uniform, mishnaic construction, of which they
formed relatively inconsequential part.

V

THE TALMUDS' MESSIAH

We now need hardly belabor the fact that the rest of the
rabbinical canon saw matters otherwise. Our tables require no
substantial amplification. What we do not find in the Mishnah,
we find everywhere else. What we discern in particular are
answers to two questions. First, which facts specifically
serve the larger (Talmudic) system at hand, and which ones
simply occur at random in the documents? The answer, as we
shall see, emerges from a larger theory about the character of
the rabbinical system. Second, what was rabbinic in particular? That is to say, that theory, to begin with, has to
explain the relationship between what was distinctive to the
schools, on the one side, and what was part of the general
heritage of the Jewish nation overall. Let us begin with this
matter, since the answer to our question is right on the
surface.

When the Talmuds treat the structure of the liturgy, they
take for granted that rabbis bore responsibility for the
organization of the prayers and arranged them in accordance
with their standard mode of thought (exegesis of pertinent
verses of Scripture). Hence, we need not doubt that the
liturgy speaks for the rabbinical estate. The use of the
liturgy in synagogues beyond rabbinical influence cannot be
demonstrated. But we need claim no more than that the liturgy
served people in synagogues -- whether or not all synagogues --

and so spoke out of common national-religious heritage. When viewed in such a light, the prayers tell us what formed part of a generally-accepted heritage of conviction about the Messiah and about Israel's history. That heritage presents common-places about the Messiah's bringing God's rule, on the one side, and his restoring Israel's Land, holy city, and holy place, on the other.

Distinctive to rabbis, then, are two sorts of views about the Messiah. First, they express in their particular way what were generally held convictions. Second, some of their formulations constitute doctrines in fact distinctive to their own estate. In the present context, we may point to the notion that Israel can hope for just government only when God rules. That belief, though stated in a way peculiar to rabbis, in fact expresses what must have been a widespread yearning. But the doctrines that, to prove worthy of God's rule, Israel must accept the dominion of gentiles, must demonstrate its humility in order to make itself worthy, and that rabbis provide the model for the way in which Israel at large must live -- these and parallel points derive from, and express, the larger system of the rabbinical canon. They do not stand upon a single continuum with the generally-held beliefs of the nation at large. They make the rabbinical canon as distinctive, different from the literary-theological heritage of the people in general (if, beyond Scripture, such a thing can be said to have existed at all). So they express part of what made the rabbi rabbinical.

Bearing in mind this distinction between what was part of the antecedent, universal heritage of Israel, and what emerged from the distinctive system of the rabbis, we may rapidly review our catalogue of topics. If I may point to those I should regard as falling into the two categories just defined, they are as follows [(?) - Not certain]:

Generally held elements of the Messiah-myth (including biblically-supplied information)			Facts particular to the rabbinical canon and expressing its distinctive conceptions		
1	11	33 (?)	5	19	40
2	20	34	9	21	43 (?)
3	23	35	12 (?)	22 (?)	44
4	24 (?)	38	13	25	48 (?)
5	26 (?)	41 (?)	14	31 (?)	49 (?)
6	27	42	15	32	
7	28 (?)	45	16	36 (?)	
8	29	46	17	37 (?)	
10 (?)	30	47 (?)	18	39 (?)	

Obviously, the range of uncertainty overspreads the whole. Were we to be able to consult sources beyond those at hand, moreover, we should find reason to treat as generally-known (if not demonstrably believed) facts a far broader, perhaps different, range of conceptions from those listed here. But all we have beyond the writings of the schools are the writings of the synagogue.

When we ask about the canonical context of conceptions of the Messiah that emerge from the formative centuries of Judaism as we know it, we nonetheless can point with some certainty to elements congruent to broader national convictions, on the one side, as well as to some elements distinctive to the rabbinical system on the other. Indeed, we may claim to distinguish, among the latter, two systems -- mishnaic, and talmudic. We may point to that rather small set of facts deemed by the former to be systemically important, as distinct from the much larger set of facts, (including the small set) utilized by the latter. Why can we not specify that all facts found in the Talmuds play some clear part in the articulation of the rabbinical system exposed therein? The reason is that the Talmuds make no attempt to frame a complete and exhaustive statement of their viewpoint, a messianism including everything relevant, while excluding the irrelevant and, finally, systematizing the whole.

It remains to point out that this set of questions may not apply to our catalogue of components of the canon's picture of Israel's history and destiny. My impression is that virtually the entire corpus may prove distinctive to rabbinical circles. But the Prayerbook provides no control. So we have no way of knowing what ideas proved congenial to elements of the nation at large, and which ones served to express viewpoints particular to rabbis. Concepts deriving from the apocalyptic tradition -- e.g., the four kingdoms as represented by four animals -- clearly come from people who lived prior to the formation of the rabbinical movement. How these symbols were revised to serve the rabbinical system, I cannot now suggest.

VI

THE MISHNAH AND THE TALMUDS COMPARED

We see two clearly differentiated sections within the rabbinical canon. One is well defined in its interest. We can offer a plausible explanation of the way in which, consonant

with those larger systemic points of insistence, the Messiah-
myth makes its modest contribution. The other, more encompassing section of the canon also yields a coherent viewpoint.
In accordance with that larger viewpoint, we can discern the
systemic usefulness of parts of the larger representation of
facts about the Messiah. But a number of facts referred to in
the second (Talmudic) sector of the canon do not clearly relate
to the systemic interests of that sector as a whole. If, then,
we take seriously the differentiation of the larger canon of
formative Judaism into two separate, though related, sectors,
we may tell the story of the Messiah in the present context in
just a few words.

1. The Mishnah's framers formulated a world view and a
way of life for the Jewish nation in which historical events
played little part. They insisted on uncovering the ongoing
patterns of life, eternal laws of nature and supernature. To
these points of insistence, the concept of the Messiah and of
the meaning and destiny of Israel among the nations proved
irrelevant. The framers of the Mishnah spoke of other things.
We do not know to whom they wished to address their vision.

2. The continuators of the Mishnah in the Talmuds
constructed their exegetical essays both through, but also
around, the Mishnah. They explained and expanded upon the
Mishnah's points. But they also made provision for expressing
their own views, as distinct from those stated in the Mishnah.
Do these other, extra-mishnaic, views come later in time?
Obviously the answer is partly yes, partly no.

On the one hand, the facts, in the main, can be shown to
have circulated before, during, and after the time of the
Mishnah's formulation. The first and second centuries, after
all, encompassed the greatest messianic explosion in the
history of Judaism. Coming at the end, the Mishnah expressed
its implacable judgment upon that age of messianic expression.
Its authors cannot have failed to know what everyone else in
Israel knew full well. So what the Talmud knows about the
Messiah, in the main, derives from a heritage of facts earlier
circulating in Israel.

On the other hand, much that the Talmud's authorities wish
to say about these ancient facts and to express through them
speaks to a range of conceptions peculiar to the talmudic
rabbis themselves. In its particular form and point of insistence, what is distinctive also comes later in the formation of
the canon.

So some ideas are general and early and some are particular and late. The governing criterion is special to the canon
at hand. What is distinctive to the Mishnah, namely its malign
neglect of the Messiah-myth, reaches expression early in the
canon at hand. What is expressive of the rabbinical perception
of the Messiah reaches its present condition later in the
formation of the canon, even though the facts that are reshaped
are of ancient origin.

VII
THE MESSIANIC IDEA IN JUDAISM?

We find in the rabbinic canon no such thing as the Messianic idea. The sources reveal no such harmonious, encompassing
construct. Once we differentiate among stages of a given canon
of sources -- the rabbinical one -- on the one side, or among
type of canonical writings -- school, synagogue -- on the
other, we discover distinctions among assertions about the
Messiah. More important, we discern diverse ways in which the
Messiah-myth serves some of these several compositions. It
follows, as I said at the outset, that the conception of a
single prevailing construct, to which all assertions about the
Messiah by definition testify, does not exist. When we look at
the origins of statements about the Messiah (as about any other
topic), we turn out to deconstruct what has been invented whole
and complete, in our own time.

Klausner[2] and Scholem[3] provide portraits of a composite that, in fact, never existed in any one book, time, or
place, or in the imagination of any one social group, except an
imagined "all Israel," and a made-up "Judaism." That is why,
once we distinguish one type or system of Judaism or one group
of Israelites from another, recognizing commonalities and
underscoring points of difference, we no longer find it possible to describe and analyze the Messianic idea at all.
Indeed, in the present context, we can no longer even comprehend the parallel categories, the...idea, and in Judaism. The

_____

[2]Joseph Klausner, The Messianic Idea in Israel. From
its Beginning to the Completion of the Mishnah (N.Y., 1955:
Macmillan). Translated from the third Hebrew edition by W.F.
Stinespring.

[3]Gershom Scholem, The Messianic Idea in Judaism. And
Other Essays on Jewish Spirituality (N.Y., 1971: Schocken).
In particular, "Toward an Understanding of the Messianic Idea
in Judaism," pp. 1-36.

upshot is that a new classification is required, new categories must be defined. These appear, I have shown, in two ways. First, they emerge from the differences between one book and another, related book. Second, they arise from the recognition that categories of books reflect different life-situations. Both of these types of categories form commonplaces in contemporary humanistic learning.

The figure of the Messiah serves diverse purposes, defined by the framers of the larger systems in which the Messiah-myth will find a place. We know that the authors of the Mishnah assigned an insubstantial role to the Messiah. But did the framers of the ultimate rabbinical system, in particular the great encyclopaedists of the Talmud of Babylonia, simply open the gate to admit "the Messiah" at large? I think not. What we find in the talmudic sector of the formative canon of Judaism is not merely an established, general conception of the Messiah, now invited to serve (as it had so well elsewhere) as the principal teleological justification also, of the rabbinical system. True, the Messiah enters. But he does so only on the rabbis' terms. So he is incorporated into the rabbinical realm through a process of assimilation and (from the viewpoint I think dominant among the Mishnah's philosophers) also neutralization.

Under the circumstances, it is difficult to see that the Talmudic rabbis had much choice. The vivid expectation of the imminent advent of the Messiah could hardly continue indefinitely. For instance, decades after Paul's declarations on that matter, people were still dying, the people of God still suffering, as the Gospels' authors realized. So the Messiah had to find secondary, long-term embodiment in some form: rabbi, priest, master and divine model on earth -- God-with-us, the word made flesh, Son of Man in the image of God -- and in heaven, yet other tasks. So the ahistorical Christ of Paul, lacking all biography, then become the Jesus of Q, Matthew, Mark, and Luke, ended up as the Jesus Christ of John and of everyone beyond: no longer merely the celebrant of the end of time, but now the center and pivot of all time, all being, all history. Shall we then conclude that the established, inherited conception of the Messiah, as termination of life and time, defined for the heirs and continuators of Christ in the church what they would see in him and say about him? Quite to the contrary. They inherited, but also reshaped the inheritance. Whatever happened in the beginning, Christ as Messiah

continued to serve long after the moment that should have
marked the end of time. Now as the ever-stable focus and pivot
of Christian existence, the Messiah became something other and
far more useful. So far as the apocalyptic expectations were
not realized, indeed, could not have been realized, the Messiah
had to become something else than what people originally
expected. True, he will still be called Christ. But he will
be what the Church needs him to be: anything but terminus of a
world history that -- up to now -- has refused to come to an
end.

So too was the case of the Messiah in the formative canon
of Judaism. That is, if we take for granted that people to
begin with imagined the Messiah in accordance with the promises
of old, we must assume that at the outset they saw the Messiah
as an apocalyptic figure, coming at the end of time. As
dominant and definitive pattern, that version of the Messiah-
myth then passed from the center of the stage of the Messiah.
Other patterns -- attempts to explain the same unclassifiable
figure -- came into use. As to the Mishnah's part of the
canon, at the beginning the authors wished so far as possible
to avoid all reliance upon the Messiah as apocalyptic figure.
Even the language was given a meaning not primary in the prior
writings, "messiah" as (mere) high priest, "messiah" as something other than eschatological savior, whether priest or
general, whether from David's line or the house of Joseph. But
then in the Talmud's sector of the canon, the figure of the
Messiah, and the concerns addressed through discourse about
that figure, came to powerful expression.

So, to state the argument briefly, just as established
conventions of the Messiah-myth served the Church merely to
classify Jesus at the outset, but later on other taxa came into
play, so the Messiah-myth found no consequential place in the
rabbinical canon at the outset, that is, in the Mishnah. But
later on that same myth became the moving force, the principal
mode of teleological thought in the Talmudic sector.

If I had to guess why the Talmuds gave prominence to a
concept ignored in the Mishnah, I should have to appeal to the
evidence of what the nation, Israel at large, had long had in
mind. It seems to me self-evident that a Judaism lacking an
eschatological dimension must have contradicted two established
facts. First, the people read Scripture, which told them about
the end of days. Second, the condition of the people, deteri-
orating as it was, called into question the credibility of the

ahistorical construction of the Mishnah.[4] So, I should imagine, for the Mishnah to be of any practical use, it required not only application to diverse circumstances, which the rabbis gave it. Its system also required expansion, not only by augmenting what was there, but also by exploring dimensions not contained therein at all. By reshaping the ahistorical teleology of the mishnaic system into an eschatological idiom -- indeed, by restating the eschatology in the established Messianic myth -- the rabbis of the Talmud made the Mishnah's system over.

But if the Mishnah was thus forced into that very grid of history and eschatology that it had been formulated to reject, the Mishnah's ontology in turn drastically modified the Messiah-myth as the Talmuds would portray it. For the Messiah was recast into the philosophical mode of thought and stated as teleology of an eternally-present sanctification attained by obedience to patterns of holiness laid out in the Torah. This grid is precisely the one that the framers of the Mishnah had defined. So by no means may we conclude that what changed, in the end, was the Mishnah's system. Its modes of thought intact, its fundamental points of insistence about Israel's social policy reaffirmed, the Mishnah's system ended up wholly definitive for Judaism as it emerged in the canon at the end of its formative centuries, the "one whole Torah of Moses, our rabbi."

How so? The version of the Messiah-myth incorporated into the rabbinic system through the Talmuds simply restates the obvious: Israel's sanctification is what governs. So if Israel will keep a single Sabbath (or two in succession), the Messiah will come. If Israel stops violating the Torah, the Messiah will come. If Israel acts with arrogance in rejecting its divinely-assigned condition, the Messiah will not come. Everything depends, then, upon the here-and-now of everyday life. The operative category is not <u>salvation</u> through what Israel <u>does</u>, but <u>sanctification</u> of what Israel <u>is</u>. The fundamental convictions of the Mishnah's framers, flowing from the reaction against the apocalyptic and messianic wars of the later first and early second centuries, here absorbed and redirected precisely those explosive energies that, to begin

---

[4]I have tried to place the formation of the earliest compilations by rabbis of exegeses of Scripture ("midrashim") into this same context, in my <u>Midrash in Context. Exegesis in Formative Judaism</u> (Philadelphia, 1983: Fortress).

with, had made the critical concern Israel's salvation through
history. So while the Talmuds introduced a formerly neglected
myth, in fact in their version the Messiah became precisely
what the sages of the Mishnah and their continuators in the
Talmud most needed: a rabbi-Messiah, who will save an Israel
sanctified through Torah. Salvation then depends upon sanctification, so was subordinated to it.

To summarize: The Mishnah then proposed to build an
Israelite world view and way of life that ignored the immediate
apocalyptic and historical terrors of the age. The Mishnah's
heirs and continuators, who produced the other sector of the
formative canon, did two things. They preserved that original
policy for Israelite society. But they also accommodated an
ongoing social and psychological reality: the presence of
terror, the foreboding of doom, and Israel's ironclad faith in
the God who saves. Israel remained the old Israel of history,
suffering, and hope. The Mishnah's fantasy of an Israel beyond
time, an Israel living in nature and supernature, faded away.
It was implausible. The facts of history contradicted it.

Yet Israel's condition, moral and social, must govern
Israel's destiny, in accordance with the Torah's rules, but
also precisely as biblical prophecy and Mishnaic doctrine had
claimed. What then could Israel do about its own condition?
How could Israel confront the unending apocalypse of its own
history? Israel could do absolutely nothing. But Israel could
be -- become -- holy. That is why history was relegated to
insignificance. Humble acceptance of the harsh rule of gentiles would render Israel worthy of God's sudden intervention,
the institution of God's rule through King-Messiah. What the
canon set forth at the end, in its rich eschatological-
messianic myth and symbolism, states precisely what the Mishnah
at the outset had defined as its teleology, but in the idiom of
life and death, nature and supernature. The rabbinical canon
in its ultimate form delivered the message of sanctification,
garbed in the language of salvation.

INDEX TO BIBLICAL AND TALMUDIC REFERENCES

BIBLE

MISHNAH

TOSEFTA

Berakhot
    5:25   160-162
Moed Qatan
    2:9   128
Negaim
    6:7   94

BABYLONIAN TALMUD

Berakhot
    51b   162
    55a   91
    62a   35
Menahot
    65a   9
Moed Qatan
    20a   128
Qiddushin
    66a   74
Shabbat
    31a   9

PALESTINIAN TALMUD

Berakhot
    7:2   74
Hagigah
    1:7   48-49
Horayot
    3:5   47
Megillah
    4:1 II   50
Taanit
    3:8 II   52

SIFRA

Emor
    16:9   130
Mesora
    5:9   94

Philo

Abba Saul, 128

Abbaye, 72-73

Abot, 15, 38, 40, 52, 56, 175, 181; authority of Torah, 43-47

Abot de R. Nathan, 175, 181

Abraham, I., 101

Abtalion, 149

Agricultural tithes, 125-126

Albeck, H., 109

Alexander Jannaeus, 65-66, 72-74, 76-77, 79, 81

Alexandra Salome, 65-66, 71-72, 79, 81; and Pharisees, 75-78

Amemar, 119

Antigonus, 149

Antiochus Epiphanes, 72

Antipater the Idumean, 65

Aqiba, 18, 43, 125-128

Aretas the Arab, 77

Aristobulus, 65-66, 76-78, 81

Azariah, 94

Babylonian Talmud, commentary on Mishnah, 162-165; messianic
     idea, 184-186; Mishnah compared, 186-188; religious and
     literary document, 147-172

Bogoas, 78

Bannus, 62-63, 69

Ben Azzai, 125

Ben Sira, 139

Ben Zoma, 125

Berakhot, 159

Bickerman, E.J., 64

Bloch, Renée, 103

Bousset, Wilhelm, 102

Brüll, N., 14, 18

Caligula, 86

Caro, Joseph, 157

Charles, R.H., 102

Christianity, Christian Jews, A.D. 70-135, 86-90; and fourth-
     century Judaism, 9-10